THE
DESIGN
PROCESS

THE DESIGN PROCESS

ELLEN SHOSHKES

WHITNEY LIBRARY OF DESIGN
AN IMPRINT OF WATSON-GUPTILL PUBLICATIONS/NEW YORK

First published in 1989 by Whitney Library of Design
an imprint of Watson-Guptill Publications
a division of Billboard Publications, Inc.
1515 Broadway, New York, N.Y. 10036

Library of Congress Cataloging-in-Publication Data
Shoshkes, Ellen.
   The design process : an illustrated guide for architects and
interior designers / Ellen Shoshkes.
      p.   cm.
   Includes index.
   ISBN 0-8230-1312-X
   1. Architectural practice.   2. Interior decoration.   3. Design
services.   I. Title.
NA1996.S56   1989   89-9177
720'.68—dc19   CIP

Manufactured in Singapore
First printing, 1989
1 2 3 4 5 6 / 94 93 92 91 90 89

Senior Editor: Cornelia Guest
Editor: Sydney LeBlanc
Designer: Jay Anning
Production Manager: Ellen Greene

ACKNOWLEDGMENTS

I would like to thank, first of all, the nine design firms whose work is included in this book for their contributions. In addition, I would like to acknowledge Anderson/Schwartz, Koetter Kim Architects, and Joseph Wetzel and Associates for their willingness to share their experiences. I would also like to thank the architecture and interior design firms who invested in my work developing the "design process book" and related concepts as an aid for communication with their clients: ISD Incorporated, where Harry Lassiter was the first to come up with the idea; Fox & Fowle Architects; Clark Tribble Harris and Li; Interspace; and Ward-Hale Design Associates. Julia Moore guided the development of the ideas, supported the evolution of the concept through major changes at the last minute, and provided invaluable criticism of the manuscript. Cornelia Guest also deserves credit both for her help in shaping the ideas and illustrations, as well as her insightful editing of the manuscript. Jane Thompson provided early encouragement, and friends in the profession, in particular, Karen Phillips, Herb Oppenheimer, and Michael Sorkin, read the manuscript and supported my work through the lonely periods. In addition to the principals, many individuals within the organizations whose work is presented here helped document the case studies, including William Lennertz, Monica O'Neal, James Garrison, Lisa Odyniec, Susan Strauss, Alan Joslin, Jim Batchelor, Karen Bronikowski, Dennis Carlone, Roger Boothe, John Diebboll, Allen Prusis, John Vallance, Gerard Geier, Timothy McGinty, John Meunier, Douglas Kuzmicki, Steven Izenour, James Collins, Howard Litwack, and Kathy Wilson. Thanks are due to Sydney LeBlanc, who helped ease the book through the production process, and to Jay Anning, who allowed me to participate in his book-design process. Lastly, thanks to my parents, whose support made writing this book possible.

CONTENTS

DESIGN IN PROCESS

The idea of the designer as artist has been a prevalent one in the past decade as aesthetic preoccupations have focused on style. But the process of design is seldom simple or direct: It involves much more than applied fashion or style for its own sake. Designers do not work in a vacuum. They have a social responsibility as well as an aesthetic one, since good design can be the catalyst for growth and change in a community. Design solutions must respond to diverse pressures, including both formal ideas as well as human, environmental, and technical realities. The design process thus evolves out of the interaction of people, events, problems, ideas, and images. By describing how nine innovative projects—ranging from buildings to interior renovation to large-scale developments—progressed from concept to reality, this book attempts to shed light on the actual process of design.

The design process has a certain mystique. It is hard to describe moments of inspiration. But architecture is both an art and a science. The architectural design process (which in this book refers to the full range of architectural concerns from interior to urban design) integrates analysis with intuition. Architect Robert Geddes has described the architect as a composer: Indeed,

getting almost any project built today requires a collaborative effort orchestrated with as much innovation and imagination as the creative act of design itself. Design is decision making, and the key to successful projects lies not only in the final form but in the process leading up to it. Poor design decisions can be costly to correct or have lasting social implications. The design of the process must be as carefully considered as the design of the form. An understanding of what takes place during a project and why can demystify design and provide a shared vocabulary for clients, designers, and other participants whose collective actions guide the design process.

THE CHANGING PROFESSION

Architectural education today focuses on theoretical and aesthetic explorations that have little to do with professional practice. As a consequence of the profession's specialization in the art of design, architects are losing control over the building delivery process as well as their authority over issues of concern to society. Recently the pendulum has begun its return swing and designers are reawakening to concerns of social responsibility, human values, and the content of design. This

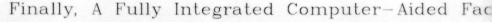

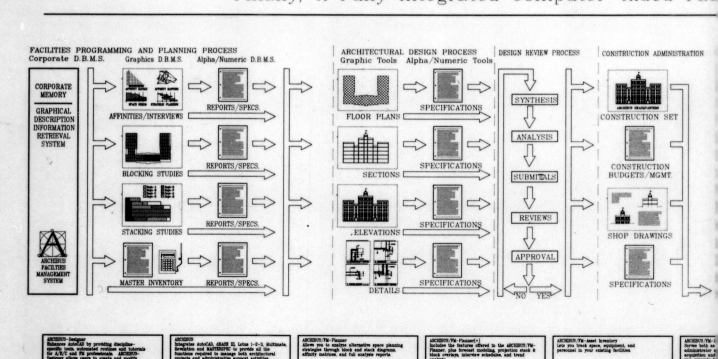

suggests that the time is ripe for architects and designers to reflect on what they do and why.

In his book *Architectural Practice: A Critical View* (Princeton Architectural Press, 1988), Professor Robert Gutman describes how the current economic environment is affecting the demand for architectural services, the characteristics of clients, and the role of the architect. For one thing, he observes that institutions—rather than individuals—have become the predominant type of nonresidential client. Corporate clients often have a prescribed way of organizing building projects and in-house facilities management staff to run them. The role of outside consultants is limited to supplying specialized services such as interior design or feasibility studies. The client's project managers and facilities staff, on the other hand, play a wider range of roles starting before the design process begins and continuing after it has been completed.

Another trend noted by Gutman and others is that projects are becoming larger and more complex than in previous decades, thereby demanding new technical and organizational skills. Factors contributing to this change include the high cost of real estate, new building technologies that make it possible to construct taller towers and longer spans,

and the expanding range of activities and equipment needs within organizations caused both by changing institutions and automation. The need to coordinate the large, multidisciplinary teams required for complex projects itself adds to the complexity of the design process. Numerous decisions by many players must be made as a project evolves, new information is generated, and needs change.

The computerization of all aspects of the design process is now a reality that design firms can no longer afford to ignore. As corporations automate their business operations, it becomes more efficient for them to link up with firms using the same technology. The computer enables firms to enhance contract drawings with a knowledge base and so integrate many functions, such as cost estimating, procurement, and project control. Computer services and training have emerged as service areas for many firms. Other new service opportunities based more on the analysis of information than on design include facilities management, strategic facilities planning, and research on topics ranging from building performance to environmental psychology.

Whether public agency, private corporation, or commercial developer, clients are looking for help in determining what the next generation of projects

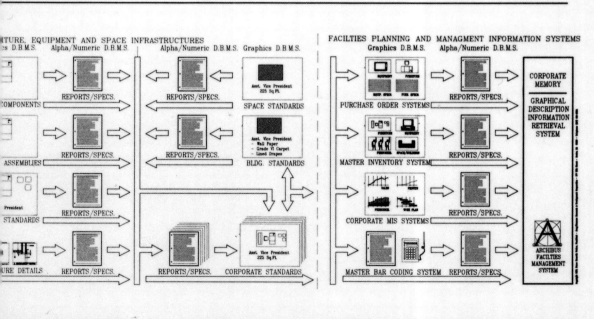

The diagram from Jung/Brannen Associates illustrates how computers enable design firms to provide a broad yet integrated range of additional services, from programming to cost analysis to facility management.

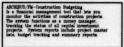
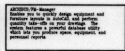
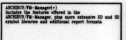

will be like in terms of mixes of uses, building technologies, and types of properties. Designers must work more closely as part of the client's team to address a broader range of problems, incorporate new technology, and rethink the design process to meet these new challenges with innovative responses. "The traditional model of the master builder where the owner provides money and design consultants provide all services hasn't existed in a long time," says Deborah Poodry, Director of Programming for the Massachusetts Division of Capital Planning and Operations. "Whoever is managing the design process must have a sense of the complexity of the process and a clear understanding of the goal."

LEARNING FROM CASE STUDIES

In this context of change and complexity, what are the factors that contribute to successful projects— those that satisfy the needs of the client, the community, and the designer? How do creative ideas survive the process of give and take and the maze of constraints that tends to reinforce conventional design solutions? The case study approach addresses these questions by observing the experience of others and examining how, in practice, issues arise and problems are solved. The nine projects profiled in this book are exceptional, but not unique. They provide a window onto issues that are faced by many firms in similar situations across the country, enabling generalizations to be made by comparing the particular lessons in each case.

The first three cases look at familiar building types in suburban, rural, and urban settings: The Village Center, a shopping center in Brewster, Massachusetts, by William Rawn & Associates; Firestation Five, in Columbus, Indiana, by Susana Torre; and Washington Court, an apartment house in New York City by James Stewart Polshek and Partners. Each of these buildings had to undergo a form of public review and each met with objections that led to delays and changes in the original design.

The next two cases are educational facilities: The Lewis Thomas Laboratory at Princeton University, by Payette Associates with Venturi, Rauch & Scott-Brown; and an expansion of Arizona State University's College of Architecture and Environmental Design, by The Hillier Group. These projects illustrate two ways in which architects who specialize in design are teaming up with technically oriented firms to achieve a client's high standards for both aesthetics and performance.

The sixth case study is of the renovation of the Aetna Life & Casualty home office, by Jung/Brannen Associates and Aetna's facility management team. It addresses the issue of how the design of older office buildings must be altered to accommodate changes in the nature of a company's work. The case also illustrates how computerization of the planning and design process can support facility management.

The last three case studies are of master plans for large-scale developments: CambridgeSide, a mixed-use mall complex in Cambridge, Massachusetts, by Arrowstreet; Metropolis, a mixed-used complex and office tower in Los Angeles, by Michael Graves, Architect; and Kentlands, a new town in Gaithersburg, Maryland, by Andres Duany and Elizabeth Plater-Zyberk, Town Planners. These cases show three approaches to the design of major new construction that will be built over many years and designed by various architects.

An accurate diagram of the design process would be more like a board game than a straight path according to Susana Torre. Design is an iterative process: You go back and revise assumptions if they do not work out or if conditions change. In practice, however, design services are organized as a logical sequence of steps. All projects follow the same process within a broad scope, although each has its own logic and rationale. The type and amount of work completed in similar phases differs, as does duration. The case studies in this book illustrate this variation. By comparing the graphic timelines that summarize the sequence of work in each case study, the differences among them become clear. For example, Duany and Plater-Zyberk used a seven-day charrette to produce a master plan for the Kentlands project (pages 226–53). In contrast, it took Arrowstreet four years to negotiate a master plan for the CambridgeSide complex that satisfied both the developer and the city (pages 172–95).

PHASES OF WORK

The standard project phases typically consist of planning, programming, schematic design, design development, contract documentation, and contract administration. Additional services may include obtaining public agency approval, feasibility studies, or facility management. Each phase refers to a clearly defined set of issues, procedures, types of deliverable item, and participants. Equally important, phases correspond to a level of decision making (and decision maker, in some organizations), proceeding from the most conceptual, such as defining corporate values or growth strategy, to the most detailed, such as the brand of hardware.

During the planning stage goals are defined, nondesign issues are addressed, past lessons are evaluated, and the location of the project is

PROJECT	ARCHITECT	CLIENT	PROGRAM	ISSUES
The Village Center Brewster, MA	William Rawn Associates	Developer: Corcoran & Jennison Corporation	Shopping center in a rural setting	Historic district guidelines as planning tool
Firestation Five Columbus, IN	Susana Torre in association with Wank Adams Slavin Architects & Engineers	Municipality: City of Columbus, Indiana	Civic building for new suburb	Client participation; town's architectural heritage
Washington Court New York, NY	James Stewart Polshek and Partners	Developer: Philips International Holding Corporation	Infill housing in a historic district	Historic district guidelines; public review; difficult site
Lewis Thomas Molecular Biology Laboratory, Princeton, NJ	Venturi, Rauch & Scott-Brown, with Payette Associates Inc.	Private institution: Princeton University	State-of-the-art research laboratory to help recruit a new department	Collaboration to achieve high standard of design and technical performance
Addition to the College of Architecture and Environmental Design, Tempe, AZ	The Hillier Group, Alan Chimacoff, Director of Design, with Architecture One, Ltd.	Public Institution: Arizona State University	Significant addition to existing building in urban campus setting	Competition to speed up the process; tight budget and schedule; role of construction manager
Aetna Home Office Renovation, Hartford, CT	Jung/Brannen Associates, Inc., with the Aetna Home Office Renovation Team	Corporation: Aetna Life & Casualty	Renovation to modernize headquarters complex	Large scale; standardization; computerization; role of facility managers
CambridgeSide Cambridge, MA	Arrowstreet Incorporated, Architects and Planners	Developer: New England Development Corporation	Master plan for mixed-use complex to revitalize urban waterfront	Urban design guidelines; commercial mall and parking requirements
Metropolis, Los Angeles, CA	Michael Graves, Architect	Developer: Parkhill Partners	Master plan for mixed-use complex in central business district	Competition for high-profile design; redevelopment guidelines
Kentlands, Gaithersburg, MD	Andres Duany and Elizabeth Plater-Zyberk	Developer: Joseph Alfandre & Co., Inc.	Master plan for new town on site of last large farm in the county	Alternative to suburban sprawl; integration of mall and housing

determined. Programming defines the specific objectives of a project and describes the functional, physical, social, and budget requirements to be met. Schematic design includes evaluating alternative design concepts and developing a preliminary layout that satisfies both the program and formal concepts. In the design development phase, the design is refined: The sizes, shapes, and relationships of various components are defined and revisions are made based on an analysis of alternative materials, methods, and costs. Contract documents describe how to build the project on a trade by trade basis, set standards of quality of workmanship, and specify information necessary for the procurement of furniture and equipment. Contract administration ensures that the project is built as specified in the documents and coordinates changes and corrections as they arise during construction.

As the case studies show, the role of the designer today, in many project teams, is to be somewhat involved in programming, heavily involved in design, involved in a limited way with documentation, and not very involved with construction.

BACKGROUND

Each case study begins with a discussion of the context in which the project took place, that is, the environment in which the interaction of people, events, and ideas occurs and the design solution evolves. This is particularly relevant for large projects, as the balance of power now seems to favor those who oppose what *New York Times* architecture critic Paul Goldberger described as the "virtual carte blanche" builders have enjoyed in the past. Both local and regional efforts to control growth are playing a large role in monitoring new construction. Communities are using whatever means they have to prevent uncoordinated growth and the traffic congestion and environmental degradation it brings. As the case of William Rawn's design for The Village Center in Brewster, Massachusetts, shows, where planning regulations do not exist, the broad powers of historic districts are being used for land-use planning as well as to control aesthetics.

Both The Village Center (pages 22–47) and Michael Graves's Metropolis (pages 196–225) are commercial projects that took place when developers wanted to build as much as possible legally before impending restrictions to curb growth went into effect: The pace of both developments was slowed, however, by public review of the projects' impact on the environment. Similarly, Arrowstreet's ten-acre CambridgeSide project was stalled until the

developer decided to work within the framework of the City of CambridgeSide urban design plan. Metropolis and CambridgeSide are the kind of mixed-use projects that many cities hope will help revitalize blighted districts. The cities of Cambridge and Los Angeles encouraged these projects with zoning bonuses as incentives. When a booming economy caused pressure for growth that exceeded expectations, these cities used bonuses to leverage private development to provide public amenities that fit the city planners' vision.

While these projects illustrate some solutions to the problems of how to fit new construction into existing communities, the Kentlands case study describes the design of a new town on virgin land. Duany and Plater-Zyberk have formulated a set of planning principles aimed at solving the problem of unplanned suburban sprawl. Their plan for the new town of Kentlands goes beyond local ordinances in terms of preserving the environment and providing open spaces. While the Kentlands plan evolved in response to the characteristics of the specific site, DPZ's radical seven-day-charrette approach to the planning process is an alternative to conventional practice that could be applied anywhere.

The cultural environment can also be an important factor in setting the stage for the design process, as the case of Susana Torre's Firestation Five in Columbus, Indiana, shows (pages 48–71). Largely due to the sponsorship of the Cummins Engine Foundation, Columbus has acquired a distinguished collection of buildings by noted architects that is a great source of civic pride. Torre's design for the firestation had to both live up to this civic tradition of innovation as well as provide an image that suited the community.

THE CLIENT

In every project, clients play an integral role in the design process. "You are only as good as your clients are" is an often-heard comment among designers. The question is, What is the ideal client? For some it may be one with a clear vision and a willingness to work as part of a team toward that common goal. For others it may be a patron who does not get intimately involved in the process. As the case studies show, there is no one answer. Different kinds of organizations have different decision-making styles and agendas. Methods that make sense for a large corporation may not work for a developer or a municipality. However, regardless of the type or size of project, the best clients are those who have a good understanding of the complexities of the design process and provide clear direction to the designer at the beginning of a project.

A client who involves the public in the design process can help ensure that a building will be perceived as part of the community. This is particularly important for civic buildings, where the public is, essentially, the client. A client can encourage participation from the public sector by including them in the development of explicit guidelines before design begins or by involving them during design through review panels. One drawback of the review method is that these panels can become overly fussy and sometimes weaken a design. In the case of Firestation Five, for example, the client—the City of Columbus—acknowledged that participation of the public review committee in design decision making might not lead to the best architecture; however, the city feels it does provide a valuable learning experience for the town and develops a shared sense of ownership. The entrepreneurial developer of Kentlands in Gaithersburg, Maryland, Joseph Alfandre, also recognized the political reality that community input

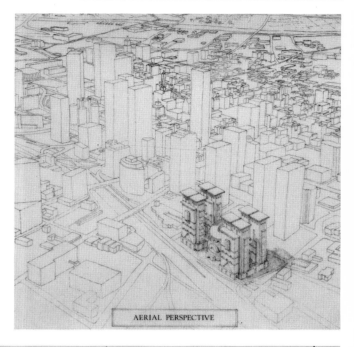

AERIAL PERSPECTIVE

Top: Metropolis, a mixed-use project by Michael Graves, was planned to satisfy Los Angeles's guidelines to control growth and revitalize the central business district.

Bottom: Andres Duany and Elizabeth Plater-Zyberk design new suburban towns to conform to their own copyrighted building standards, which often go beyond the requirements of local ordinances.

Princeton University's 240-year-old campus is steeped in tradition. Over the past decade, the University has initiated numerous construction projects with new architectural styles, evincing a changing institution.

can help overcome resistance to a potentially controversial development. His decision to use a charrette approach to planning was to stimulate interaction and discussion and to build support among various levels of government, builders, and local residents. However, while public clients might admire this type of participatory process, it is a difficult model for a bureaucracy to emulate without cutting through a lot of red tape.

A private institution such as New Jersey's Princeton University, the client for the Lewis Thomas Laboratory (pages 96–123), is another type of client in the patron mold. Yet an interesting aspect of the Lewis Thomas Laboratory case study is that two very different client/architect relationships emerged in the same project. Venturi, Rauch & Scott-Brown developed the façade design with little client input or supervision, while the molecular biology department head was an active partner in Payette's process of planning the interior spaces of the building.

In contrast to Princeton, a public institution such as Arizona State University in Tempe has to be more accountable for how it spends the taxpayers' money. As mandated by state law, ASU hired a construction manager to oversee the expansion of the College of Architecture and Environmental Design (pages 124–47). Architect Alan Chimacoff says, "A lot of the success of the project is on account of the construction manager's careful, thoughtful, crafty management." The expertise of the users— architectural faculty and staff—was another factor influencing the final product. They were active

participants in writing the building program and refining aspects of the design.

Another case where the client's expertise made a major contribution to the final product is Jung/ Brannen's renovation of the Aetna Life & Casualty Insurance headquarters complex in Hartford, Connecticut (pages 148–71). In the midst of a decade of capital expansion and corporate reorganization, Aetna's facility management department had acquired a solid understanding of the design and construction process as well as how facility planning could support the company's long-range objectives. The facility management group applied the lessons it had learned from past projects in planning the renovation and led the team effort, which included a construction manager who also served as the general contractor.

Even the role of the commercial developer is changing. Once the least likely type of client to commission good design, such developers are being forced to rethink conventional formulas and short-term solutions in the face of increased competition for projects, a shortage of easily buildable sites, and the spread of no-growth sentiments. New England Development (CambridgeSide), Parkhill Partners (Metropolis), Corcoran & Jennison (The Village Center), and Philips International (Washington Court) are examples of savvy developers who responded to these challenges by teaming up with talented architects to produce better quality buildings that include noncommercial features and that are sensitive to the community in which they exist.

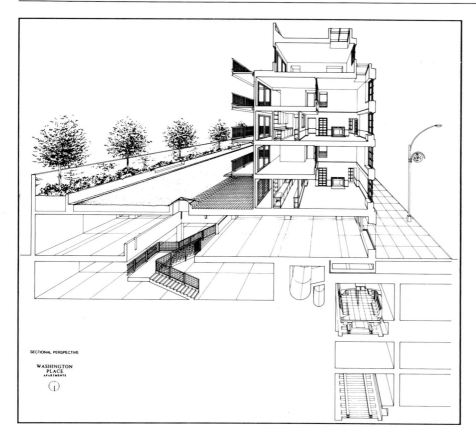

SECTIONAL PERSPECTIVE

WASHINGTON
PLACE
APARTMENTS

The Washington Court Apartments were designed by James Stewart Polshek and Partners in response to the traditional architectural context and to the physical constraints of building over the subway and sewer tunnel below the site.

THE SITE

Site selection and planning are often the first steps in the design process. Frequently a project coalesces around a particular site or a client's need to expand or renovate an existing facility. Robert Geddes has written (in *Process: Architecture #62*) that the "site is not only the setting but the stimulus for architectural form." However, what can be built on a given site is conditioned by a number of constraints, including zoning, codes, restrictions incorporated in historic or redevelopment districts, covenants attached to deeds, engineering difficulties, and community social values.

As Geddes points out, context is both a function of time and place. Buildings are only one element in a continually changing landscape. A major issue addressed to some degree in all nine case studies is how to harmoniously unify architecture, landscape, and the community. For example, both The Village Center in semirural Massachusetts, and Washington Court in urban New York (pages 72–95) are located in historic districts where new construction must be "appropriate" to the context of the area's heritage as well as its vision for its future. Village Center architect William Rawn produced a design that referred literally to the context of Greek Revival style buildings, but it was initially rejected by the historical commission for being out of scale with the

rural setting. Washington Court architect James Stewart Polshek proposed a smaller building than legally allowed for its parking lot site in order to patch the urban fabric. The scheme responded not just to the site's historic context, but also to a physical constraint: the challenge of building over the city's subway and sewer tunnel. However, Polshek's design was opposed by the community at first for its lack of traditional details.

The prominence of the Lewis Thomas Laboratory on Princeton's campus prompted the university administration to team up Robert Venturi (an alumnus of the school who had demonstrated a sensitivity to the campus with a previous building), who was responsible for the appearance and impact of the building on the site, with Payette Associates, experts in the building type, who designed everything else. Similarly, ASU's expansion of the College of Architecture and Environmental Design occupies a prominent site on the edge of the campus bordering the City of Tempe. The design had to present the public face of the university as well as embody the educational values of the institution. The visibility and importance of the building led ASU to conduct a competition to select a better architect than could be found through standard procedures.

For large-scale developments the site is often the

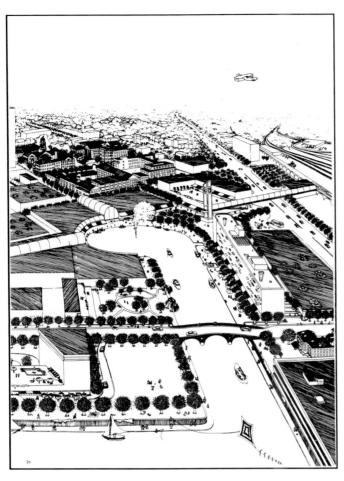

CambridgeSide had to fit the City of Cambridge Community Development Department's urban design plan—an open-space network focused around a rehabilitated canal—to revitalize the blighted waterfront district.

single most important factor affecting the design process. The former Kent Farm, on which the master-planned community of Kentlands will be built, is the last large tract of farmland in the Gaithersburg area. The city's desire to prevent piecemeal development or even a typical subdivision encouraged developer Joseph Alfandre to adopt a comprehensive approach. Individual buildings in a large-scale development can be similarly affected. Firestation Five is located in a planned community in Columbus that was also built on the last large farm in the city limits. Because the firestation site was donated by the subdivision developer, Susana Torre's design had to respond to both the developer's criteria and the city's aesthetic aspirations in the context of the surrounding farmland.

Both CambridgeSide and the Metropolis projects had to satisfy redevelopment district guidelines to qualify for density bonuses and public approval. The site for CambridgeSide was part of a large expanse of abandoned land on the East Cambridge waterfront for which the city had formulated its own urban design as a framework for private development. The actual boundaries of the developer's parcel shifted many times during the four years it took to negotiate a master plan that satisfied both the guidelines and the developer's economic requirements.

In contrast, the site for Metropolis is a full block in the central business district of Los Angeles. If the project met the city's design guidelines, the developer would qualify for increased density and assistance in assembling the parcel. However, the guidelines were only articulated in detail in response to Michael Graves's master plan. This approach reflects the difficulty of making specific plans for the design of new construction in the midst of downtown areas, where it is hard to predict which parcel of land will be developed, when, and for what purpose.

ARCHITECT SELECTION
One of the most crucial steps in the design process for clients is to select the right architect. The client must decide what it really wants both from an architect and for the project. Once a project's goals and the architect's scope of services have been defined, they will serve as the framework for communication between client and architect throughout the design process. Obviously, working with a "star" designer to create an attention-getting building, as in the case of Michael Graves and Metropolis, involves a different set of expectations than working with a service-oriented firm as part of

a corporate team, as in the case of Jung/Brannen Associates and Aetna.

In three of the cases clients used competitions to commission distinctive designs for high-visibility sites. The Metropolis competition was a sort of "style war" among leading architects aimed more at selecting a designer than a design. Graves had to revise his submission before actually winning the commission. The Arizona State University competition was used to elicit applications from a wider pool of architects than would otherwise respond to an RFP (request for proposals), due to the state's low cap on design fees. The competition process achieved better quality design for less money than such a complex program normally would entail. In both of these cases the competition served to accelerate the design process as well. The competition used by the City of Columbus was a hybrid in that no submission of a proposed design was required; the competition was solely to select the architect. This case illustrates how a competition can increase public awareness of design.

Aetna facility managers designed an entirely different type of competition to select an architect. Their aim was to test their own ideas against leading design firms as well as to simulate actual working conditions to test how well the firms would work as part of the Aetna team. The submission requirements included both a master plan and working drawings for two full-scale mock-ups.

In the other cases designers were selected specifically for their expertise in the particular problems posed by a project, either on the basis of past work for the client, as with Arrowstreet, Payette, and Venturi, Rauch & Scott-Brown; from a short list of qualified firms, as with James Stewart Polshek; or through word-of-mouth referrals, as with William Rawn and Andres Duany and Elizabeth Plater-Zyberk. Developer Alfandre was convinced to go ahead with DPZ's unconventional charrette process during a precontract trip with the architects to England, ostensibly to look at models for the new town but actually to test their "chemistry."

As with any other relationship, good chemistry is often the deciding factor in putting together the right team. When the participants in a project enjoy working together it is always a good sign, but, on the other hand, to choose an architect on the basis of how easy he or she will be to work with may not be the best yardstick. Tom Harrison, consultant to the Cummins Engine Foundation's architectural program, says, "There are too many dominant clients, too many architects willing to please. You can end up with a mishmash. After all, they say that Frank Lloyd Wright was a very difficult man to work with."

Architects Alan Chimacoff (right) and Gerard F. X. Geier (left) of The Hillier Group display part of their winning presentation in the competition to design an expansion of Arizona State University's College of Architecture and Environmental Design.

PROGRAMMING

During the 1960s and 1970s programming as a separate activity was a central focus in design. In the 1980s, however, there has been more emphasis on style and end product than on building performance or users' needs. Programming remains an essential part of what the designer does, but has been absorbed into the design process to a greater or lesser degree, depending on a firm's philosophy. The nine case studies in this book illustrate a variety of ways to combine program and design, ranging from total separation to an integrated approach. Whatever the method, a good program should communicate clearly, put all the issues on the table, and set the scope—and therefore cost—of a project.

The Arizona State University case is an example of one end of the spectrum, where the programming process was totally separate from the design, and where the client supplied the program. Faculty and students researched the space needs and worked with the construction manager to estimate costs. The project's scope and budget was based on negotiations over what the users wanted versus what the owner felt was needed. (In discussing a client's involvement it is important to make the distinction between the owner and the users.) Competition submissions were carefully evaluated in terms of how they satisfied the program's stated goals as well as the list of functions and cost constraints. The first

real meeting of architect and client did not take place until after the competition, however, in schematics, which architect Alan Chimacoff felt was a real drawback.

The Lewis Thomas Laboratory is an example of the opposite extreme, in which programming was an iterative process linked to design that continued throughout the project. Payette Associates began work by researching similar buildings and discussing the users' needs with the molecular biology department head. The result was a two-page program summary that set the basic size and scope of the building. Programming continued during schematic design, as the specific sizes and relationships of spaces were worked out during meetings through sketches and diagrams, which the client signed off on. In this sense, schematic design is programming. Payette was as concerned with the behavioral and social side of the building as with technical issues. Working closely together, the architects and the department head defined the activities of the department as they planned the space.

The case studies of Firestation Five and Aetna's home office renovation show that programming can also be thought of as up-front planning to address the important nondesign issues that affect a project. Susana Torre began researching the program even before she had the job to design Firestation Five. To

Susana Torre's approach to designing Firestation Five in Columbus, Indiana, began during the architect selection process, an informal competition for which she prepared by researching firefighting history.

prepare for the first interview with the client, the architect became familiar with the history of the institution of firefighting and considered how its changing goals might be embodied in the form of the building. For the second interview Torre analyzed the site. After winning the commission, Torre incorporated programming in the design process as the first phase of work, adding an analysis of user, space, and equipment needs to the broad framework established during the initial studies. The final program was documented in a booklet, which marked the end of analysis and the beginning of synthesis—design. The City of Columbus had already targeted a budget for the project, which had to be revised once the actual scope of work and level of quality were defined.

Programming can also be master planning, as the Aetna case study shows. Aetna's facility management staff studied the requirements for the renovation of its headquarters in the context of such broad issues as the decentralization of the organization, the impact of new technology on the work environment, frequent relocation of personnel, and the need for a shared corporate identity. This macro look was complemented by a micro analysis of workstation requirements, which led to the master plan concept of a standardized system that could be applied on a large scale (the facility is the size of a small town), with the flexibility to grow and change over time. Jung/Brannen's ability to computerize the master plan and link it with programming information allowed Aetna to integrate all aspects of the design process, from space planning to furniture procurement, and created a "living data base" out of the contract documents that serves as a facility management tool.

Client involvement early in a project can be as important to the ultimate design as is the contribution of the architect, according to architect Joseph Esherick, in practice for over fifty years. In the case of Aetna, the in-house group not only developed the basic planning concept but also involved the users (who actually were the clients for the renovation of their departmental areas) in the process. By building a mock-up of the standardized workstation before the master plan was finalized, the facility planners were able both to get valuable feedback and to build support for the idea. By participating in the mock-up evaluation, the client/ users felt personally involved in the process and approved radical changes from the status quo.

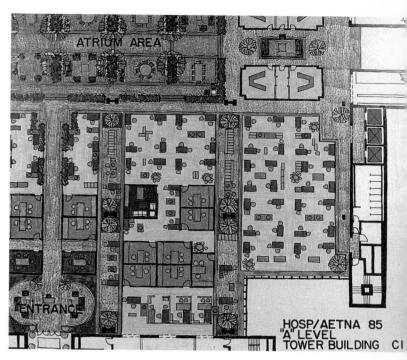

Aetna Life & Casualty's facility management team began planning their headquarters renovation years before construction. A master plan addressed major issues, including decentralization, new technology, frequent staff relocations, and the desire for a strong corporate image.

SCHEDULE

Two major areas where problems arise between clients and architects are when designs exceed projected costs and when they go beyond anticipated schedules. A common problem that derails the design process is when an inappropriate level of detail is addressed too soon or when goals established at the outset of a project do not guide subsequent decisions. Clients have different levels of understanding of construction costs and schedules, requiring different levels of responsibility from the architect. As shown in the case study of Firestation Five, the architect may need to educate the client about the economic feasibility of program and design decisions. On the other hand, the client may be quite knowledgeable; large corporations and institutions such as Aetna and Arizona State University, for example, are very sophisticated about construction. In either case, the key issue is that careful planning early in a project can help avoid costly mistakes later on.

With the growing complexity and cost of projects, corporate clients and developers are increasingly including professional construction managers on the project team, often bringing them on board before selecting an architect. At ASU, for example, the construction manager consulted on the evaluation of the competition submissions and helped the school write up a comprehensive scope of services that demanded an unusually high level of completion for each phase of work. This efficiency paid off. When the need for a new utilities tunnel created a major setback, the project was able to absorb both the cost overrun and the delay without postponing the anticipated date for the completion of construction.

Economic factors pressure many projects to get under construction quickly. As cases such as the ASU addition, the Lewis Thomas Laboratory, and Metropolis show, a tight schedule is not necessarily a negative constraint on the design process, however. Speaking at a symposium on "Public Agencies as the Catalysts of Good Design," planner Poodry suggested that such schedules can actually benefit a project: "A project designed to a schedule and especially an accelerated schedule, when properly organized, can be far superior to a project that proceeds in an erratic fashion. Time that is not lost changing one's mind and redirecting energies of the entire team improves decisions. Well-organized projects are more fun to work on, more profitable for the architect, less costly for the client, and the clarity of this organization is reflected in a more successful design solution."

Princeton's Lewis Thomas Laboratory is a good example of how a fast-tracked construction schedule along with the constraints of a collaborative process helped promote an intensity of commitment among the project team members. A schedule of overlapping project phases was devised so that Payette Associates could begin design development of the building systems while Venturi continued to explore the schematic design of the facade. This approach demanded excellent coordination of consultant work, as mechanical systems were built into the exterior skin.

The public review process can introduce an unpredictable element in a project schedule. As a result, this phase of work is often handled as an additional service on an hourly basis, as in the case of Washington Court in New York City. Feeling under pressure by the owner to get the project under construction quickly, architect James Stewart Polshek submitted plans for public review while they were still in the schematic stage. Yet the necessary approval was delayed month after month by community opposition. During this time the comments of the community were "unconsciously absorbed" in the design. In the case of The Village Center in Brewster, working drawings were nearly complete when due to a technicality historic commission approval was denied. The design process started all over again, and a smaller scheme was developed, approved, and documented.

Most large-scale projects take years to plan. The more complex a project is and the more public interests it must represent, the more likely it is to become controversial. The process of negotiating trade-offs among the various interests can result in design by default. In some cases, though, the longer the time for study and refinement, the better the final product. The CambridgeSide mall in Cambridge is a good example of this. Over the course of four years, the project's master plan went through numerous iterations, during which time the participants in the design process earned each other's respect and became a team working toward a common goal.

In the Kentlands case study, the element of time is a vital factor in the design process. By gathering the key decision makers in a project for a charrette on the site, architects Andres Duany and Elizabeth Plater-Zyberk reduce the amount of time it takes to plan a large-scale development from several years to seven high-energy days. DPZ believe that the charrette approach is not just faster and more efficient, but better. Andres Duany says it allows them to "compress history." In this case, the process may very well be as important as the product. The dramatic, interactive experience is an exceptional means for educating the public and generating enthusiasm. The real value of the process is not in the details of the product (which can be worked out later) but in the shared vision it generates, which in this case will guide the community and the developer through the many years it will take to implement the ambitious project.

DPZ's charrette offers an intriguing alternative model for planning practice, but one that is hard to follow. Not every architect has the charisma of DPZ's Andres Duany and not every developer has the vision of Joseph Alfandre. The Kentlands project dramatizes a lesson that applies to many innovative projects, particularly large-scale developments: The design process is a catalyst for change, not just in the built environment, but in people's lives, the way a community sees itself and works together.

The process of design is a learning experience: It can focus people's attention on the possibilities for change or present a new way of looking at the environment. It provides an organizational framework that enables the synthesis of multiple and conflicting factors and channels the contributions of many people. It stimulates innovative solutions to problems. As the case studies that follow show, there is no formula or secret technique for good design. However, the final result is inextricably tied to the process that produces it. By understanding this important relationship, the participants in a building project—architects, designers, developers, clients, and others—can work to creatively integrate the process to produce superior design.

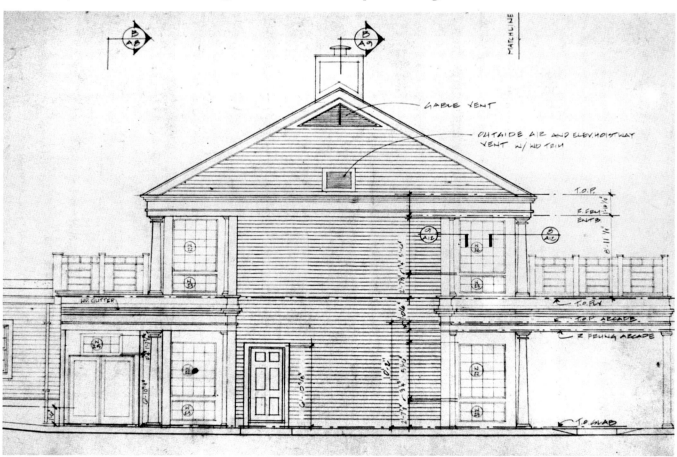

Working drawings by William Rawn Associates for The Village Center in Brewster, Massachusetts, were nearly complete when the local Historic District Committee revoked the Certificate of Appropriateness they had issued the previous year. Antigrowth sentiments forced redesign of the project at a reduced scale.

William Rawn's Greek Revival style design for a retail complex in the village of Brewster, Massachusetts, was considered "appropriate" according to the local historic district's design guidelines one year and "inappropriate" the next. New committee members, representing local concern about unplanned growth, did not object to the quality of the design, but to the size of the project. The process whereby Rawn found a formula that satisfied the developer/client, the historic district commission, and his own aesthetic principles, is the focus of this case study. The study illustrates how historic districts are being used to control development in the absence of other land-use planning regulations. However, when public design review is based on ambiguous criteria, its effect on the final product depends more on the interpretation of the individuals involved than the stated guidelines. Public resistance to the project led to significant changes in the scheme and lengthy delays, but the final product manifests both its own architectural integrity and respect for the community in which it exists.

PROJECT OVERVIEW

Project A 50,000 sf shopping center in Brewster, Massachusetts.

Architect William Rawn & Associates, Boston, Massachusetts.

Client Corcoran & Jennison Corporation, Quincy, Massachusetts.

Charge To serve as a gateway for a 250-acre resort and as a link to the town.

Issues ✔ Satisfying the requirements of historic preservation regulations and responding to a shifting interpretation of them.

✔ Design of individual buildings to shape the character of the public realm.

✔ Need for design that is sensitive to the historic character of its context without being imitative of historic styles.

✔ Implementation of historic preservation regulations as land-use planning controls.

✔ Retail centers as civic places and an urbanizing force.

Duration Three years from start to completion of working drawings (September 1985–September 1988).

Budget $3,000,000.00.

TIMELINE

YEAR 1

- PROGRAMMING
- CONCEPTUAL DESIGN
- SCHEMATIC DESIGN
- DESIGN DEVELOPMENT
- 1st HISTORICAL COMMITTEE REVIEW (Approval granted)
- WORKING DRAWINGS

YEAR 2

- BUILDING PERMIT APPLICATION (Zoning variance denied)

YEAR 3

- 2nd HISTORICAL COMMITTEE REVIEW (Approval denied)
- APPEAL (Appeal denied)
- REDESIGN
- 3rd HISTORICAL COMMITTEE REVIEW (Approval granted)
- CONSTRUCTION DOCUMENTS
- CASE STUDY ENDS

YEAR 4

- ANTICIPATED CONSTRUCTION

YEAR 5

BACKGROUND

Increasing anxiety over how to manage growth has become a political issue throughout New England. The debate between conservationists and developers has heated up in recent years as a rapidly expanding regional economy has intensified the pressure for new construction, threatening the great natural beauty for which the area is famous. Yet New Englanders of a traditionalist cast have generally resisted the imposition of government planning. "Planning" is viewed as being at odds with "free enterprise." This case study of William Rawn's design for a shopping center on Cape Cod illustrates how some towns are using the design guidelines written into historic district legislation to control development in the absence of land-use planning regulations.

When Rawn designed the shopping center for a site in Brewster, Massachusetts—a site that is within the Old King's Highway Regional Historic District— he created a traditionally detailed, Greek Revival style building. The local Historic District Committee approved the scheme and the architects proceeded to the working drawing stage. Due to an oversight, the same design had to be resubmitted for approval the following year, and, this time around, new members on the Committee rejected it as "inappropriate" for the semirural site. At issue was not the quality of the design (which was praised), but the size of the building and the urbanizing effect it would have on the town.

Although zoning laws for the site allowed a building of the proposed density, the Historic District Committee was using its populist mandate to preserve the quality of the environment and to serve in a planning capacity in the absence of any other agency to do so. The developer, Corcoran & Jennison, could have contested the legality of the historic committee's restrictions on the scale project, but was concerned itself about the issue of unplanned growth, and agreed to a compromise. The final structure is a response not only to the immediate site, but also to the larger community, for which it provides an urbane public meeting place.

OLD KING'S HIGHWAY REGIONAL DISTRICT HISTORICAL COMMISSION

The issue of unplanned growth is particularly insistent on Cape Cod. The population of the Cape's fifteen towns grew by 18 percent between 1970 and 1980—as compared to a 2 percent growth rate for Massachusetts as a whole during that period. The Cape has experienced so much land development that the stretch between two once-small towns, Falmouth and Hyannis, is now covered with urban sprawl. By the early 1970s, planners saw signs that the margin of development was pushing eastward along the main traffic artery, Route 6A, also known as Old King's Highway.

State law enacted in 1973 set up the Old King's Highway Regional District Historical Commission (the Regional Commission) to preserve the historical character of the five villages in that area, including Brewster, and to protect them from strip development. In Yankee tradition, each town administers the law independently, through its own historic district committee, comprised of four elected members and one architect appointed by the town selectmen. The Commission, which consists of the chairmen of the five town committees, only interprets the law and hears appeals.

The law endowed the Commission with a broad mandate—"to promote the general welfare of the inhabitants of the member towns." The town committees assess the appropriateness of exterior features of new buildings based on a broad range of factors that include not just historical value, but also the general design, arrangement, texture, colors, and signage of a structure, and the relation of these elements to the context. The committees are authorized to evaluate the relative sizes of buildings, but not details of design or portions of the building not visible to the public.

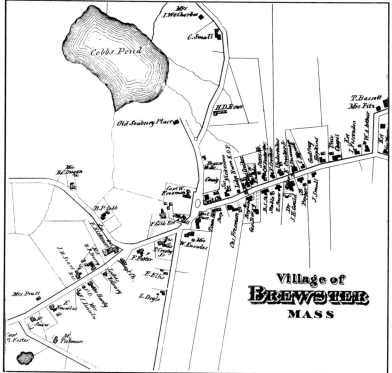

Above: Rendering of the view from The Village Center retail complex arcade.

Left: A map of the historic village center, Brewster, Massachusetts.

THE CLIENT

Developer Joe Corcoran is one of the largest landowners in Brewster. He founded his development company, Corcoran & Jennison Corporation (C&J), in 1971. In 1976 the company started a contracting division in order to gain more control over the whole construction process. C&J specializes in housing, and in 1980 it had recently completed a 250-acre planned unit development (PUD) in Brewster, called The Ocean Edge Resort.

The resort includes a conference center, 900 condominiums, a golf course, tennis courts, swimming pools, and restaurants. Corcoran & Jennison hoped that the conference center, a converted turn-of-the-century monastery, would extend the business season beyond the summer months for the resort.

After completing the Ocean Edge, however, the firm of Corcoran & Jennison was not on the best of terms with the Brewster Historical Committee. The developer had been previously turned down on various project proposals at least a dozen times by the board. Initially, these rejections had been overruled by the Regional Commission. Construction is one of the biggest industries on the Cape, a factor that for a long time had mitigated resistance to development. By 1984, however, antigrowth sentiment had grown to the point where a building moratorium, proposed by former senator Paul E. Tsongas, was gaining wide public support. Corcoran's proposals began to be met with firm local opposition that the Regional Commission would not veto.

THE SITE

Corcoran & Jennison bought an irregularly shaped piece of land filling in the area stretching from Route 6A to its Ocean Edge housing complex. Although the site was on the edge of town, the setting was semirural. Corcoran's plan was to develop the land and build a shopping center, which he hoped would also serve "as an interesting entry to the resort, as its jewel."

Corcoran conceived of the shopping center as an urbane place where people would congregate, and he named it The Village Center. In fact, Brewster does not have a "main street," and the project was to be a link between the town and the resort. But after a sales office was constructed on the site in the ersatz Colonial Cape Cod style popular with local builders, Corcoran realized that the idea was not coming out as he had envisioned. He wanted something "unique," which he could be proud of and which the town would want.

Corcoran greatly admired the stately homes built for sea captains who settled in Brewster in the 1820s and 1830s. He decided that the Greek Revival style of these houses would be appropriate for the shopping center he wanted to build. More importantly, he thought the town would welcome a commercial development if the design were harmonious with its architectural heritage. However, he was going to have to find a new architect, as the ones he had worked with in the past were not qualified for the job.

The developer read an article about the Boston Society of Architects' presentation of an award to

The old Nickerson Carriage House and former monastery became a conference center.

William Rawn for his design of a Greek Revival house. "It was obvious that Rawn had done a lot of research on the style," Corcoran observed. He telephoned the architect's office for an appointment. The meeting took place the following morning and by 10:00 A.M. they had signed a contract.

THE ARCHITECT

William Rawn studied architecture at MIT, after having earned a degree in law and having served as assistant provost for the University of Massachusetts. This career switch was "not a radical one because architecture was present in everything else anyway," Rawn explains. At law school he specialized in housing and land development law, and at the University of Massachusetts one of his responsibilities was campus planning.

Rawn started getting attention soon after opening his own office in 1983, when a Greek Revival style house he designed became the focus of author Tracy Kidder's best-selling book *House*, an account of that project from the points of view of owner, architect, and contractor. Since then, the work of Rawn's firm has continued to win recognition for its sensitivity to context, attention to detail, and appreciation of traditional planning and design principles.

With a staff of twelve, Rawn is directly involved with each project in the office. Key members of the team for this project included Rawn, as the project designer, and associate Alan Joslin, as project architect.

Two views of the site, with the real estate office at top left.

PROGRAMMING
September 1985

C&J anticipate construction to begin the following summer, although they are aware of the possibility of delays during the approval process. The architects create a schedule, and completion of design development is projected for early summer. The developer's enthusiasm for a design based on architectural themes belonging to the University of Virginia becomes a driving force in the process.

The architects' work began with an analysis of the project's constraints. These included, in addition to the need to have the design fit in with the historic context, the developer's requirement to phase construction, programmatic issues, and zoning restrictions.

HISTORIC CONTEXT

Brewster's architectural context is traditional, yet broad. Although more working-class in character than neighboring towns, Brewster is particularly proud of its collection of Greek Revival ship captains' houses that line the highway. Together with the Greek Revival-inspired farm buildings found in the area, they give Brewster its venerable character.

SITE

The parcel has an irregular shape with a "panhandle" projection on one end. It is also diagonally sliced by a road stretching from the highway to the resort. When the State of Massachusetts designed the road, C&J did not own the land and thus had not considered the road's potential impact on the future development of the site. Road realignment would require a long approval process, and so was ruled out of the question.

ZONING

The site was zoned for commercial use only. It was adjacent to open land also owned by C&J but zoned for residential use only. As for any commercial project, the number of building square feet allowed by code is determined by the number of parking spaces to be provided. To appropriate land in the residential zone for parking use, the developer would need to obtain a zoning variance.

Determination of the overall number of allowable square feet, with and without the zoning variance, was a key issue.

PROGRAM

The new building would have to be integrated with the existing real estate office, which had been functioning as a sort of lobby to the resort. The office would have to be visible but not prominent. There would be no anchor stores. Shops would be medium-sized boutiques.

C&J did not insist that vehicular circulation take place between the highway and the buildings, as in strip shopping centers. Pedestrian and bicycle access from the neighboring residential area were to be provided, as well as benches and other pedestrian amenities.

Beyond these intentions, there was one more, expressed by Corcoran: "It should be the kind of place where people go because they feel comfortable just sitting and not having to buy anything, but hopefully they will want to anyway. The Greek agora was a market and meetingplace, so this type of place is in keeping with the Greek Revival theme."

Rawn's early doodles

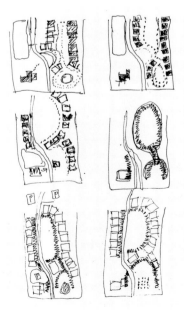

8seats
5seats

PHASING
The complex would be built in two phases. Phase One, consisting of construction extending over 20,000 sf, would be built immediately. Phase Two, consisting of construction extending over 25,000 sf, would be built after the first building was "absorbed" (about 80 percent rented)—which could take up to three years, according to the developer.

Local homes in the Greek Revival style, which developer Corcoran suggested Rawn refer to in his design.

CONCEPTUAL DESIGN
October–November 1985

The architects have some specific ideas about the kind of space they want to make. They are interested in exploring the architectural and site planning characteristics of the Greek Revival style in an abstract sculptural way. They want to express the place's civic role as a public meeting place as well as its commercial function.

Joe Corcoran recalls, "It was my idea to base the design on Greek Revival, but Bill Rawn took that idea one step further and brought it to conclusion." For Rawn, Thomas Jefferson's University of Virginia (UVA), with its arcades connecting Greek Revival buildings, immediately came to mind as a model for The Village Center. Rawn's idea was not to reproduce the buildings, which are brick, but to capture some of the themes of the campus, which he has described as "urban, beautiful, and subtle." Arcaded walkways connecting many two-story pavilions, each one different from the others but clearly part of a whole, became the motif for the scheme.

Rawn felt that the connection between the shopping center buildings ought to be retail as well as an arcade, but that the second stories ought to be leased as office space. The mixture of retail space with office space was already a common practice in

The University of Virginia campus, with Greek Revival style buildings. Each features a unique façade, connected by an arcade surrounding a central green.

small commercial buildings in the area, but no American shopping center or mall had been built along those lines since the 1940s.

As a first step, the architects had to sell the client on the design concept. To convince Corcoran that their idea could work, the architects showed him photographs of the University of Virginia campus. Corcoran's first reaction was skeptical; however, he was quickly won over. "After all," Corcoran said, "Jefferson was my favorite president. I admired him because he was so many things—a politician, a philosopher, an academic, an architect, even a planner!"

By coincidence, shortly after his introduction to the UVA idea, Corcoran picked up an airline flight magazine and found an article on Jefferson and the University of Virginia. Something clicked; he'd always wanted to visit the campus. When Rawn also suggested to him that he go and see the place, Corcoran realized that this was a good excuse to plan a trip. Corcoran and his partners went to Charlottesville and toured the campus, absorbing its detail, seeing how it worked. Suddenly Rawn's idea was no longer just an abstraction, and they were completely converted. The developer's desire to achieve an authentic Greek Revival style building modeled on Jefferson's campus was now a force directing the design process.

SCHEMATIC DESIGN
December 1985–March 1986

After studying site planning alternatives, the architects design an authentic Greek Revival scheme with elaborate wood molding and trim. Cost estimates come in high, so they revise the scheme to express the spirit of the style, but in a more stark, abstract manner. The developer prefers the original version despite the extra expense.

The architects developed a scheme that would evoke the authentic Greek Revival atmosphere that the developer wanted, by creating a highly articulated form with copious ornamental wood molding and trim. "We tried not to be imitative and came up with a somewhat freewheeling interpretation of Greek Revival," says Rawn. The architects began by regarding the building as a system of components: arcades and simple volumes. Rawn directed his staff to use models for these components and to explore massing and site planning alternatives, pushing and pulling with the components to create various kinds of public spaces relative to the highway. The best ideas were presented to the client as a series of schemes exemplifying how the buildings could relate to the highway and to each other.

One day Rawn assigned a sketch problem (a quick drawing exercise) in his office. He asked his colleagues to come up with ideas for building elevations using the system of component parts. The result was a collection of vignettes of arcaded pavilions, which allowed the architects to step back from their model and to gain some sense of how the pieces, represented in blank white cardboard, would eventually look. After considering numerous possibilities, they finally decided to wrap the arcades around a lawn that people could spill onto. Rawn pointed out that such a commons is a typical Greek Revival element and that it dignifies structures by setting them back from the road.

The "commons scheme" turned to advantage the presence of the road crossing the site, by allowing cars to drive past the arcade and lawn. The architects felt that while orienting the backs of buildings to the road would be more convenient for parking, this would isolate the front arcades from the animating flow of movement. Rawn says, "This situation is similar to the typical interior covered mall, where you have to penetrate the megavolume before you are aware of the lively retail environment. Contrary to our initial concern, the road crossing the site didn't destroy the University of Virginia image, but adds a new layer of meaning to it and changes its function." One disadvantage of the scheme was that in setting the buildings so far back on the site, parking had to be located partly on the land zoned for residential use.

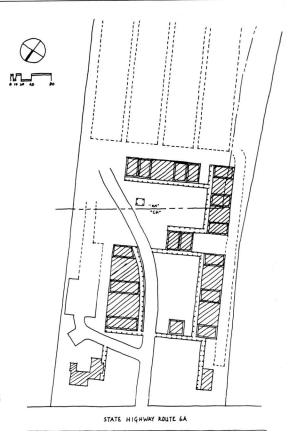

STATE HIGHWAY ROUTE 6A

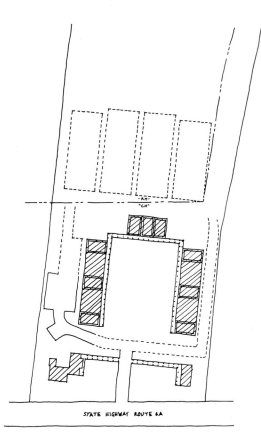

STATE HIGHWAY ROUTE 6A

Site plan alternatives

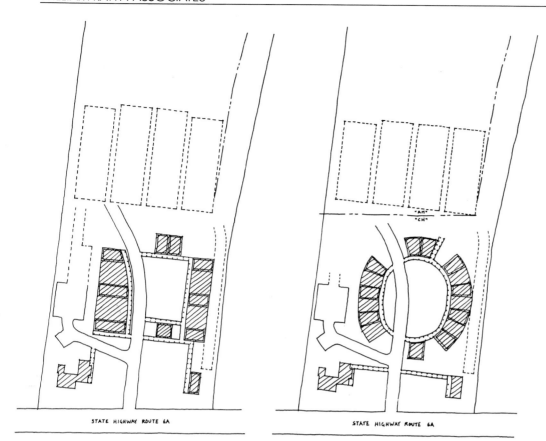

STATE HIGHWAY ROUTE 6A

STATE HIGHWAY ROUTE 6A

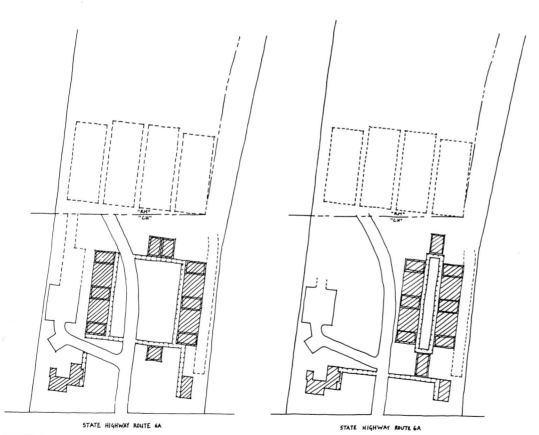

STATE HIGHWAY ROUTE 6A

STATE HIGHWAY ROUTE 6A

COST ESTIMATES

C&J's construction division prepared preliminary cost estimates. The builders said construction would exceed $100 per square foot. This figure seemed high to Rawn, and he offered to put together a "less articulated version" to save money. The architects also saw this standstill as an opportunity to get away from an approach they considered too historicist. To reduce the price, they simplified both the forms and the materials, creating a sparse but strong sculptural attitude for the buildings' front façades. They wanted to create effects that would be true to the spirit of the style without imitating specific ornamental details.

The architects presented these sample elevations to Corcoran, but he was not interested in the simplified version. They had eliminated so much detail that the scheme looked plain to him. Rawn declared, "We would have been willing to pursue it as an idea if the developer had wanted us to, but I had to admit that the alternative was not as interesting as the more articulated scheme."

Studies for simplifying the elevations

Design as a Tool for Competitive Edge.

Corcoran did not want to tone down the idea, despite the cost. The developer believed that the added component of historic detail at The Village Center would give his project an edge. The original scheme had become both a matter of pride and of business competition, as many other housing developments were also angling for conference business. He also felt that a better-quality project would convince more upscale businesses to locate there, even if the rents were slightly higher.

"A marketing consultant would have advised us to bring the project in for less, maybe $60 a square foot, and ask for less rent," he stated. "But we've learned that if you really try to do the right thing from a design point of view, it usually will pay for itself (as long as it's appropriate to the market you're in). I'm going to do the best that I can."

The developer directed the architects to stay with the University of Virginia design concept, even to the point of including a dome at one end, as in the original. However, this particular feature later proved to be too expensive to include.

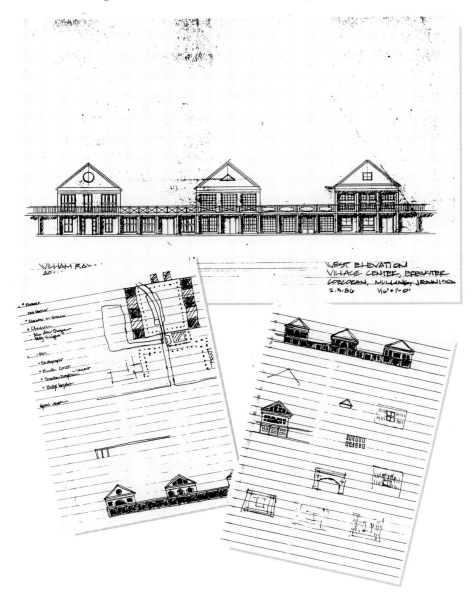

DESIGN DEVELOPMENT
March–June 1986

The design is revised to keep costs down while preserving the concept. To initiate the town Historical Committee's review, a submission has to include fully developed elevations of each building surface. The architects create a set of presentation drawings that form the basis of working drawings, if approved.

The architects revised the original scheme only slightly to keep costs down, while maintaining the proportions and the modulation of surfaces favored by the developer. They achieved this by:

• Reducing the amount of molding (to limit their reliance on complex carpentry).

• Making simpler patterns of openings in wall surfaces.

• Using geometric forms to create pediments with large, straightforward columns and eliminating complex entablatures and fascia pieces.

Next, the team studied in detail the architectural ramifications of the scheme. Still to be resolved were questions such as:

• How to integrate the two parts of a commons (divided by the highway).

• How to treat special building corners.

• How to link the project with the housing development.

• How to build the arcade interconnecting the quadrangle of buildings.

A rendered site plan showing the quadrangle of buildings linked by an arcade, integrating the two parts of the site.

The architects then changed their focus and began to consider the larger picture; they evaluated whether the posture of the Center should be picturesque or monumental. Traditional Cape Cod town centers date back to eighteenth-century villages and feature quaint, meandering paths that seemingly get lost among small buildings. Residents and tourists alike treasure this environment. Yet both C&J and Rawn were seeking an image that was going to distinguish this project from the others. And the "new traditional shopping village" was itself becoming so common as to constitute a new stereotype.

The architects resolved to use formality "to create a perceivable, larger order." They

realized that the creation of a strong set of building walls would yield a backdrop against which they could play off special buildings within the bulk. This site-plan approach was also well suited for the stately Greek Revival architectural style. The final design consisted of two parallel buildings on either side of the commons, each with a clear rectangular volume for the lower floor. Inside each was an open column grid. Above this uniform base, a second story was placed at six intervals, to create the appearance of six pavilions.

For reasons both economic and form-related, the pavilions were built with repeating structural features; five of them incorporated identical service

cores (stairs, bathrooms). The sixth was designed to be more elaborate—it would serve as an eatery as well as a link to the sales office. The arcade defined a ten-foot-deep zone, an area of special treatment that has helped to give the ensemble of buildings its unique character. The highly articulated decoration that was applied to the front façades wrapped around the building corners at the second-story levels. Altogether the complex included about 30,000 sf of retail and office space and 15,000 sf of basement and storage space.

One objective of the overall design was to achieve as much transparency as possible for the walls near to the sales office/check-in center, to support its function as a "lobby" for the

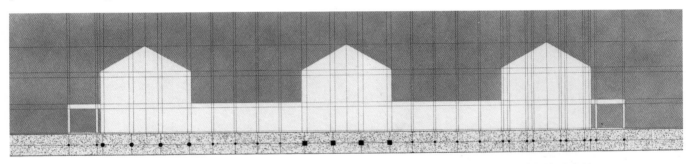

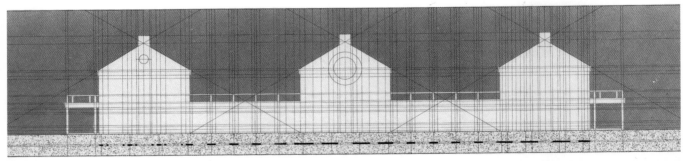

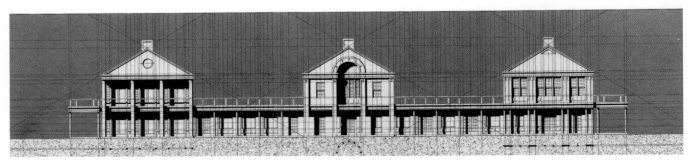

resort. At first, the architects tried placing a courtyard between the two main buildings, but they subsequently felt they needed a strong mass in that position in order to make the quadrangle work. The solution was a pavilion having a two-story volume composed mostly of glass on its side and front face. Visitors are able to see into the pavilion from the parking area and sales office, and can also see through it onto the quad. Although mostly transparent, the volume provides a solid mass that anchors the corner. The parking lot for the sales office is located in back of it; therefore, the buildings present a grand facade to Route 6A passersby and screen the view of parking from the road.

Renderings of the geometric framework show how the architects used formality "to create a perceivable larger order."

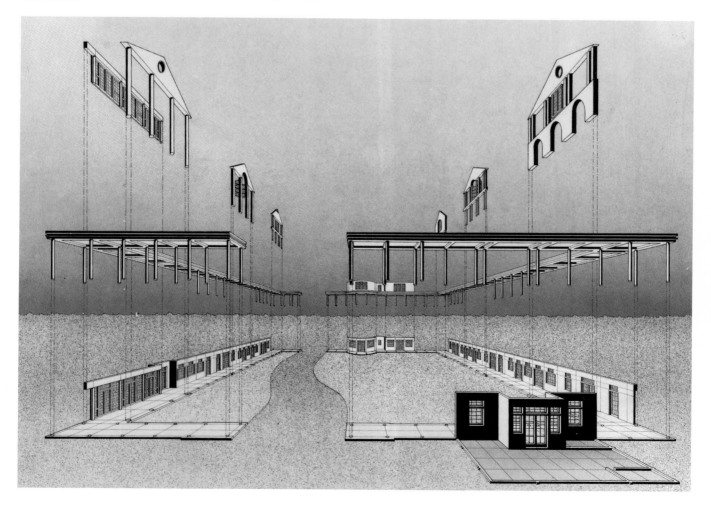

HISTORICAL COMMITTEE REVIEW
July 1986–July 1988

The Historical Committee approves the scheme on the first try but the parking layout is denied a zoning variance. When the one-year approval expires and the scheme is resubmitted, the Committee, which has new members, rejects the project as too massive for the site. Eventually the developer agrees to a smaller building. The revised scheme maintains the original design concept and is approved.

FIRST HISTORICAL COMMITTEE REVIEW: July 1986

Bill Rawn defended the proposal to the Committee, along with project manager Joe Corcoran, Jr., representing the developer (his father), and Jim Tobin, president of The Ocean Edge Resort. To everyone's amazement, given the developer's past rejections by the Committee, The Village Center was approved after the Committee's first review by a vote of four to one.

One minor change was negotiated—the addition of windows to the back sides of the buildings. The Committee felt it was too harsh on neighboring property owners to turn a windowless back on them. Otherwise, Committee members had nothing but praise for the quality of the design. Rawn was pleased to make the change, which he agreed improved the design. The approval was good for one year.

WORKING DRAWINGS: September–December 1986

Rawn's office began work on the construction documents in September. The two buildings, to be on facing sides of the road leading to the resort, were planned for phased construction, but the plans would be submitted as a package to the building department for construction permit application. Over half of the required parking spaces extended onto C&J's abutting parcel zoned for residential use only. This meant that the project would require a zoning variance, an appeal process that is initiated once the building permit request is rejected for noncompliance with the zoning code.

C&J's construction division was the general contractor and had been involved throughout the design process, developing details, choosing building systems, and coordinating the landscaping. This phase of the process went quickly, and was completed by the end of the year. The working drawings and permit set were handed over to C&J, who would be handling the building department approval process since they had a friendly relationship with the department.

However, in May 1987, the zoning board of appeals denied the developer's request for a variance to build the parking lot. This unexpected turn of events caused a delay, while the developers debated among themselves whether or not to proceed with the construction of Building One with only the portion of the parking that was in compliance, or to pursue another strategy. Somehow during this period, the necessity of renewing the historical commission approval was overlooked, and the architects had to return to the Committee for another review.

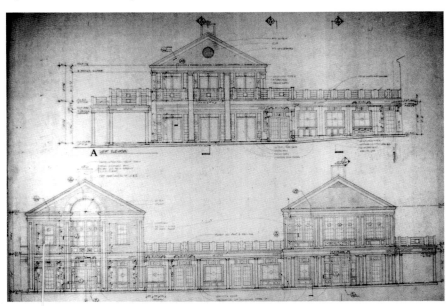

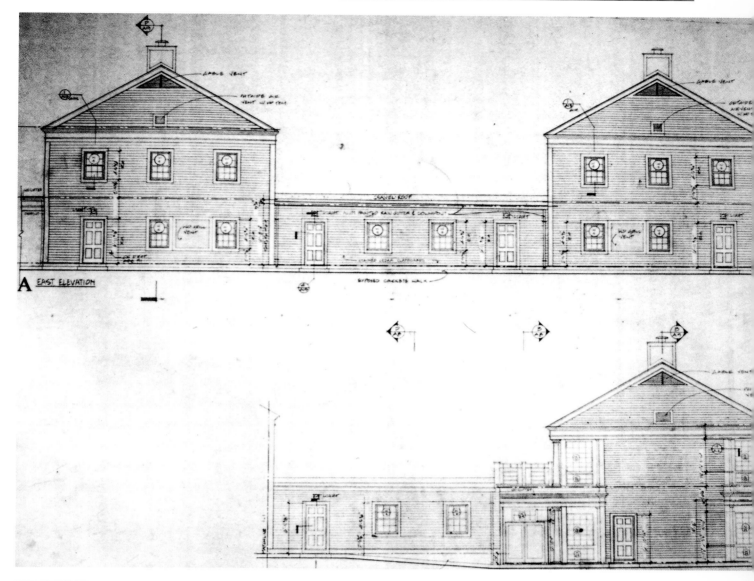

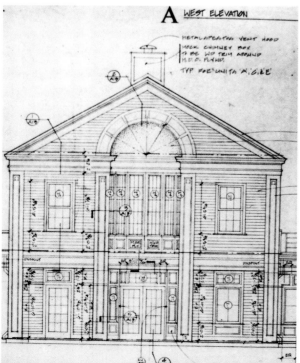

Opposite page and left: Working drawings of the west elevation.

Above: East elevation as approved by the Historical Committee in July, 1986.

SECOND HISTORICAL COMMITTEE REVIEW: September–November 1987

In September, on behalf of the developer, Rawn and colleagues resubmitted the previously approved scheme for what they believed would be an automatic renewal. But this time the Committee rejected their application by a vote of three to two. What had happened?

In the intervening year, two new members had been elected to the Committee, and both were in favor of measures limiting growth in the town. The design was commended, but with a proviso: it would need to be in an appropriate context. Opposition to the project boiled down to three issues:

• The size of the complex (two 176-foot-long buildings, each with 64-foot-long wings) was disproportionate to that of other buildings in the area and considered to be too intrusive.
• By creating an urbanized area, the complex would alter the character of the quasi-rural setting.
• The siting of the project was considered too close to the main street of Brewster, further altering the character of the setting.

The Committee may have been under the impression that the landscaping of the site was to be a formal design. A landscaping plan had not yet been part of the submission, yet the strong symmetry of the architecture must have suggested that any planting would echo this symmetry. The Committee suggested that the developer consider a naturalistic landscape design using indigenous plants.

The developers agreed with these suggestions and authorized the architects to draw up a

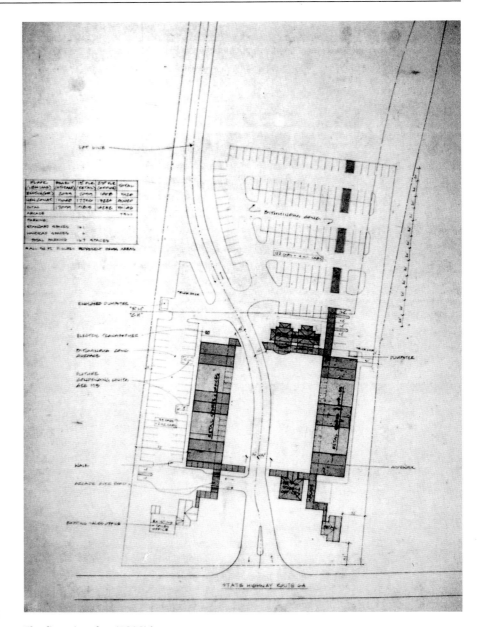

The first site plan (1986) included parking in the parcel zoned for residential uses.

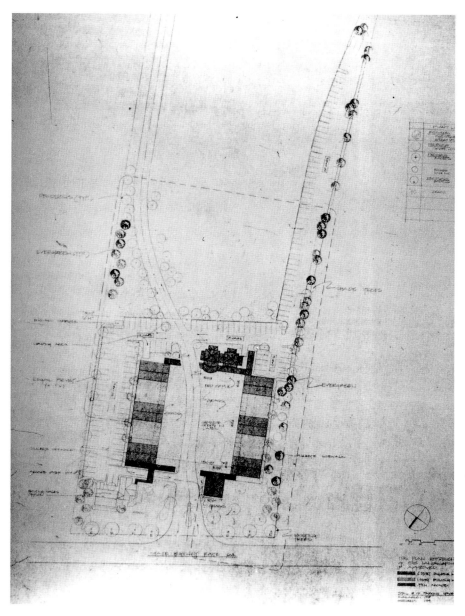

The second site plan (1987) shows revised parking and landscaping.

landscape plan. Their intent was to assimilate the buildings to their natural surroundings, and thereby soften the impact of the size of the buildings. Trees and other plants would also screen the view from the highway.

Rawn returned to the Committee in November with the new plan. But permission to build was still denied; the development, in the opinion of the Committee members, was too dense for the site. Aware of the hardship the denial would cause the developer, the Committee accounted for its decision on the grounds that construction of the project would be a detriment to the public welfare.

Appeal. This time the developer, contending that the Committee had overstepped its authority, appealed the decision to the Regional Commission. Corcoran's position was that he could, as of right, build a structure of unobjectionable appearance, and of the chosen size on the chosen site. The town Committee, in his opinion, was charged only with control of how buildings should look, not of how big they should be or where they should be. Corcoran agreed that the town needed to preserve open space, but he argued that it needed development too, if it were in good taste.

His effort was to no avail, however. The chairman of Brewster's Historical Committee, Michael Shay, sat on the Commission and was a popular and persuasive spokesman for the town's position. There had been a lot of commercial development in Brewster, and its citizens wanted to slow down the pace. The Commission advised C&J to work out a compromise with the town.

Redesign. Neither architect nor developer knew what to do next. Exploring his options, Corcoran asked Rawn to study an extreme solution locating all parking for both buildings on the commercially zoned parcel. The architects tested this plan and found that there would be enough room, but only if all available open land, including the quad, were filled with parking spaces. Rawn recalls how difficult it was to present what he knew to be a terrible scheme, but he trusted the developer and knew he would not implement it.

Developers and architects were at an impasse. Finally, Rawn recalls, Corcoran said, "OK, let's appease everyone." First, the architects looked at what they had to do to keep parking away from the residential zone and out of sight of the road. This would mean putting parking all along the "panhandle." However, even

this scheme would not provide the number of parking spaces required by code for the amount of retail space in the project. It became clear that the only solution was to reduce the density of retail.

What could be eliminated from the buildings and yet allow them to retain the integrity of the original scheme? Rawn's solution was to remove the second-story arcade, the first-story retail spaces lining the arcade between buildings, and the basement spaces under them. This would reduce the building's overall length and actual mass. A visual sense of continuity among pavilions was achieved via the arcade. Trellis landscaping was added to the now-open arcade to screen the view from the road toward the parking behind the building and to further soften the impact of the scale of the complex.

The entire wing that was to be

opposite the sales office was also eliminated. Its intended function had been formal—to be a symmetrical entry to the complex, as viewed from the highway. Later, the architects acknowledged that the removal of this portion of the building actually strengthened the design. The roof of the arcade would form an uncovered balcony linking the second stories of the pavilions. Retail space would extend to the second stories as well, originally reserved for only office space. Corcoran envisioned that this would give the place a more urban feeling, with more opportunities for people to wander and look up, out, across, or down at each other.

THIRD HISTORICAL COMMITTEE REVIEW: July 1988

The proposal was unanimously approved.

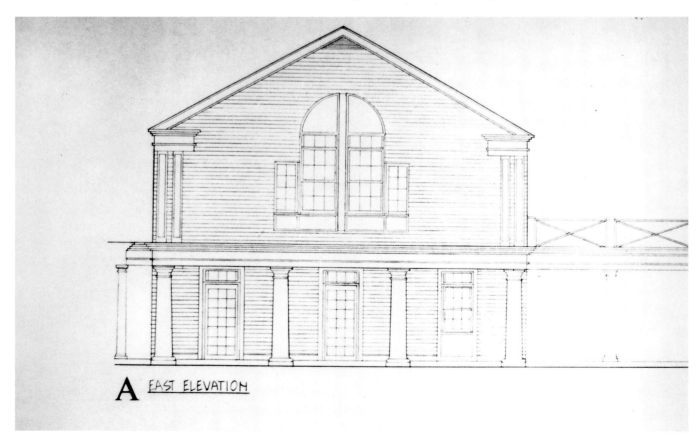

A EAST ELEVATION

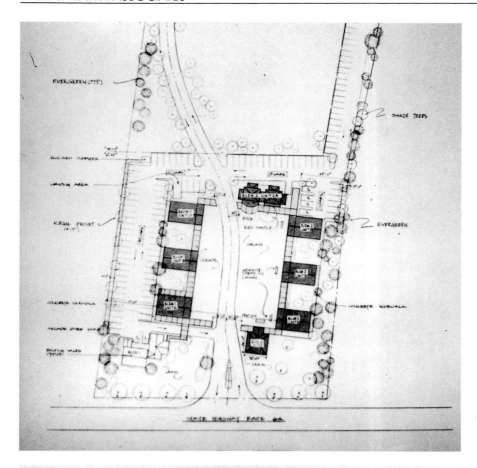

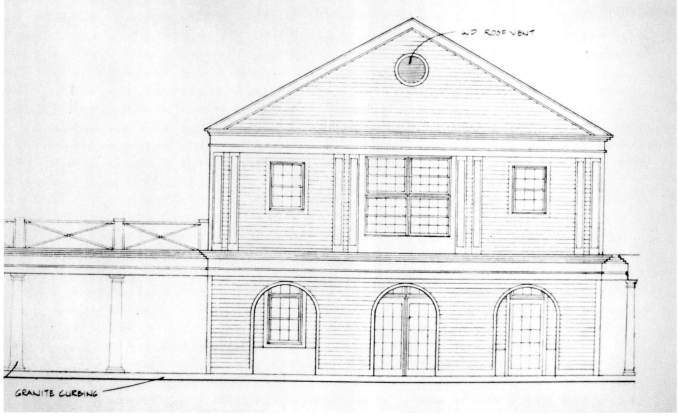

Opposite page and below: Drawings of the revised design approved by the Historical Committee in September, 1988.

The final site plan, left, shows the reduced scale of the buildings.

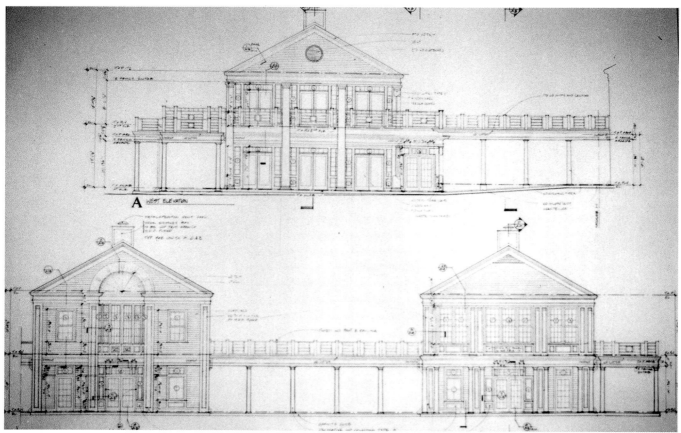

CONSTRUCTION DOCUMENTS
August–September 1988

A zoning variance was no longer necessary for either building. A set of permit drawings for Building One were completed rapidly during August and submitted to the building department soon after Labor Day. Not a day was wasted, as it appeared that a moratorium on all construction might soon be imposed in that part of the Cape until a stronger regional growth policy could be implemented. At the end of September 1988, construction documents for the project went out to bid.

Final building elevations and details, from the working drawing set.

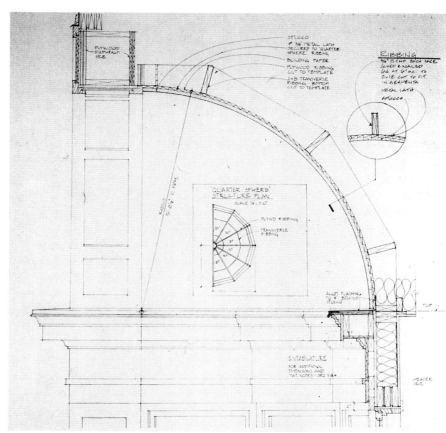

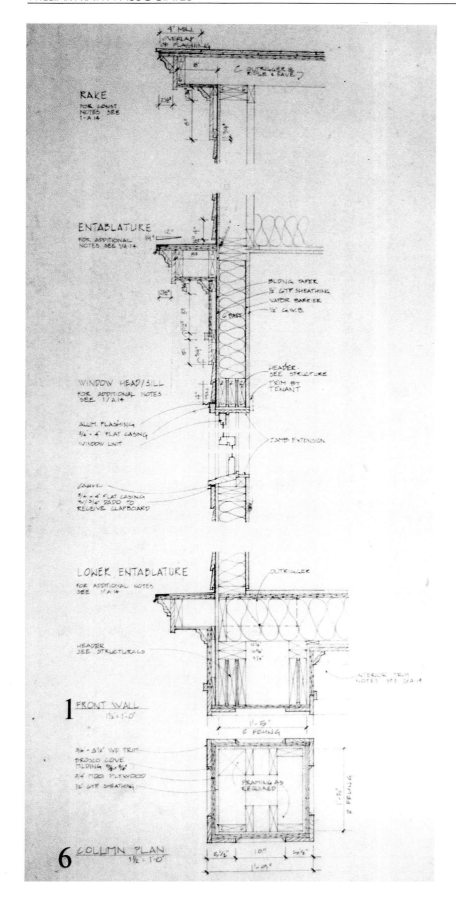

OBSERVATIONS

To function as a village center, a mall must have more than just a stately appearance; it must embody the values of the community.

- The historic district guidelines led to higher quality design by influencing the developer to hire a better architect and use better materials than are typically utilized for commercial buildings. Ironically, the design concept based on the historic model became the driving force in the process, inspiring the developer to spend money on decorative features with no commercial or functional value.

- "Through the design process for The Village Center, the developer improved his image and reduced animosity between himself and the town," says Rawn. "Corcoran's willingness to cooperate with the historical committee put to rest the town's fears of being overwhelmed by large scale, honkey-tonk development." These fears are not ungrounded—C&J owns so much land in Brewster that anything it does has a strong impact on the town's growth. Brewster already suffers intense traffic jams during peak vacation months, and developments such as the C&J conference center threaten to make such congestion a permanent fact of the town's life. So it is not surprising that the historical committee would want to protect any power it had to control this developer's activities.

- Prompted by the sense that unplanned growth was getting out of hand, the historical committee acted "to promote the general welfare," and used the design review process to evaluate not just the architectural merits of the building, but also how and where it could fit into the community. The committee had assumed the role of town planner, but its authority to make land-use planning decisions was ambiguous. For any municipal agency review to be meaningful, the ways in which new buildings are going to affect the public welfare must be spelled out in advance. Evaluation of development plans on a site-by-site basis is not a substitute for comprehensive planning.

- The urbanization of many rural and suburban areas is not the result of planning policy, but, in part, due to the proliferation of malls. In suburbia, where, proverbially, there is no place to go, malls provide a community focus and serve as de facto town centers. With the increased competition among malls, many developers now see the benefits of creating places where people are going to visit and might end up shopping too. But to develop a building with public-minded qualities requires a design process that looks beyond short-term profit and respects both the integrity of the architecture and the community in which it is going to exist. "To do so," says Rawn, "not only requires a long-range perspective, but also a sensibility that distinguishes between architectural fashion and what is appropriate in a specific context." The creation of shopping centers with public amenities is more expensive, as it involves quality materials and details, and the inclusion of noncommercial features. "If you try to do the right thing, to build tastefully," proclaims Corcoran, "it will pay for itself in the long run."

- One reason for the success of this project, according to Rawn, is that Corcoran is a visionary developer and takes the long view. When C&J successfully converted an obsolete public housing project to a mixed low- and moderate-income community, it also provided a new commercial mall on a public open space, resembling a village green, where people could congregate. "You have to think about how people are going to live," says Corcoran. The role of such developments as catalysts for the revitalization of urban neighborhoods is certain. As developers increasingly include subdivisions with malls, they will play a similar role in shaping the urbanization of suburban areas.

VILLAGE CENTER □ BREWSTER, MASSACHUSETTS

Perspective views of The Village Center as seen from Old King's Highway.

FIRESTATION FIVE

A CIVIC BUILDING IN THE COUNTRY

The process by which noted architect Susana Torre was commissioned to design a new firestation in Columbus, Indiana, and the way in which the eleven-member building committee's participation in the design process affected the final building is the focus of this case study. Columbus's collection of sophisticated buildings by internationally known architects is a source of civic pride. The design of this building had to acknowledge the city's unique architectural context, its history of innovation in firefighting equipment and facilities, and the rural qualities of the site in a subdivision at the city's edge. The building also had to satisfy the subdivision's design guidelines. Although Columbus may be a unique place, this case illustrates that an institution or group needs to understand what it means to be a client on a project that aims at something beyond utilitarian structure. While there are many participants in the creative process, it is the role of the architect to ultimately give the project coherent form.

PROJECT OVERVIEW

Project A 6,000 sf firestation for a suburban subdivision.

Architect Torre Beeler Associates (formerly Susana Torre), New York, New York, in association with Wank Adams Slavin Associates, New York, New York.

Client The City of Columbus, Indiana.

Charge To create a state-of-the-art firefighting facility with an appropriate civic image.

Issues ✔ Use of a limited competition to commission a distinctive design and qualify for foundation support of design fees.

✔ Creating a framework of communication between the eleven-member client committee and the architect. Determining who makes design decisions.

✔ Using design to support the goals of the institution, such as encouraging equal opportunities for women firefighters.

✔ Accommodation of both equipment needs and the residential image desired by the client in a form that expresses the building's public importance and is integrated with the natural setting.

✔ Renegotiation of a fixed budget in light of the subsequently developed program and design concept.

Duration Sixteen months from competition to completion of working drawings (September 1983–December 1984).

Cost $1,000,000.00 for construction.

TIMELINE

YEAR 1

PREPROJECT PLANNING
(Architect selection)

PROGRAMMING

SCHEMATICS

DESIGN DEVELOPMENT

DOCUMENTATION &
CONSTRUCTION

YEAR 2

CASE STUDY ENDS

YEAR 3

YEAR 4

YEAR 5

BACKGROUND

Being invited to design a building in Columbus, Indiana, is like being enrolled in an architectural hall of fame. With the help of the Cummins Engine Foundation, this southern Indiana agricultural community (population: 32,000) has acquired a collection of over fifty public buildings by internationally known architects. Over half of these are public institutions—schools, firestations, and libraries. "The town has become a sampler of modern architecture," says Teree Donoe, planning director for the city. Columbus may be unique, but much can be learned from this community's experience of working with well-known architects to produce distinguished civic architecture. In this case study, the city's learning process was perhaps more important than the finished building itself.

When Susana Torre was selected as the architect for a new firestation in a subdivision of Columbus, she soon discovered that the commission was not a mandate for design freedom. The client, an eleven-member committee, played an active role in deciding what the final appearance of the building would be. This raises questions about the role of the client in the design of a building meant to be more than just a utilitarian structure. Who makes the final decisions about aesthetics: client or architect? To understand the context for this project, it is necessary to first describe the role played by the Cummins Engine Company and the Cummins Engine Foundation in having made this project possible in the first place.

THE CUMMINS ENGINE FOUNDATION

The Cummins Engine Company, a manufacturer of diesel engines and the largest employer in Columbus, has played a major role in cultivating the architectural richness of this community. Since 1957, the company has through its Foundation provided $10 million in architectural design fees for public buildings, and has inspired the raising of an equal amount by private efforts, undertaken without Foundation assistance. Under the direction of the Cummins chairman, J. Irwin Miller, this effort began with the payment of the design fees for new public schools, in order to provide an alternative to postwar prefabricated facilities.

The philosophy behind this philanthropy has been, "Hands off design and construction." What has evolved is a heightened public appreciation of quality architecture, both old and new. Tom Harrison, a consultant to the Foundation, has said, "This [appreciation] started out with one person, but the thing has rubbed off on many members of the community, affecting the way people think about design and how to do something better." However, with innovation comes experiment and risk. Design flaws in some of the new school buildings left the citizens of Columbus wary of "celebrity" architects from "outside" who leave their small town with huge bills for repairs and maintenance.

The town learned that the answer to this predicament was not to do without these architects (as one school board tried to do), but to learn how to work with them to get better results. As one resident observed about the schools in a recent interview, "I see architecture as an evolution of how the community views its schools. Over time, people in education became more sensitive to how design works and how structures are maintained. That evolution, that learning process, puts Columbus at the forefront in creative learning environments for children."

This statement could just as easily have been made regarding Columbus's firestations. The city has a tradition of innovation in firefighting equipment and facilities, having been one of the first to use diesel aerial-ladder trucks and pumpers. In 1941, the city's Central Station introduced a U-shaped floor plan ("wrapped around" the apparatus room) that set a national standard for facility layout, still in use today. Recent stations, such as the one designed by architect Robert Venturi, indicate the city's appreciation of the fact that the design of these structures can address symbolic as well as the functional concerns.

The architectural context of Columbus. Clockwise from top: View of main street; City Hall, by Skidmore, Owings & Merrill, San Francisco, 1981; Firestation Four, by Robert Venturi, 1967; First Christian Church, by Eliel Saarinen, 1942.

THE CLIENT

The need for a another municipal firestation was created by the development of Tipton Lakes, a 1,200-acre residential community, owned in part by the Cummins Engine Company's Miller family. According to Will Miller (the son of J. Irwin Miller), during the 1970s the Miller family decided to undertake residential development in Columbus for two primary purposes: to address a perceived housing problem (which was subsequently solved by slowed growth in the 1980s), and to expand the community to the west and thereby strengthen the downtown.

Downtown Columbus sits on top of a bluff overlooking a river. Across the river to the south and west is floodplain. As the city grew, to the north and east, the downtown was left at one corner—not the city's center. The Miller family planned Tipton Lakes for the part of the floodplain nearest to the downtown, to encourage future growth of the community in that direction. Nonetheless, Tipton Lakes is separated from the city by two miles of floodplain, and cut off from it even further by railroad tracks.

The city had to extend fire protection services to the subdivision, and the Millers donated land for a new firestation with the condition that its design meet Tipton Lakes's guidelines. In this context, the mayor formed a building committee that decided to take advantage of the Cummins Engine Foundation Architectural Program, in order to commission an outstanding architect for the project.

The building committee consisted of eleven members. During the course of the long-term process of architect selection, design, and construction, there were many changes among the members, including the turnover of two mayors and three fire chiefs. Other committee members included city planning director Teree Donoe, city council members from both administrations, the executive vice-president of Tipton Lakes Development, and Tom Harrison, who served as liaison with the Foundation.

THE SITE

At its inception, Tipton Lakes Development consolidated several farms. Although the surrounding land use is still agricultural, the area is being rapidly suburbanized. Strip commercial developments have proliferated along the highway leading to downtown Columbus. The triangular site for the firestation is bounded by two major roads. The geometry of their intersection reflects the two cultures: One is on axis with the city grid, while the other follows the street pattern of the old farms.

Although the land was given to the city, as with any other building in the development, the firestation was subject to the development's design review process. According to developer Will Miller, "The review is not meant to produce architectural masterpieces; it's not a viable mechanism for that. But it prevents individual houses which will lower the overall quality of the development by controlling material selection, colors, the shape of roofs, setbacks, and other kinds of restrictions—to promote harmony between the building and the surrounding context." According to Miller, the city agreed that a representative from the Tipton Lakes design review committee needed to be on the firestation building committee to flag potential problems before they incurred great cost. Miller himself became personally involved toward the end of the process. Miller points out that, "What was unusual about this project was the developer's own design review requirement, and since the developer's family was involved in the Foundation, it looked as if the city had more direction from the Foundation than usual. I tried to be sensitive to this and not intervene more than necessary."

THE ARCHITECT

Susana Torre's New York-based firm, Torre Beeler Associates, was founded in 1988 and enjoys a mixed practice, including commercial, institutional, and residential projects. With a staff of seven, Torre plays an active role in each project, generally working with a design team of two to three staff architects. Torre established her first independent practice in 1978, and has combined practice with teaching at Columbia University, where she organized a symposium on "Hispanic Traditions in American Architecture." She also compiled and edited a collection of essays, *Women in American Architecture* (Whitney Library of Design, 1977). Torre's work reflects her wide range of interests and an aesthetic that expresses a combination of function, structure, and theory.

Aerial view of the site

PREPROJECT PLANNING
September–December 1983

As part of the competition/ selection process, Torre prepares a set of design guidelines and an analysis of the site to determine the location, orientation, patterns of circulation, and image of the building.

ARCHITECT SELECTION

In September 1983, Torre received a letter informing her that she was among seven architects invited to compete for the design of the new firestation. There were no formal requirements and no program was included. According to city planning director Teree Donoe, "The committee wasn't looking for design ideas, but to get a feeling for the person in general. Each architect was experienced with small buildings and had a record of completing projects within budget. Since all of them were qualified, the choice boiled down to intangibles."

At the interviews, the architects showed slides of their work and talked about themselves. Donoe recalls that much of the selection depended on whether or not the committee liked an architect's past projects. Donoe continues, "One brought in slides of very imaginative buildings, but they looked like something that would fit better in Southern California or Florida than

Indiana. It was hard to imagine that person's buildings looking good in a small town in the Midwest." The committee was also very concerned with the architects' philosophies of firestations—did the architects view them as monumental or residential-type buildings?

SUBMISSION #1: DESIGN GUIDELINES

Torre put together a booklet to introduce her firm and describe her design approach for the mid-November interview. Her preparation included the study of the firestation as a building type, visits to both urban and suburban stations, conversations with firefighters, and research at the library of the New York City Fire Department. Her objective was "to extend the city's tradition of innovation in firefighting techniques and facilities to the new building, in terms of state-of-the-art equipment, as well as the internal layout, relationship to the site, energy conservation, and aesthetics."

The criteria listed below were proposed by Torre and intended to provide a durable framework for the development of the design.

Site:
- Integration of building and landscape features.
- Preservation of existing trees.
- Utilization of "drive-through" potential of site.

Program:
- Efficient layout, with easy entry and exit of apparatus.
- Easy access to apparatus room from the living areas.
- Living areas zoned for visual and acoustic privacy.
- Provision of bedrooms and bathrooms for both men and women firefighters.
- Promotion of social interaction via group cooking and leisure facilities.

Energy Conservation:
- Taking advantage of passive solar design.
- Maximization of building's energy performance.

Construction:
- Use of durable materials and simple building details and systems to minimize cost and maintenance.

Aesthetics:
- Expression of the public importance of the building, without resorting to monumental scale.
- Acknowledgment of local vernacular styles.

The committee could not reach a decision, and asked to talk to three of the applicants again: Torre, Peter Eisenman, and Robert A. M. Stern. Tom Harrison pointed out that the Foundation would have given the committee another list of seven names, if necessary. So far that has never happened.

Above, left: A typical farm-house. Clockwise from upper right: a "model" firestation in a nearby town; Fire Station No. 14 in Atlanta, 1913; Fire Station No. 18 in Shreveport, 1973; Boston's Engine 33/ Ladder 15, 1888; and the York, Pennsylvania firestation, c. 1799.

SUBMISSION #2: SITE ANALYSIS

For the second presentation, in early December, Torre drew a set of diagrams to explain her analysis of the problems and options related to placing the firestation on the site. The design guidelines developed previously provided the basis for evaluation of each alternative. Key issues were:

- The public image of the building.
- Easy entry and exit for the apparatus trucks.
- Accessibility to the apparatus room from the living areas.

Torre's study also addressed the character of the living environment. Drawing on her research, Torre concluded that the two prevailing models were inadequate. One, a barracks, seemed too cold. The other, a home, seemed too intimate. As an alternative image, Torre proposed a "clubhouse," which she described as "a place that provides physical comfort and psychological support for the individual within a shared institutional setting that includes leisure activities as well as training."

THE COMMISSION

Late in December the committee selected Torre, by a one-vote majority. Planner Donoe recalls that they were impressed by her systematic approach to the problems at hand, and, given the candidates' equal qualifications, some felt it was time for Columbus to have a building designed under the program by a female architect.

Another important factor was the committee's sense that Torre would be flexible and easy to work with.

BUDGET

Based on the fact that the new firestation was to be approximately the same size as one recently built by the city and designed by local architects, the Mayor contended that the construction costs should be about the same—a maximum of $500,000. However, this figure did not take into consideration any building program, other than the number of firefighters and trucks, or that this site would require more grading and landscaping than the other.

SCOPE OF SERVICES

Torre was hired as the architect in charge of design and was expected to develop the program with the city fire chief. Wank Adams Slavin Associates, a firm with which she was associated at that time, was to provide the construction documents, as well as design the mechanical system.

Torre also hired a local architect, Charles Budd, as a site representative and as a consultant to review code issues.

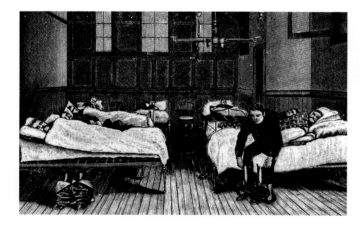 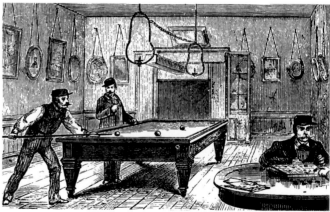

A firestation bunk room, New York City, 1889, left, and a sitting room, c. 1877, right, illustrate the alternative images of bunkhouse and clubhouse associated with firestations.

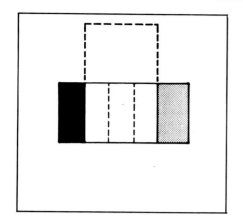

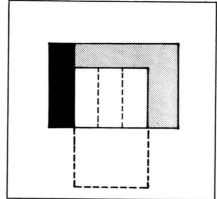

Studies of alternative building plans

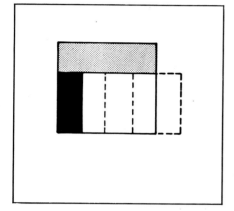

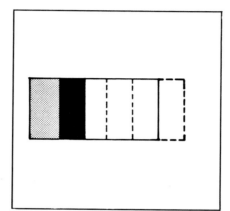

Diagrams of the site analysis: alternative building plans and access.

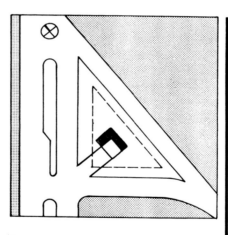

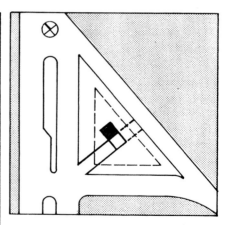

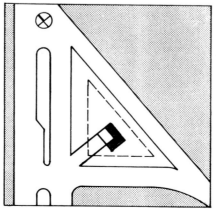

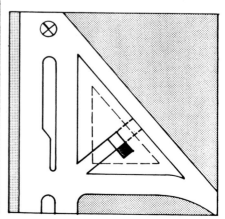

PROGRAMMING
January 1984
In putting together the program, Torre and fire chief James Miller analyze a range of issues, including functional necessities, qualitative factors, and matters such as the building's role in supporting the goals of the institution, e.g., promoting teamwork and equal opportunities for women firefighters.

Working closely with the fire chief, Torre spent a month developing the building program. They observed and analyzed the buildings and activities of three other firestations in town, and interviewed firefighters and staff that worked in them. Then they compared the strengths and weaknesses of typical stations in terms of layout, architectural features, environmental qualities, and maintenance factors. They also evaluated the program for the firestation the town had recently built.

PROGRAM SUMMARY
The final program summarized space requirements by category and function, and listed detailed requirements for each program element, specifying its location in the building, the other functional areas it should abut, desirable architectural characteristics, and support services required.

Torre notes, "Firestations are machines that have to work. The program is a very regulated set of relationships. Where things are in the building was dictated absolutely by how the machines functioned."

Lists of detailed requirements included:

- Items permanently connected to the building.
- Items related to building services.
- Items that were to occupy floor space, but would not be permanently attached.

Key Features. A basic description of the building emerged. It was to have a three-bay apparatus room, with accommodations for a staff of eighteen sharing three shifts.

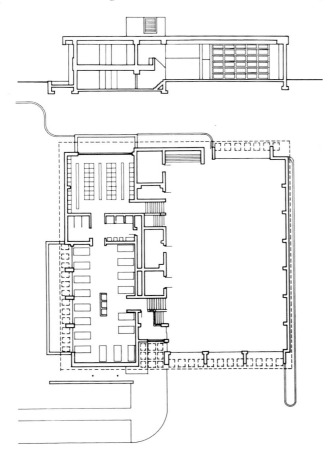

Plan showing clear separation of service areas and apparatus rooms

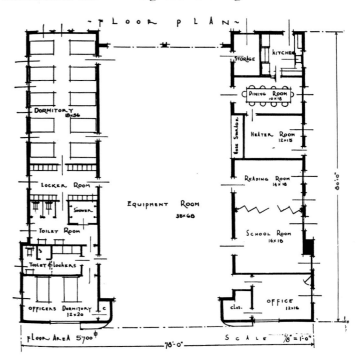

Plan of "drive-through" station in Burbank

Living quarters were to have a residential layout, with separate bedrooms for each firefighter per shift (a total of six bedrooms, each with three beds). One of these rooms was to have a private connection to the bathroom, to accommodate one woman firefighter. To test this plan, the architects developed a schematic layout of the dorm/bedroom before the rest of the building had taken shape.

Character. The programming study concluded that the building should have a residential character for two reasons: First, it was in a residential area, and second, firemen were to live there on short-term bases. Another conclusion was that although the

facility was to be state-of-the-art, many old-fashioned methods were still the best. For example, alternatives to the hose-drying tower, such as burying the tower shaft or eliminating the need for the tower altogether by using expensive, fast-drying hoses, were considered and rejected. The design did allow for the future expansion of equipment, however.

Zoning. Public and private activities were split into two zones—a fairly innovative decision at that time. Recognizing that at this site the firestation would be used as a community facility, the architects included in their design a room large enough for community meetings. Outdoor space was

also zoned for a range of public and private activities, including basketball and barbecues.

Budget. When the building committee reviewed the program in mid-February, it soon became clear that the project was turning out to be more costly than projected. At this stage, however, cost constraints were not carved in stone. The project was funded by Federal Revenue Sharing money, so as the design evolved, explains planning director Donoe, "the decision to raise additional funds did not require going back to the taxpayers, but was more a matter of shifting priorities and was negotiated through budget discussions between the mayor and city council."

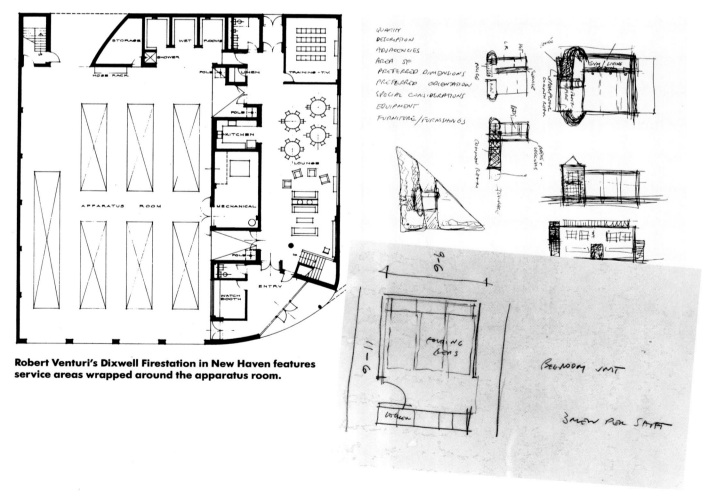

Robert Venturi's Dixwell Firestation in New Haven features service areas wrapped around the apparatus room.

Organization of program activities on the site, top; early studies for the bedroom module, bottom.

SCHEMATICS
February–March 1984

Torre's initial design is a modular masonry building with a simple curved roof that will achieve the objectives of keeping cost down, preventing the roof from leaking, facilitating future expansion, and incorporating the vernacular style of local buildings. This scheme has negative associations for some committee members and they ask the architect to revise the design.

Torre chose to work with a modular building system. The architects set up a planning grid based on a four-inch module and began studying alternative floor plans. Based on the site analysis, the building was located in one corner of the lot. Preliminary diagrams explored how to connect the two basic parts: house and garage. Torre's research on the building type showed that the relationship between these two parts was intrinsic to the institution—the designer cannot invent a new firestation floor plan but only explore variations on a theme.

At first, the sketches showed house and garage as separate, adjacent zones. However, this scheme required too much space. Next, the architects pulled the parts together, by trimming the excess space from around the vertical core and overlapping the squares. This basic strategy remained unchanged.

In mid-March the architects submitted the schematic design package, which closely followed the design criteria established in their initial proposals.

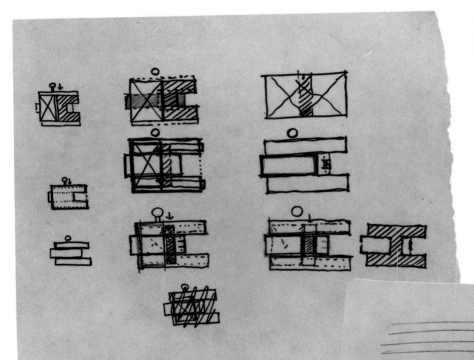

Planning grids, above, show alternative ways to connect the two basic parts of house and garage; sketch, right, studies locating the building to facilitate expansion.

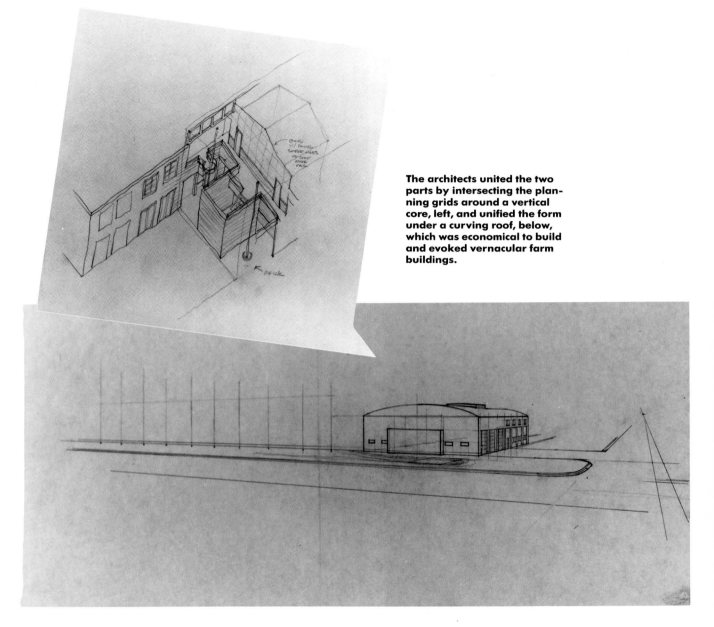

The architects united the two parts by intersecting the planning grids around a vertical core, left, and unified the form under a curving roof, below, which was economical to build and evoked vernacular farm buildings.

SITE PLAN

Integration of the building and the site was an important concern of both the developer and the design team. Landscape architect Cassandra Wilday developed a proposal for landscaping that acknowledged the differences in the scale and patterns of vegetation associated with the site's dual (rural and suburban) setting. The concept was to combine sturdy species of trees in large clusters, similar to those on farms, with more particularized planting along the main street-edge of the site.

The plan limited parking to one edge of the site, to preserve the site's natural character and to leave existing vegetation in place. A row of ginkgoes along the driveway would serve as a windbreak and continue the formal planting fronting the street-edge by creating a ceremonial wall along the entry.

Walkways from the parking lot were laid out in reference to the city street grid, while magnolia trees planted around them would be aligned with the planning grid of the building. Torre says that the juxtaposition of the two grids was intended "to create an informal landscape with an underlying formal order, suitable to a public building in a rural setting."

Another conceptual gesture was the conversion of an existing drainage ditch that cut across the site to a stone-lined channel, leading to a circular, stone catch basin with, possibly, a water jet.

BUILDING DESIGN

Hard-lined drawings illustrated the schematic design: a long, narrow building with masonry block walls, a simple curved roof, and a silo-like hose tower. This solution actualized the client's objective to express an "ordinary" rather than monumental style. Proposed materials included ground-face and glazed concrete blocks, insulated translucent panels, and standing seam metal roofing with a color finish.

The "house" portion of the building is split between two wings, and further zoned with public areas on the ground floor and in the living spaces above. Each bedroom has three pull-down beds and a small terrace. The yard between the wings (modeled more after a barnyard than a courtyard) provides firefighters with a private place to relax outdoors, as the building has no backyard.

The "house" is linked to the "garage" by a service core with stairs and the pole—a layout loosely modeled on a museum plan by Louis Kahn. The core provides privacy in the living areas as well as direct access to the apparatus room; it includes an indoor exercise room overlooking the apparatus room. According to Torre, "These functional elements were used to shape the spatial qualities of the building and therefore its form."

CLIENT RESPONSE

Although the eleven committee members made no immediate comment, planner Donoe recalls that Torre's first design "was generally disliked by the committee. Several members decided to go to New York to tell her about their concerns." Torre arranged to meet them at a restaurant that has spectacular views of Manhattan at night. As

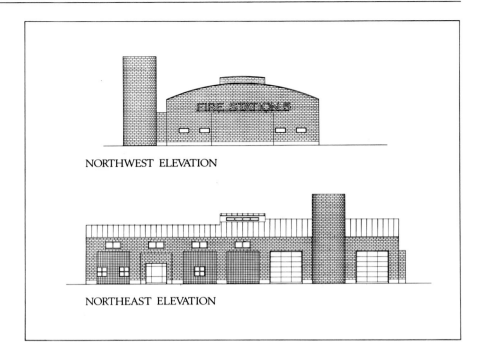

NORTHWEST ELEVATION

NORTHEAST ELEVATION

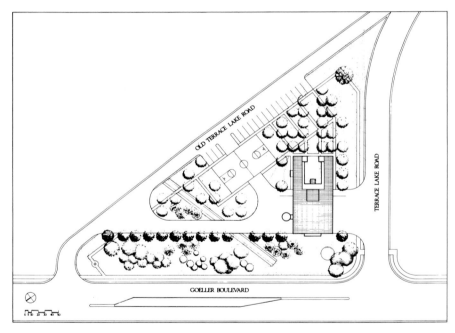

The schematic design submission consisted of a set of hard-lined drawings, clockwise from top left: Northwest elevation; first floor plan; second floor plan; site plan.

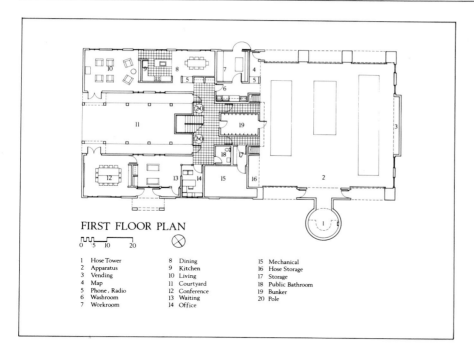

FIRST FLOOR PLAN

0   5   10   20   ⊗

1   Hose Tower   8   Dining   15   Mechanical
2   Apparatus   9   Kitchen   16   Hose Storage
3   Vending   10 Living   17   Storage
4   Map   11 Courtyard   18   Public Bathroom
5   Phone , Radio   12 Conference   19   Bunker
6   Washroom   13 Waiting   20   Pole
7   Workroom   14 Office

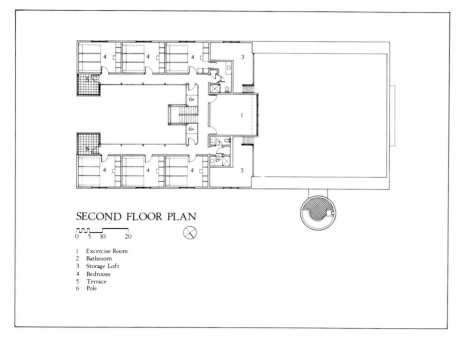

SECOND FLOOR PLAN

0   5   10   20   ⊗

1   Excercise Room
2   Bathroom
3   Storage Loft
4   Bedroom
5   Terrace
6   Pole

luck would have it, the committee members came to New York on a day when President Ronald Reagan was visiting. Torre was stuck in traffic, arrived late at the restaurant, and, due to heavy fog, there was no view—just a reflection of anxious faces.

"The mood was definitely uncomfortable at first," says Torre. "The members of the committee were worried that the scheme looked too finished. They didn't know how willing I'd be to make changes, how adamant I'd be about some things. Over dinner I reassured them that I was flexible and they finally relaxed. Then, the fog parted and there below us was this incredible view. It was like a sign!"

Two design features that disturbed committee members were the shape of the roof and the masonry block walls. The broad, curving roof reminded them of industrial buildings in the area, according to Donoe, evoking images "of those temporary buildings with corrugated metal roofs."

"Up close, you could see the ground-face block was more beautiful than brick," Donoe says, "but from a distance it looked like the inside of somebody's basement." When Torre pointed out to committee members that the material was similar to that used by architect Richard Meier for one of the city's public schools, she was informed that they did not like that school.

Donoe suggested that although architects find beauty in these materials, they generally hold negative connotations for people in the Midwest. Torre has said that, looking back, the experience taught her a lesson: to keep schematics looking schematic.

DESIGN DEVELOPMENT
April–June 1984

The key event of this phase is the transformation of the image of the building in response to the client's objections. The building committee and architect engage in a lengthy process of agreeing on the aesthetics of the exterior, in particular the size and color of the brick. With less client involvement, the internal layout is refined to improve efficiency.

In response to the client's concerns, Torre agreed to change the roof and to use brick instead of block for the walls, but she insisted that the brick be a larger size than typical. Still to be solved was how to reconcile the large scale of the garage and the smaller scale of the residential parts of the building.

"The garage is the major piece of the building, so you can't put it in the back, as in a house, and in this case the building doesn't have a back—sitting on a triangular lot, it's exposed on all sides," Torre explains. Having reconciled the two parts in plan, the problem now was how to integrate them in elevation. Her solution was to interrupt the facade by using the hose-drying tower as a transitional piece, juxtaposing the larger and smaller scale elements on either side of it.

CHOOSING A BRICK

The use of a large-sized masonry unit was a way of dealing with the scale of the entire building, Torre felt. She also liked the rich surface texture of the material. Her preference was for an 8″ (high) × 16″ (long) brick. Members of the building committee objected to that brick, as it is the same size as concrete block. They preferred a yellowish 8″ × 8″ brick. Torre objected, because that brick recalled the aesthetic of projects by another firm.

Client and architect met many times to discuss the size and color of the bricks, which were of particular concern to the developer. "It was a lengthy, involved process" recalls Donoe. To resolve the issue, the architects studied the alternatives in great detail. They considered nearly any brick that conformed to the module, and they looked at combinations of large and small bricks, comparing the visual characteristics of each pattern.

By the end of May, they had agreed on a pattern that combined a 4″ × 8″ with an 8″ × 16″ brick, but it turned out that the larger brick was unavailable and that the labor needed to create the pattern made the choice too expensive. Finally, they settled on a 4″ × 8″ gray brick, set in a standard running bond pattern.

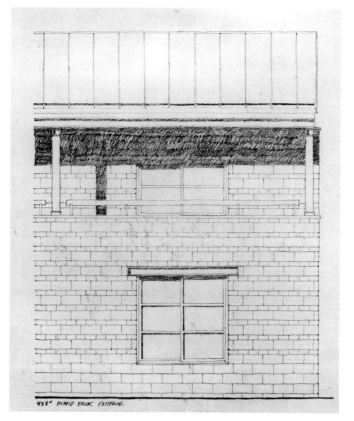

Brick studies. Opposite page: The 8″ × 16″ running bond jumbo brick pattern first proposed was rejected by the committee. Above: The 4″ × 8″ and 8″ × 16″ hybrid brick pattern of the second proposal, left, was approved and then rejected for cost reasons. The 4″ × 8″ running bond modular brick, right, is the pattern actually used.

This public entrance facade study with hybrid brick pattern combines running and stacked bonds.

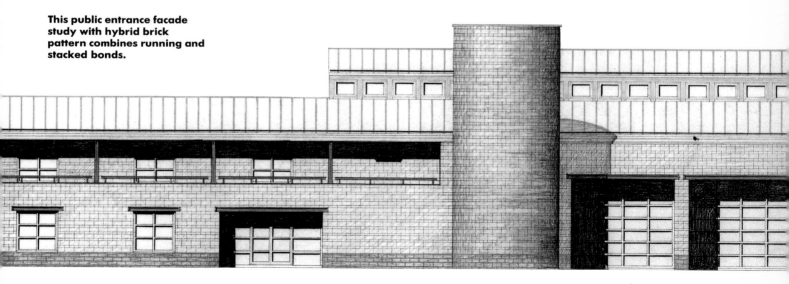

**Study for the
assembly of
column, metal
panel wall,
and roof in the
courtyard.**

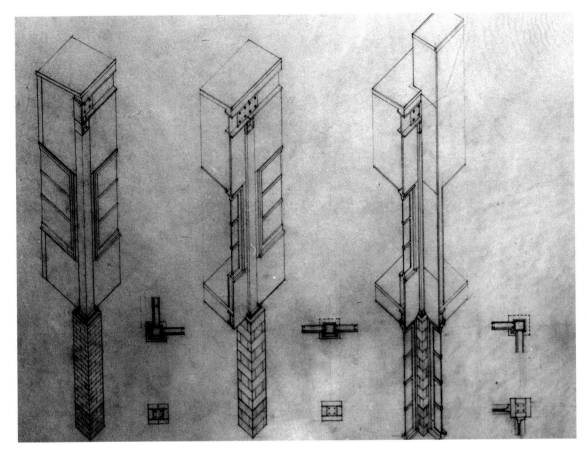

THE FAÇADE SYSTEM

Torre's aesthetic manages to
express both structure and
function, as well as purely visual
compositions. Just as the
building's two wings reflect the
organization of activities inside,
the details of the façade, such as
the exposed column capitals, are
an authentic articulation of
structure.

To expose the steel frame to
the outside, fireproofing is
applied to the inside wall of the
building, enabling the structure
to be technically outside. The
columns pass through the wall
and support the roof, clearly
showing that the masonry wall is
just providing enclosure and not
bearing any load.

Aesthetic considerations
prompted the relocation of the
entry; the decision had nothing
to do with programmatic
concerns. Likewise, the
architects' decision to clad the

hose-drying tower in brick rather
than metal was intended to
strengthen the composition of
the predominantly masonry
façade, not to signal a continuity
of either structure or function.

Torre explains the process of
arriving at the final design: "First
you have to go through
cumbersome, fussy studies to
finally get to the simple and bold
statement. There are things one
needs to draw to see what's
actually going on. I was looking
for an economy of means,
striving for the simplest, boldest
laconic expression—to be
eloquent with just a few things."

COLOR

Initially, Torre wanted to use
metal panels in two colors, red
and blue, to set off the hose-
drying tower, the stair tower, and
the walls facing the courtyard,
and to serve in contrast to the
gray bricks used everywhere

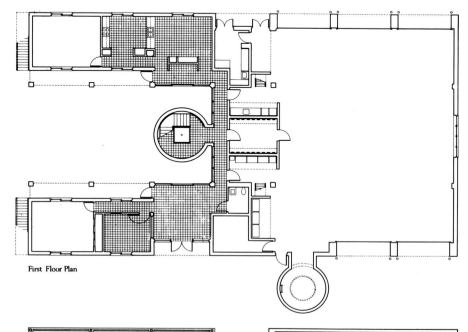

First Floor Plan

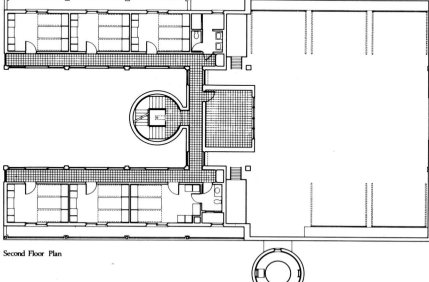

Second Floor Plan

From the design development presentation: Model showing the yellowish brick color scheme, top. First and second floor plans, bottom.

else. The area enclosing the trucks was to be clad in red, the hose-drying tower in blue—symbolizing fire and water.

When the developer objected to the color scheme because of the patriotic associations, the architects decided to use just the blue panel. They also changed to a yellowish brick color when they learned that the gray brick was not available in the size they had selected.

CUTTING COSTS

Towards the end of design development, a contractor was hired as a preconstruction consultant, to provide cost estimates. It was at this point clear that the initial budget had been unrealistic. Although more money was ultimately allocated by the city council, the overall size of the building had to be reduced, and some design features, including the formal landscaping, were lost. The architects trimmed all "fat" off the interior spaces, and essentially scraped inches off the entire length of the building.

Earlier in the year, fire chief James Miller had resigned. The next fire chief was not as enthusiastic but tried to work with the architects to tighten up the layout without sacrificing key components of the program, such as the bedroom with private-bath access for a female firefighter, or the large-sized kitchen for group cooking.

This meant paring down the dorm rooms to the functional minimum, as determined by the size of the beds. Torre points out that the design process started with the development of the schematic dorm concept during programming, based on the need for three, side-by-side pull-down beds; and it ended at the same level of examination—the dimension of the beds.

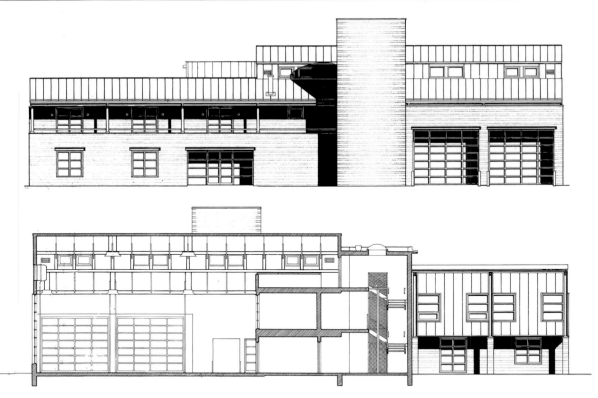

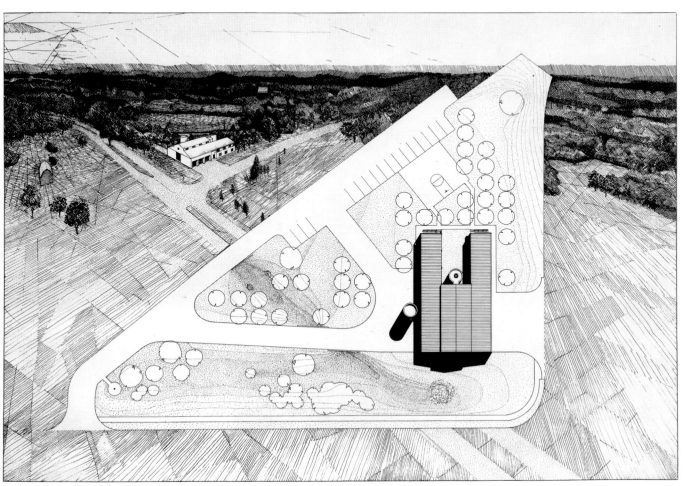

DOCUMENTATION AND CONSTRUCTION
July 1984—December 1985

The first bids come in too high and Torre has to revise the plans. But the key issue to be focused on in this phase of the project is not that changes are necessary, but the importance of cooperation and teamwork throughout the design and construction process.

Torre was the architect in charge of design, and Wank Adams Slavin Associates (WASA) was to develop the construction drawings.

Architect Charles Budd represented Torre in the field; his responsibilities included supervision, code review, and acting as a mediator on issues that impacted on the design, as they came up during construction. Torre found his contribution invaluable, especially after she ended her association with WASA partway through this project to start her own firm.

Foundation advisor Tom Harrison explains: "The project was nearly finished before Susana Torre was aware that there were something like twenty-seven items on the punch list. These were items which she couldn't settle alone, because the decisions had been made by the engineers at WASA. We finally got together and resolved things, but there were moments that were very uncomfortable."

Despite the moments of tension during design and construction, the final building is a source of great pride in the city. It is among a select group of buildings included in the itinerary of an architectural walking tour of the city and a popular destination for visits by school groups. Architect Torre was also invited to be among the first instructors in "Design Legacy," a private program started in 1986 for upper-level architecture students, to enable them to participate in a two-week seminar in the city. The topic of the 1986 workshop was the design of civic buildings.

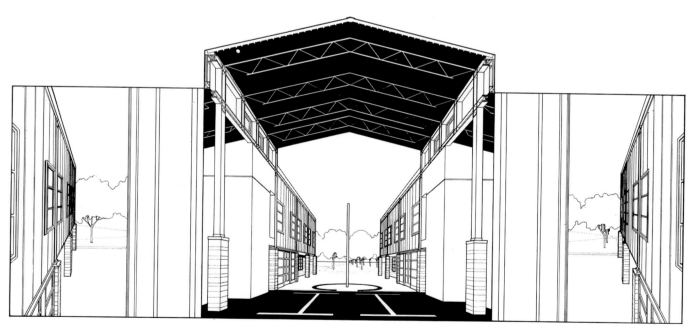

The final design: North elevation, top left; section through stair tower looking north, center left; conceptual site plan illustrating how the building bridges the rural and suburban setting, lower left; conceptual perspective through the building towards the courtyard, above.

OBSERVATIONS

A community learns about good design by participating in the design process.

- The design of a civic building, even a relatively simple one such as this firestation, can become complex, as it must represent the ideals of numerous interest groups. The push for architectural excellence in Columbus, which led to Torre's commission, has also evoked a strong response in the community—people care about good design. As a result, members of the client building committee wanted to actively participate in the shaping of the final product. However, having hired a distinguished architect to create an exceptional design, the client then needed to learn how to work with her to get a good result—how to participate in a design process that aspired to produce more than a utilitarian structure.

- Torre felt that her mandate was to contribute to the city's tradition of innovation both in architecture and in firefighting, yet the building had to respond to its small town setting as well. "Things aren't explicit, but everyone knows when something's not appropriate," Torre observes. "There are many participants in the creative process, but the role of the architect should be to provide formal coherence. Many people are concerned with the superficial coherence of a building—the building is seen as a consumer product. But participating in design is a different process from buying an item."

- The appearance of this building evolved in response to the client's concerns. "In my opinion it would have been better if we'd left Torre alone," says city planning director Teree Donoe. "The main issue is not whether I happen to like or not like any particular design or if anyone in the community does. Columbus has become a sampler of modern architecture and the architects should make the best statement of their ideas of design. The building should reflect the ideas of the architect, not the committee." Foundation advisor Tom Harrison agrees: "The client should be a part of the project, should have the right and responsibility of saying 'I don't think that will work,' but should stay out of aesthetics."

- Developer Will Miller sees it differently: "The architect does not have the right to be the final arbiter on all aesthetic issues. A good architect views himself as serving the client but also has an idea to sell. The architect has to convince the client that the aesthetic is effective. The best buildings result when the architect is skillful at communication with lay people."

- The client has an important role to play in the design process. A hallmark of Torre's approach is to base design on a thorough analysis of the building type and program. But when the client saw the schematic design, the committee members were not happy with it. Torre learned that the drawings should not have appeared to be so finalized. Design drawings have to be fairly well developed, however, before most clients can respond to them. Developer Miller observes: "Clients should take time to learn about how architects work, the pressures they're under, and what the design process is all about. On the other hand, a lot of architects misunderstand the client's point of view. It's important to know how to manage expectations and explain options."

- The value of a project can lie more within the design process itself as a learning experience than in the final product. The committee selected an architect partly on the basis of how easy it would be to work with the applicants. Tom Harrison suggested that perhaps "ease" should not have been such a consideration—that working with a committee can be difficult, and strained relationships do not necessarily produce poor results. However, Donoe points out, "A lot of care has to be taken in Columbus about who the real decision makers are. You can't keep up public support for a lot of projects if people think decisions are being dictated by the Foundation. As the Foundation liaison, Tom Harrison is skillful about letting other people make decisions and get ownership of the project. We may have got a better building if he had, but it would not have been better for the city."

The finished building, clockwise from top: View from the sidewalk; the apparatus room; view inside the stair tower; the courtyard with stair and fire pole tower.

WASHINGTON COURT

A MODERN BUILDING IN A HISTORIC DISTRICT

The design of this apartment house in New York City's
historic Greenwich Village today epitomizes contextual
urban design, but it caused an angry public debate in 1984.
Community groups saw the building—the first major new
construction since the Village became a landmark district
in 1969—as an opportunity to set a precedent for future
development. Architect James Stewart Polshek's philosophy
is that "new buildings must reflect the future as well as the
past." The architect's initial concept was admittedly
modernist, which, due to neighborhood pressure and
negotiations with the Landmarks Preservation Commission,
evolved to reflect more "historical" references, but in an
abstract way. This case study examines the issues: What is
appropriate architecture in a historic district; and what is
the purpose of historic districts?

PROJECT OVERVIEW

Project 67,500 sf low-rise housing with twenty-eight apartments and ground-floor commercial space.

Architect James Stewart Polshek & Partners, New York, New York.

Client Philip Pilevsky, Philips International Holding Corporation, New York, New York.

Charge To build new infill housing on a vacant lot in a historic district.

Issues ✔ Necessity of siting the building directly over a subway tunnel and constructing less than the allowable density in order to restore the city fabric through "contextual" design.

✔ To create a design that is "appropriate" in the historic architectural context without producing a pastiche of traditional details.

✔ To develop a socially responsive residential building type with architectural character, at a reasonable cost and in compliance with the building code.

✔ Community desire to set a precedent for future development.

Duration One year from start to completion of working drawings (January–December 1984).

Budget $9.5 million construction cost.

TIMELINE

YEAR 1 — YEAR 2 — YEAR 3 — YEAR 4 — YEAR 5

PROGRAMMING
SCHEMATIC DESIGN
LANDMARKS PRESERVATION COMMISSION REVIEW
DESIGN DEVELOPMENT/ CONTRACT DOCUMENTS
CONSTRUCTION
CASE STUDY ENDS

BACKGROUND

The process through which architect James Stewart Polshek went to build the first new housing in New York City's Greenwich Village since that neighborhood was legally named a landmark in 1969 illustrates many of the problems of designing infill projects in historic districts. With the best of intentions, the architect replaced a parking lot with a building that was accommodating to the surrounding context and provided much more amenity than the standard developer's brick box. Yet the design and the architect were reviled by community preservationists who wanted to fill the gap in the neighborhood with a building of a more traditional style.

On one level, the issue at hand was whether architecture in historic districts should embody traditional details or instead draw on them abstractly as a means to express modern social concepts. But perhaps the debate over style really masks basic political and economic conflicts and the shortcomings of city planning.

"Change is so permanent a feature of city life that one almost expects yesterday's parking lot to be tomorrow's skyscraper," a *New York Times* reporter recently wrote. Many New Yorkers feel overwhelmed by the pace of development, their lack of power with respect to it, and the sense that no one listens. Consequently, local planning and preservation efforts have gained wide support. Yet in this case, residents concerned with preserving their environment became vehemently opposed to a design that showed uncommon respect for the neighborhood context, because it did not include specific traditional elements in a particular style.

Greenwich Village residents have a reputation for being vocal participants in local planning issues, particularly regarding historic preservation. After half a century of commercial development in the area, local community groups welcomed the idea of new housing, but also saw the project in question as a potential precedent for new construction in the neighborhood. Because the building is in the Greenwich Village Historic District, the design had to be approved by the city's Landmarks Preservation

Commission (LPC). Thus, concern over the future of the site was channeled through the LPC approval process, the first step for any developer.

LANDMARKS PRESERVATION COMMISSION

The New York City Landmarks Preservation Commission was created in 1965, to preserve areas and buildings that contribute to the historical or architectural quality or cultural importance of the city. Currently, over fifty neighborhoods have been legally designated landmark districts, including Greenwich Village. The law gives the Commission the right to review all proposals for alterations and new construction in these districts, to determine if they are "appropriate." Without a certificate of appropriateness, an owner may not apply for a building permit.

One of the unusual aspects of the approval process is that applications for major works are reviewed during public hearings, at which anyone who wishes to may speak. In addition, the LPC solicits the recommendation of community boards, whose members are appointed by the city council and borough president and advise city agencies on local planning issues. In the past ten years, the community boards have come to wield significant power in land-use planning in the city.

Once an application to the LPC has been made, a public hearing is scheduled. At the beginning of each month, the community boards are advised of the projects that fall within their districts. During the month, for a particular project, the community board's landmarks committee will hold a public hearing regarding the project and invite the applicant to make a presentation. At the end of the month, the committee then presents its findings to the full board, which votes on its recommendation.

The Commission considers the community board's recommendation, but does not have to follow it. If, for any reason, six of the eleven appointed commissioners cannot agree on a ruling, or if a community group requests more time or additional information, a decision may be postponed until the following month's hearing.

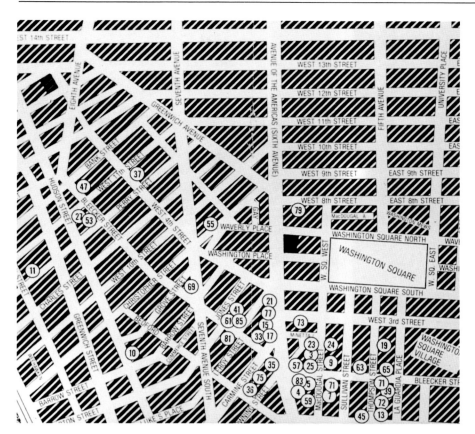

THE CLIENT

Philips International Holding Corporation, owned by Philip Pilevsky, is a New York-based company primarily involved in commercial real estate development, mostly shopping centers. The firm had acquired the reputation of being "flippers"—of holding onto properties until their value increased and then selling them without having made many improvements. However, when Philips purchased the parking lot site in Greenwich Village, at the end of October 1983, its intention was to build housing, in part because that was the only use that would be allowed without a variance.

The developer's experience with housing had been limited to renovation projects, and this was to be Philips International's first venture into new construction. The building of any structure in New York is complicated, but this project had added difficulty due to its location within the landmark district. As a result Philips International wanted to hire an architect with the sensitivity and expertise needed to handle the approval process, rather than one of the firms with which they were used to working on typical commercial projects. The developer did not play an active role during the design process, instead trusting the team it had assembled to make the right decisions.

THE SITE

The project site is on Sixth Avenue, between Washington Place and Waverly Place, in Greenwich Village, a 16,800 sf parcel occupying the entire eastern blockfront of the avenue and extending about 30 feet along both side streets. Cutting a 20-foot swath underneath the site, parallel to the avenue, is a tunnel for the city's subway and sewers. Also beneath the site is the subterranean Minetta Creek. Compounding the problem of accommodating housing to this spot is the busy street life generated by the Sixth Avenue commercial strip of shops, restaurants, and cinemas.

Before the Sixth Avenue subway was built in the early 1930s, this site contained row housing dating from the early nineteenth century. Stately row houses still line the side streets, leading to historic Washington Square nearby. For many years the site was occupied by a parking lot, frequently used by vendors as a flea market. Two reasons such a prime location remained undeveloped for so long were the technical difficulty and cost of building over the subway, and the high water table. Another reason had been the watchdog efforts of local preservationists to ensure that any structure on this prominent site would blend into the neighborhood context. A local paper commented that the community board had "turned down so many conceptual designs for proposed buildings on the site . . . that it's getting to be a habit."

One of those proposals, for a Loews movie complex, was defeated when the community board and the Village Coalition, which represents six local groups, opposed the project as an inappropriate use of the space. That battle was also fought within the Landmarks Preservation Commission, even though its jurisdiction is limited to aesthetic concerns. The Loews Corporation used four different architects in its unsuccessful bid for approval. The Village Coalition's success in that fight established it as a political force having influence in decision making related to how the site should be developed, although it had no official role in the approval process.

Margaret Moore, a local preservationist, felt any building on the site would be "a centerpiece for one of America's most important Greek Revival neighborhoods . . .," citing in particular a church built in 1834 across the avenue from the site, and neighboring row houses. Yet, according to a booklet published by the LPC, *A Guide to New York City Landmarks*, "The architecture of the [Greenwich Village] District—the . . . most heterogeneous in the city—reflects the physical growth of this section of Manhattan for over 180 years, and illustrates the changing economic base of the area in the variety of building types and functions." The variety of residential architecture includes Federal, Greek Revival, and Italianate town houses, turn-of-the-century tenements, and contemporary high-rises.

PREPROJECT PLANNING

In an unusual but increasingly common arrangement, the James Felt Realty Company, which sold the land to Philips, also served as advisor to the developer, assisting the firm in assembling the consultant team and analyzing the pro forma financial arrangements. In this capacity, according to Victor Carrega, project manager for Felt, they recommended that Philips hire an architect with special expertise in designing for landmark districts. After interviewing three or four firms considered to be strong in contextual design, Felt advised Philips to select James Stewart Polshek and Partners.

Due to the extensive technical constraints of the site, Carrega recounted, the developers decided to hire a construction manager (CM) rather than have a general contractor bid on the job. Lehrer McGovern was hired. Carrega believed that having the construction manager on board throughout the design process, to provide "value engineering" (a cost-and-benefit analysis of alternatives), would help a project like this and assist in building an alliance between the developer, architect, and contractor.

In the words of architect James Garrison, "the advantage of working with a CM is that, if you could have made a trade-off instead of losing a particular option, it's better to know sooner rather than when it's too late." Carrega adds that, in a complicated building environment like New York City, the construction manager "has a better ability to interface with the subcontractors, who often have more current information on building techniques

and costs than the engineer, since they may have just finished a similar job nearby." As developers turn more and more to difficult sites, due to the lack of more suitable urban land, the trend toward including construction managers on project teams will become even more common.

Marketing consultants were also part of the team. Their role was to advise on the mix of units, internal layouts, and the nature of amenities. The recommendations of such consultants currently carry a lot of weight with housing developers in New York City.

SCOPE OF SERVICES

In addition to the standard scope of architectural services, negotiated for a lump sum fee, the architects were also responsible for guiding the project through the Landmarks Preservation Commission approval process. As the duration and extent of work involved was hard to predict at this time, the architects billed for services on an hourly basis, with no set ceiling.

THE ARCHITECT

James Stewart Polshek and Partners was founded in 1964 and has since gained an international reputation for architecture that is both community-oriented and sensitive to site and client requirements. James Stewart Polshek, who was dean of the Graduate School of Architecture, Planning, and Preservation at Columbia University for fifteen years, leads the firm in all design matters. The seventy-five person firm is based in New York and led by four partners and seven associates. Its practice specializes in new construction, historic preservation, interior design, and urban design.

Members of this project team included James Stewart Polshek, partner in charge of design; Paul Byard, partner in charge of management; James Garrison, now a partner, as senior designer; and Gaston Silva, now an associate, as project architect.

PROGRAMMING
January 1984

From the start the architects see this project as a chance to address the problem of in-fill housing, which, they feel, standard building types are not addressing. They develop plans and use the constraints of the site to justify to the client the particular building type they believe is appropriate.

Architect James Garrison says "We always begin by defining as many constraints as possible up front." In this case, economic constraints dictated that the ground floor was to be commercial. The historical district legislation mandated only that the design be "appropriate" to the character of the neighborhood. Column loading was dictated by the weight that could be supported by the subway tunnel, which ran under

the entire blockfront area of the site. Other constraints included social concerns, zoning regulations, and the architects' own agenda.

SOCIAL CONCERNS

To determine what kind of building would be appropriate, the architects took some time to consider what this building would be giving back to the people who live in the neighborhood and proposed specific goals for the type of socially responsive housing they wanted to build. These were:

- To maintain the street edge (to repair the fabric of city and not be "a tower in a park").
- To integrate the project with the life of the community.
- To provide apartment types that allow for variant lifestyles.
- To define a transition from public to private space.

BUILDING TYPE

"Here was an opportunity to make low-rise housing that would have amenities rather than merely be a double-loaded slab, as was typical then," says James Garrison. As an architecture student during the 1970s, he had been influenced by the innovative housing then being built by the New York State Urban Development Corporation. Both Polshek and Garrison saw this project as a chance to apply some of those ideas to the problem of building new housing in older cities.

ZONING

Zoning regulations written in the early 1960s revealed their authors' modernist bias. Building measurements could exceed the allowable floor area ratio (FAR) if a given amount of space on the site were left open. This open-space ratio bonus was created with the public interest in mind, but led many developers to build towers surrounded by bleak plazas. Project architect Gaston Silva states, "We wouldn't agree to do that anywhere in the city but least of all in this neighborhood."

James Stewart Polshek comments: "Under the zoning provisions of New York City, we could have built a three-and-a-half-story building covering the entire site. In terms of bulk and volume, such a building would have been completely out of character with the elegant brownstones of the two side streets. Therefore it was decided . . . [that] the bulk of the building should come close to matching the height of the adjacent town houses. . . ."

Views of the Washington Square neighborhood, with characteristic row houses and apartment buildings.

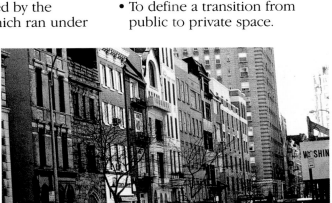

APARTMENT TYPE

Another programmatic objective was to develop special "Greenwich Village" apartment types, featuring more variety, smaller scale spaces, and distinctive character. Polshek soon determined that duplex apartments were a way to foster this. Although this solution was not dictated by either marketing or structural factors, the use of two-story spaces lightened the load over the subway, which James Garrison felt reinforced the "rightness" of the decision. However, designing the units to comply with the city's intricate building code was going to be tricky. Two means of egress are required of every floor, including the upstairs of duplex units—yet another constraint.

PROGRAM ANALYSIS

To sum up their analysis of the program and constraints, Garrison drew up a set of diagrams, illustrating the trade-off between tower and low-rise solutions. The plan to build up to the property line to reinforce the street wall meant both that the bulk of the building would be over the tunnel and that they would not be able to build a structure of maximum density. And a tower set back from the street, although legal, would never get LPC approval.

A U-shaped building configuration enclosing a private courtyard was chosen. Garrison has stressed that their intention in providing private greenspace was not merely based on an "aesthetic whim"; it was to improve the quality of life in that neighborhood, where open space of any sort is at a premium.

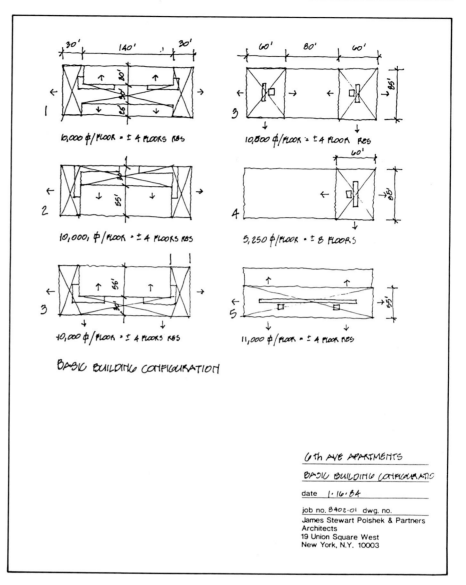

Diagram of the building configuration

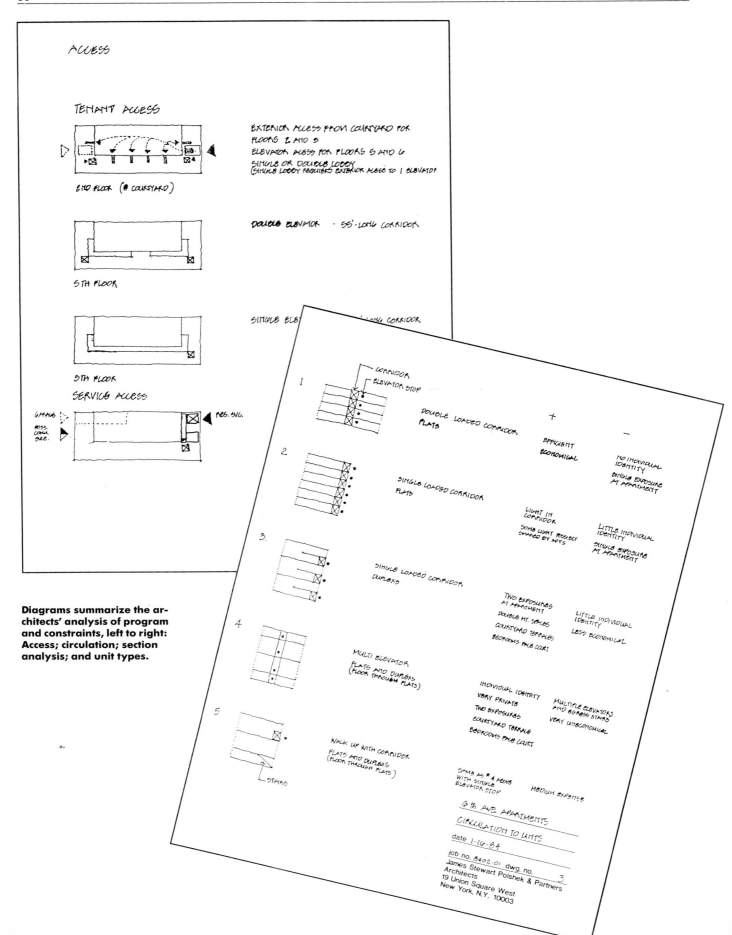

Diagrams summarize the architects' analysis of program and constraints, left to right: Access; circulation; section analysis; and unit types.

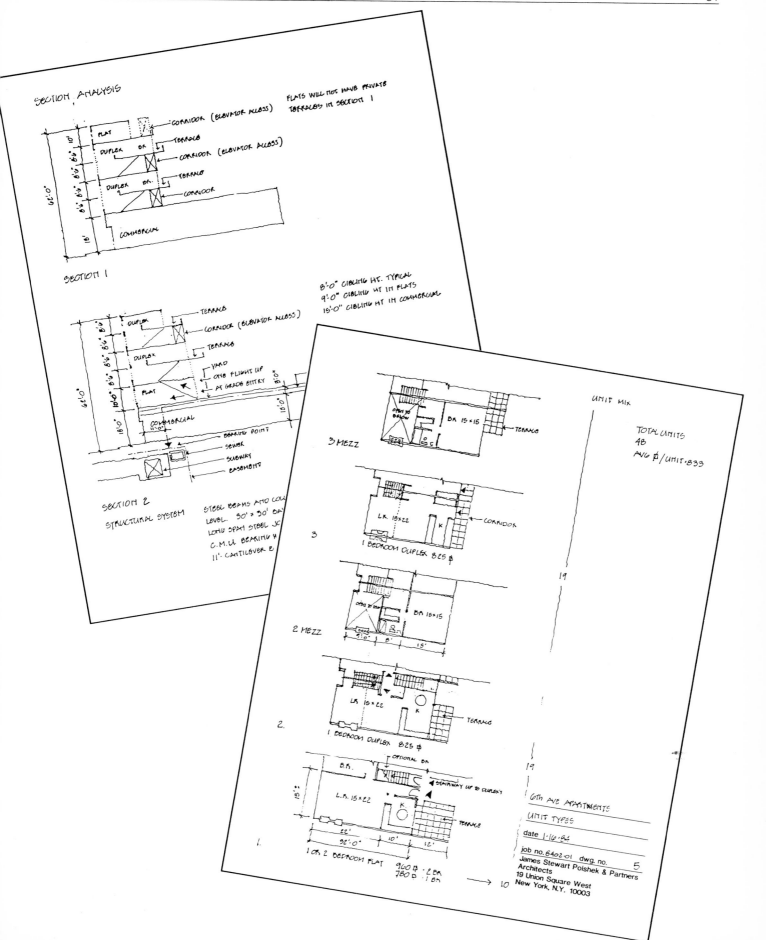

SECTION ANALYSIS

FLATS WILL NOT HAVE PRIVATE
TERRACES IN SECTION 1

CORRIDOR (ELEVATOR ACCESS)
FLAT
TERRACE
DUPLEX   OR
CORRIDOR (ELEVATOR ACCESS)
TERRACE
DUPLEX   OR.
CORRIDOR
COMMERCIAL

SECTION 1

8'-0" CEILING HT. TYPICAL
9'-0" CEILING HT IN FLATS
15'-0" CEILING HT IN COMMERCIAL

TERRACE
DUPLEX
CORRIDOR (ELEVATOR ACCESS)
TERRACE
DUPLEX
YARD
ONE FLIGHT UP
AT GRADE ENTRY
FLAT
COMMERCIAL
BEARING POINT
SEWER
SUBWAY
EASEMENT

SECTION 2
STRUCTURAL SYSTEM

STEEL BEAMS AND COL
LEVEL. 30' x 30' BA
LONG SPAN STEEL JO
C.M.U. BEARING W
11'. CANTILEVER B

3 MEZZ

OPEN TO BELOW   BR 15 x 15   TERRACE

3

LR. 15 x 22   K   CORRIDOR
1 BEDROOM DUPLEX 825 ⌀

2 MEZZ

OPEN TO BELOW   BR 15 x 15
9'-0"   8'   15'

2.

LR 15 x 22   K   TERRACE
1 BEDROOM DUPLEX 825 ⌀

OPTIONAL BR
B.R.
STAIRWAY UP TO DUPLEX'S
15' +
L.R. 15 x 22   K.   TERRACE
22'   92'-0"   10'   12'
1.
1 OR 2 BEDROOM FLAT   960 ⌀ : 2 BR
780 ⌀ : 1 BR   → 10

UNIT MIX

TOTAL UNITS
48
AVG ⌀/UNIT.833

19

19

6TH AVE APARTMENTS

UNIT TYPES

date 1·16·84

job no. 6402-01   dwg. no.   5
James Stewart Polshek & Partners
Architects
19 Union Square West
New York, N.Y. 10003

SCHEMATIC DESIGN
February—August 1984
The architects juggle the constraints to design a building that suits their intentions: one that reflects the character of Greenwich Village without sacrificing underlying order and modernity. The complex structural system required establishes a framework within which the architects develop the apartment layouts and define the image of the building.

STRUCTURAL SYSTEM

The structural frame was designed to be composed of several pieces of lightweight steel frame, densely spaced to spread the load over the subway tunnel. For economy, the lengths of steel were as repetitive as possible. These measures set up a framework, within which the designers could choose among many elements in determining the building's form. Garrison points to the setback of the

penthouses and the organization of the apartment layouts and the stairs within them, as examples of how these opportunities were used to make an orderly and rational plan.

APARTMENT LAYOUTS

Next to overall structure, the most important architectural element in housing design is the unit type, the essential building block of the plan. It took the architects approximately a month

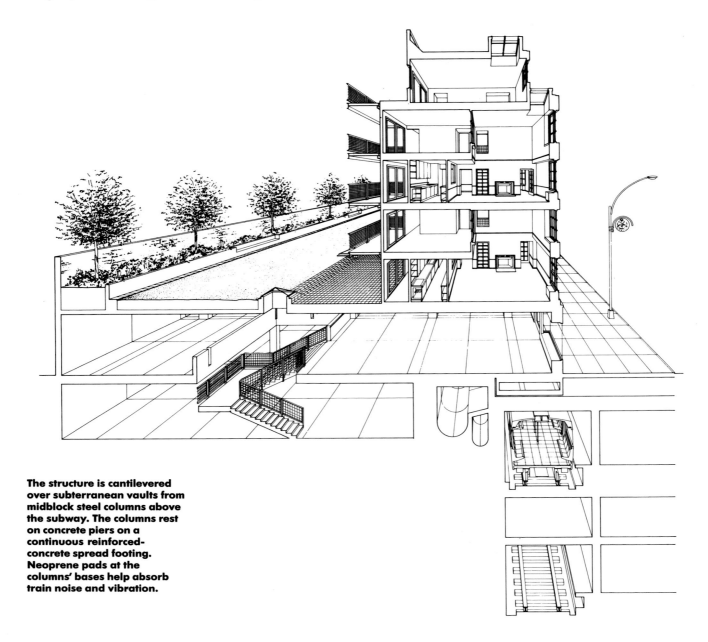

The structure is cantilevered over subterranean vaults from midblock steel columns above the subway. The columns rest on concrete piers on a continuous reinforced-concrete spread footing. Neoprene pads at the columns' bases help absorb train noise and vibration.

to come up with the basic duplex unit type. "Then everything else fell into place," says Garrison. But now, along with all other issues, the architects had to meet the building code requirements for duplexes.

Duplexes are more difficult to plan and more expensive to build than flats—there is less repetition (every other floor plate changes), each unit has internal stairs, and the overall structure is more complex. On the other hand, corridors will be needed on every other floor only. On the noncorridor floors, that space will be reclaimed by the apartments, making the overall use of space more efficient. By code, every floor of every unit needs two means of egress. A second stair corridor would have been redundant. The architect's solution to this requirement was the inclusion of fire balconies. Residents would be able to exit out a fire balcony, enter the next-door apartment through a window, and go out their neighbor's front door.

FIRE BALCONIES

But what to do with all those fire balconies? At first, the architects thought that the balconies might create a distinctive front façade feature; but after studying this possibility, they rejected it. So they reversed the layouts so that corridors and balconies faced the courtyard and living rooms overlooked the avenue. The steel-framed balconies created an architectural vocabulary for the back of the building and served as staging for planting. However, the marketing consultants saw the courtyard as a wonderful amenity, and convinced the architects that all living rooms should open onto it. This would mean running longer corridors around the outside perimeter of the building and keeping the balconies on the front façade.

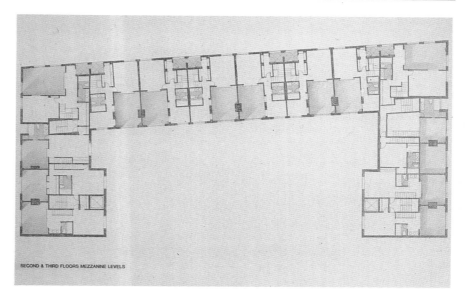

SECOND & THIRD FLOORS MEZZANINE LEVELS

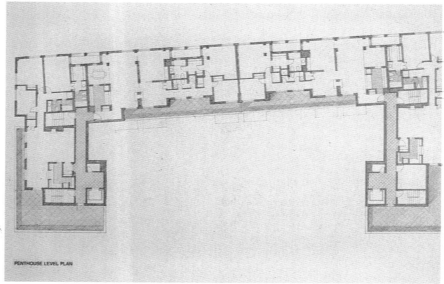

PENTHOUSE LEVEL PLAN

The second floor, top, and penthouse plan, bottom, show corridors and balconies facing the interior courtyard.

FACADE

The architects now had an agenda for what the building ought to be like. Their fundamentally modernist idea was, in James Garrison's words: "It should be a highly structured, rational building, and the façade should express the character and nature of the structure."

The building was going to take up a full block in a city where neighborhoods can change from block to block. The architects wanted to mark the corners of the building in some way to suggest that each corner had its own neighborhood identity. Polshek explains, "We broke the long facade on Sixth Avenue into three 'houses' between the two corners, each of which was defined by a tower before it turned to its short façade on the side streets." This scheme also added variety to the façade—an exclamation point to end it.

Garrison notes another rule the architects followed: "The expression of the apartment volumes inside should become part of the design of the façades." The apartment layouts and structure were based on a 12'-0" module. It would have been possible to simply lay out the apartments and allot one window per bay, but this seemed boring. So the layouts were "flip-flopped" across the face of the building, which gave the architects two elements to work with: larger and smaller windows. The pairing of these windows and their relation to other elements on the façade, such as the columns and penthouse terraces, appealed to the designers—both "as mathematical and visual gestures."

PRECEDENT

Because he lived practically next-door to the site, James Stewart Polshek was very familiar with the architectural particulars that give that part of the Village its unique atmosphere. The design team walked around the neighborhood, observing projects of similar scale and picking out their favorite features. "We examined a number of Greenwich Village buildings whose roof profiles, chimney pots, and decorative detail represented an energetic eclecticism rather than any particular style," says Polshek.

The architects rejected the Greek Revival style as a model, in part because they could not afford to construct a building of that scale with sufficiently realized details, and they knew that merely applying *faux* decorations to the surface would not work. Instead they chose to refer to the nineteenth century by using warm red brick and mullion windows and by dividing the facade into three bays, similar in scale and character to the neighboring row houses. Every apartment had a fireplace, and the numerous chimneys were used to animate the top of the building and break down the scale. Garrison

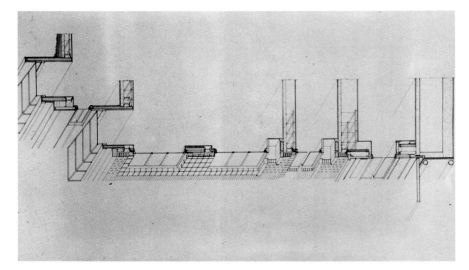

explains that these chimneys refer broadly to the industrial buildings as well as the terrace housing found in English villages during the Industrial Revolution.

MATERIALS

James Garrison points out that with the cost of construction so high, especially in New York City, the image of housing today is determined by economics much more than by structure or style—a design has to be rational in its approach to construction and materials. "The challenge we faced was how to find materials that are economical and meaningful to create a visually rich façade that relates to the character of Greenwich Village."

The architects' response, in Garrison's words, was to "take a classical vocabulary and fold it into Modernist sensibility." They used the decorative elements of the façade system—punched windows, vertical pieces, abstracted cornices—to relate back to the structural frame behind them. This allowed the architects to take full advantage of modest materials—standard brick, limestone, and terra-cotta—as Polshek explains, "not by applying them to the surface but by integrating them into the ordering system of the building."

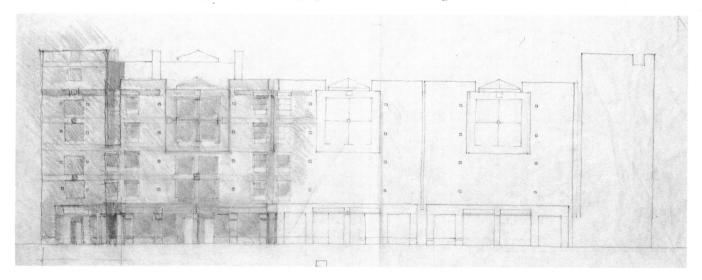

Early studies illustrate the architect's modernist sensibility. Opposite page: the facade system, top, and a study model, bottom. This page, above: The drawing illustrates how materials were "integrated into the ordering system of the building." Left: a facade sketch.

LANDMARKS PRESERVATION COMMISSION REVIEW
March–December 1984

The proposed design is opposed by local community groups as "inappropriate" to the neighborhood. They want a building in the Greek Revival style. The Landmarks Preservation Commission lacks enough votes to approve the design initially, although they find nothing wrong with the building. The debate simmers for months. The scheme is finally approved, nearly exactly as submitted.

FIRST SUBMISSION: March–April 1984

The architects applied to the Landmarks Preservation Commission in early March 1984—even though the design was still very schematic—in order to speed up the approval process. As with any developer project, there was pressure to get construction underway as soon as possible, due to the cost of financing. The first step was for the architects to make a presentation to the local community board. The initial reaction of the various community groups was that the "modern" design was too stark and institutional for the context.

Criticism was focused on architectural details, in particular the lack of ornamental cornices and projecting lintels, identified by the community board as "a local tradition of the kind the historic district is meant to preserve." In early April, before the community board vote, Polshek invited members of the Village Coalition to his office to review the design. One of the members, an architect, summarized the group's comments in a six-page letter to the community board. The main points were these:

• The institutional appearance of the façade could be improved

by smaller-scale windows or decorative treatment; a cornice could be used to break down the scale.

- The detail, including trim, lighting, and balconies, was "too large and clumsy looking" for the setting. Specific changes were suggested.
- The side elevations would benefit from more detail in the material, such as decorative terra-cotta or ornamental brickwork, rather than the "bland and flat" tile panels proposed.
- The front elevation had "too much going on." The balconies, described as "dark holes in the façade," were singled out as the weakest elements.

The letter concluded that, "it is possible to get a good building for this important site but not if the architects are pressured to move along too quickly . . . it is simply impossible to arrive at a properly refined design in so short a time." The architects acknowledged that some of the comments were valid.

By the time the landmarks committee of the community board met in mid-April, the plan had become quite controversial. Flyers for the meeting warned that "This building is to

Greenwich Village what the Beaubourg was to Paris" and portrayed James Stewart Polshek as an insensitive corporate architect and "passionate Modernist." At the meeting, the architects presented colored renderings of their scheme, along with photographs of the neighborhood showing how the design referred to the context.

The community board voted nineteen to two to ask Polshek to return with a "better design." A local paper reported that board members "heaped abuse" on the design, such as "He threw it together on a bad weekend" and "It's cold . . . an orphanage." The reporter added, "While the results may not be perfect, it might be as close as any building on the site could be expected to come. . . ."

The board, however, wanted the architect to incorporate its criticisms of detail into the design. Polshek's comment at the time was, "What we'd like is a resolution that recognizes the fact that we're agreeable to sit down with people and talk about the building . . . [so we can] proceed without the unfortunate delay of a month."

WASHINGTON PLACE ELEVATION

Community members felt the first elevation submitted to the Landmarks Commission, top left, was too "modern." A revised elevation, bottom left and above, failed to satisfy local preservationists.

SIXTH AVENUE ELEVATION

**A simplified design repropor-
tioned windows and relocated
fire balconies to face the courtyard, above, but public debate
over the lack of traditional
details raged on in the media,
opposite page.**

But the architects did have to
wait until the next month's LPC
hearing to return with a
modified design. During
preliminary meetings, the LPC
staff had been very supportive of
the original scheme.
Subsequently, preservationists
had convinced two
commissioners that the building
should be more historically
accurate, even though the
historical basis of their charges
was dubious, such as Margaret
Moore's belief that it expressed
"International Style contempt for
history." The LPC staff never
pressured the architects to add
traditional details; however, the
architects required the
commissioners' votes to move
forward with the project. At the
time there were a number of
vacant seats on the Commission.
Since six votes were needed to
approve or reject a project, if

only seven commissioners were
present and two disagreed, the
Commission could not rule one
way or the other. Many monthly
hearings would pass before they
would have a quorum.

SECOND SUBMISSION:
May–June 1984
At the end of May the architects
returned to the Landmarks
Preservation Commission with a
simplified design. Revisions
included reproportioning of
windows, the removal of many of
the terra-cotta tiles, a reduction
in the number of columns on the
front of the building, and the
elimination of the fire balconies,
which were relocated to the
inside of the "U."

These changes seemed minor,
so the commissioners scheduled
a vote on the project for their
next session, in early June. This
decision outraged community

groups, who felt that the public review process was being bypassed by not allowing them to hold another public hearing to discuss the revised design. The community board threatened legal action against the Commission and the developer if the Commission ruled on the project without considering board recommendations.

In early June the architects made another presentation to the community board, but they got the same negative reaction as before, as if no changes had been made. One member said the new design "has eliminated a number of objectionable factors," but that "it should not be approved until the architect has achieved a more coherent and balanced arrangement." The board voted to reject the revised proposal "for not trying hard enough" to fit in. Their concerns with the façade included:

- Lack of three-dimensional ornament.
- Absence of a cornice and projecting lintels and sills.
- Visual prominence of utilitarian elements such as air-conditioner grilles and skylights.
- Lack of a clear horizontal definition of a top, middle, and bottom.
- Insufficient vertical division of the façade.
- "False front" gables, which do not relate to the surrounding architecture.

APPROVAL IN CONCEPT: July 1984

When the architects returned to the Landmarks Preservation Commission at the end of July, Polshek pointed out the difficulty of responding to the community groups' "confusing and vague criteria." At various times they had labeled the design "Modernist," "Post-Modernist," "International Style," and "without style." They had criticized the front façade for being too institutional and praised the sides, and vice versa.

They had objected to the "flatness" of the façade and to the fact that it "broke the street wall," with too many openings and recesses. Polshek's position was that the community's wish to recreate an authentic historic style for the site was impossible and that the "Village's charm and historic importance has never been based on architectural homogeneity but rather on an energetic, idiosyncratic, eclectic combination of styles."

The LPC decided that the overall massing, scale, and use of materials were appropriate, and approved the project in concept. Final approval was withheld until the architects returned with more detailed drawings of some details. This decision paved the way for obtaining excavation and foundation permits, and the architects could now move into the design development phase of their work. Ground breaking was planned for the end of August, and construction scheduled for completion the following spring.

THE NEW YORK TIMES, TUESDAY, AUGUST 28, 1984

Battle Over Cornices and Lintels Rages in 'Village'

By RICHARD SEVERO

It isn't that James Stewart Polshek has anything against cornices, projecting lintels and windowsills. In fact, the architect rather likes them.

It's just that when he designed a 28-unit, $20 million residential complex in Greenwich Village, on the Avenue of the Americas between Waverly and Washington Places, he did so with the philosophy that "new buildings must reflect the future as well as the past."

And so the blueprints call for none of the usual details found on so many of the older buildings nearby — the cornices capping the facade, the projecting lintels above doors and windows, and the windowsills below.

Their absence from Mr. Polshek's plan is, in great measure, the cause of a battle in Greenwich Village, where people are used to seeing cornices, projecting lintels and windowsills, and think that if the new is properly going to relate to the old, such things are necessary. In some neighborhoods in New York City, people might wonder if a new building was ugly, or too big. But the Village is one of those areas where critics are concerned about "horizontality," rusticated stone bases and cornices.

Or, as Mr. Polshek himself says, "As many Villagers as you scratch, as many architectures will you receive."

"No cornice? That's like going to the Easter Parade without an Easter bonnet," said Ruth Wittenberg, the former chairman of the Landmarks Committee of Community Board No. 2 in the Village.

Letter-Writing Campaign

Quite a number of Villagers seem to agree, with the result that an organization called the Village Coalition, representing five block groups, is trying to persuade the city's Landmarks Preservation Commission not to grant final approval to the project. Many letters have been written to the commission supporting the coalition's stand.

The coalition goes into this with some experience. Two years ago, its members led the fight against plans to build a cinema on the site that is to be occupied by the Polshek apartments.

In the 19th century, that part of the avenue contained row housing which was knocked down when the Sixth Avenue Independent subway was built in the early 1930's. A Kinney System parking lot has occupied the site for many years.

The Landmarks Preservation Commission, whose approval is required because the project is in a historic district, plans to meet in executive session today. Mr. Polshek anticipates no problems.

"I expect approval," he said.

'Too Institutional'

But the co-chairman of the Village Coalition, Dr. Diana Tendler, a retired professor of social work at Hunter College, and a coalition member, Margaret Moore, said he should not be so sure.

Dr. Tendler said she thought the building would look "too institutional." Mrs. Moore, who used to be an editor on Glamour Magazine, said the building "ought to be against the law" because "it looks like a factory and is in conflict with our historic district."

Christobel Gough, chairman of the Historic District Committee of the Christopher East Block Association, also said the building plan is "a failure in that it is not contextual." She said she was unhappy with Mr. Polshek's intention to use blue tiles around windows.

Despite their reservations, most Village critics said that they approved of the basic scope of the structure and that it would undoubtedly begin the avenue's renaissance as a residential area, after roughly half a century of being developed commercially.

"On the whole, it is a good use of space," said Mrs. Wittenberg of the Polshek approach.

"The building itself isn't a startling example of great architecture but it isn't bad," she said. "There are certain details that could be rearranged."

Too Much 'Horizontality'

Aside from lacking cornices, projecting lintels and sills, the Polshek building also emphasizes its "horizontality" too much, Mrs. Moore said.

She would like Mr. Polshek, whom she described as "intractible," to add a rusticated stone base to the structure. Rusticated stone, containing a rich assortment of grooves, was widely used in Renaissance Italy.

Mr. Polshek, who was reached on vacation in Maine, said his building "was designed in a manner that I personally feel is appropriate to the nature of the Village, which is idiosyncratic."

Continued on Page B7

However, when the LPC met at the end of August to consider revised façade details, it became apparent that the "battle over cornices and lintels" was far from over. (The former chairman of the landmarks committee of the community board was quoted as saying, "No cornice? That's like going to the Easter Parade without an Easter bonnet.") Community groups still hoped to convince the LPC to reject the details of the design in order to force basic changes. With one commissioner firmly opposed to the design, the Commission still could not issue the final approval and instructed the architects to return the following month.

When Polshek returned to the LPC in September, the developer had already begun excavations for the building's foundation. The changes at this stage mostly involved "decorative elements," including removal of some terra-cotta tiling, redesigning the window configuration, and substituting standard brick for the jumbo brick generally used in new construction.

This time the commissioners did grant the certification of approval, which legalized the foundation and excavation work, but were still unable to approve the facade details. Meanwhile, the public debate continued. Paul Goldberger, architecture critic for the *New York Times*, wrote: "The point is not to question the process of public review as to wonder, as community activists continue to put pressure on the Landmarks Commission to reject this building, how and where that process is to end."

APPROVAL:
December 1984

Eventually, the mayor broke the stalemate on the Commission by appointing three new members to fill the vacancies. With a quorum, a vote was finally possible, and the design was approved. Some community members objected that the new commissioners should not have been able to cast the deciding votes since they had not been involved in the entire decision-making process.

In the end, however, the project was accepted with two minor changes in the façade: the addition of limestone sills and a few feet of brick in soldier courses near the top of the building.

Changes at this stage mainly involved "decorative elements."

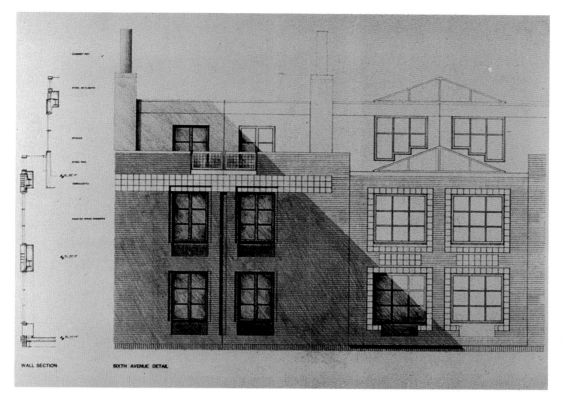

WALL SECTION   SIXTH AVENUE DETAIL

The approved façade is substantially similar to the original design and does not include a traditional cornice.

DESIGN DEVELOPMENT/ CONTRACT DOCUMENTS
September–December 1984

Since the architects' fee is low, as is typical for developer projects, they do not want to spend too much time in design development. Their approach is to set up the simplest set of working drawings possible and develop the scheme throughout documentation.

During the ten-month approval process, the comments of the community were "unconsciously absorbed" by the architects, explains project architect Gaston Silva. Drawings were constantly being revised and presented in various forms. As a result, schematics and design development overlapped. Detailed construction drawings had to be approved by the LPC, and for this reason, as well as for economic ones, the design development and documentation phases happened simultaneously.

Although to come up with the design for the basic apartment unit took the architects only one month, finalizing the plan layouts took much longer. Working around the structure was difficult. Many of the units had complex plans with multiple bedrooms, and the building floor plate changed from corner to corner. According to Gaston Silva, many decisions were based on the marketing consultants' advice on the types of amenities buyers request: For instance, most people prefer Jacuzzis to better windows, and customers like diagonal flooring as it makes small units look larger.

The marketing consultants' advice was also followed on the design of the lobby and the entry sequence from street to apartment, the detailing of which was left until last, during the contract document phase. Working with the construction manager made this method less risky, since the cost of the project was constantly being monitored.

Finally, there was the interior courtyard to design. At first, Polshek saw the garden as a romantic place with meandering paths. On the other hand, Garrison saw it as a chance for residents to have a lawn. Private open space with clean grass is a real luxury in New York City. So the architects compromised— the courtyard would be partially

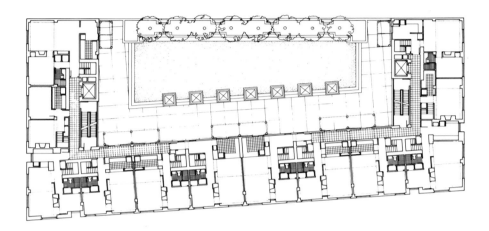

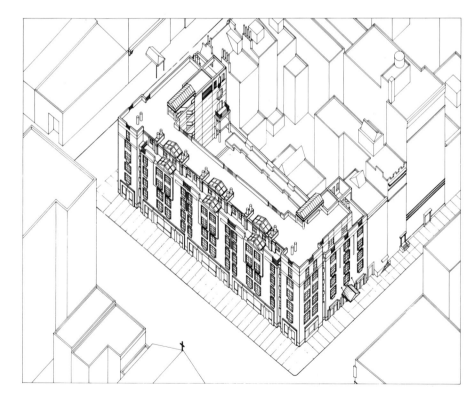

lawn, with trees and planting along the back, modeled on a plan by Mies van der Rohe.

James Stewart Polshek wrote in *Context and Responsibility* (Rizzoli, 1988): "If the outer façades were inspired by the Karl Marx Hof in Vienna, the inner façades with their stucco walls

and steel balconies owe more to Stuttgart's Weissen-hof. The entire composition, including the twelve-foot spacing of columns, the arrangement of egress stairs on the inboards side of the courtyard, and the configuration of the small but well-proportioned apartments,

resembled an academic project that had been based on the traditional mews housing type."

The developer went on to hire the architect to design a similar building in another neighborhood. The mayor later appointed Gaston Silva to serve as a landmarks commissioner.

Opposite page: Second and third floor plan, top; an axonometric view of the final design, bottom.

This page: Typical apartment floor plans, top. Below: Interior views. High ceilings and large windows make the small units seem more spacious. Some apartments have balconies over-looking the court-yard, lawn, and planted border.

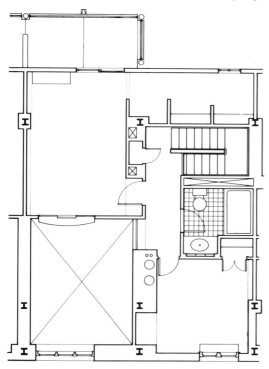

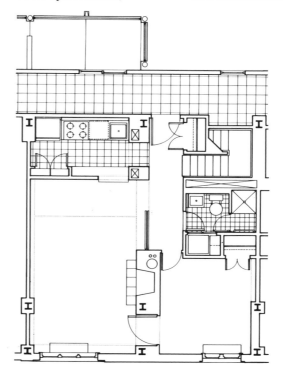

OBSERVATIONS

"We must not be dominated by nostalgia for a past we cannot recapture."—James Stewart Polshek

- "The issue is not really Mr. Polshek's building or even Greenwich Village," observed *New York Times* architecture critic Paul Goldberger. "The question is whether . . . behind all of the preservationist zeal that motivates so many people today, there is not some real confusion over just who should be designing buildings and what the whole point of having a historic district is." In Goldberger's opinion, Polshek's design was "vastly better than most new architecture in New York." If such design is not "appropriate," then what is? Although the Landmarks Preservation Commission staff did not want to dictate aesthetics, some preservationists used the public review process to try and perfect the design rather than to protect the built environment.

- Design quality cannot be measured against a narrow set of criteria without risking reducing the architectural review process into overly simplistic terms. New York City's landmark law acknowledges that such rules could stifle creativity and thus relies on the broad standard of "appropriateness." Without a full complement of commissioners, however, the system broke down and unduly favored the minority opinion and vocal activists. The stalemate goaded the city into correcting problems in the approval process, and in the appointment of commissioners. As a result, both architects and the Commission learned how to better implement the regulations.

- People want a sense of control over their environment. Diane Tendler, one of the leaders of the Village Coalition, explains that members of her group became adversarial because they felt left out of the process of deciding what should be built in their community. "To vent their frustration they wrote a lot of letters." Tendler wishes there had been some mechanism to bring the architect and community groups together as the situation polarized, to help them resolve their differences. James Stewart Polshek said he would have been willing to discuss the design if the community had only been "unified and specific in their comments." Clearly, part of the problem was caused by a breakdown in communications, rather than design issues.

- Despite the greater creative freedom it gives the designer, the review panel system has certain dangers. Many people find it difficult to read architectural drawings, and in this case, the concerned community groups had not seen the abstract connection between Polshek's design and traditional elements. Also, although it had been too early in the process to show too much detail, the architects had been under pressure to develop a design to the point where it could be reviewed. The architects later realized that the community groups had regarded these initial presentation drawings, although schematic, as too finished.

- The struggle to control the building's appearance mirrored the neighborhood's anxiety over the impact of the large scale of the project. One resident complained that the building "perpetuates the monstrosities that have already been inflicted on us." Someone else claimed to prefer the parking lot. One reporter observed at the time "The [community board's] attention to design and detail reflected [its] conviction that the fate of the site will have a crucial bearing on future development—residential as well as commercial— in the Village." Where city planning policies seem ineffective, preservation issues have become the battleground for local efforts to control the actions of powerful developers. This situation sets up an unrealistic set of expectations for the design review process and introduces nondesign issues in the debate over building projects.

- Despite the difficulties of having to work within the limitations of the review process, it did have a positive effect on the final design. The Landmarks Preservation Commission guided the process to achieve higher quality design. The developer hired a better architect than he otherwise might have, built less density than he could have, and used better-than-standard materials. The review process also forced the architects to improve and refine their ideas over a long period of time, even though the basic design concept took shape early on.

- The developer was accused of having hired a "name" architect to "sell" an unpopular project, but this was not the case: He had hired expertise. It takes both patience and skill to work through the maze of public approvals. During the controversy, a reporter observed that "Polshek . . . has persevered with his design where others have withered under community opposition," and quotes the architect's philosophical perspective: "Some people like hot fudge and others like butterscotch." James Stewart Polshek had been willing to listen but not to compromise his principles under public pressure and even personal attacks.

**The finished building, above,
and a roofline detail, top left;
skylights and stairway,
top right.**

LEWIS THOMAS MOLECULAR BIOLOGY LABORATORY
HIGH TECH WRAPPED IN HIGH STYLE

The design of Princeton University's molecular biology research facility in Princeton, New Jersey, represented a special challenge for three reasons: It was to serve as an enticement in recruiting highly sought-after research scientists; it would need to incorporate special technical requirements; and it would be one of the biggest structures to go up on the Princeton campus. To achieve this, the client put together a team of architects: Venturi, Rauch & Scott-Brown, to design the building's exterior, and Payette Associates, to orchestrate the rest of the process. While such collaboration is not yet common, it is sure to become more typical as government investment in new multidisciplinary science and technology centers in universities increases the demand for facilities that integrate design and technology.

PROJECT OVERVIEW

Project A 110,000 sf research and teaching facility for a new molecular biology department at a private university.

Architect Payette Associates, Boston, Massachusetts, with Venturi, Rauch & Scott-Brown, Philadelphia, Pennsylvania, design consultants.

Client Princeton University, Princeton, New Jersey.

Charge Provide a state-of-the-art facility that would attract top researchers in the field to join a newly created department.

Issues ✔ Integration of the new building's scale, materials, and character with the existing campus.

  ✔ The need to develop a program on behalf of the eventual users.

  ✔ Balancing site planning objectives, aesthetic criteria, integration of complex building systems, handling of hazardous materials, and users' needs.

  ✔ Tight, fast-tracked construction schedule mandated by the university's need to provide a focus for recruiting efforts.

Duration One year and a half from start to completion of working drawings (February 1983–July 1984).

Budget $22 million for construction, of which $2.5 million was for the exterior.

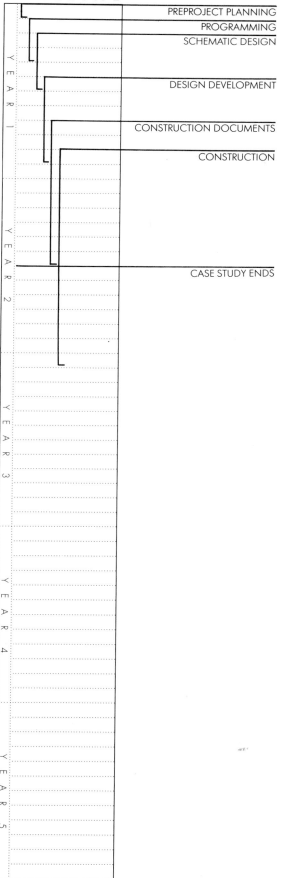

TIMELINE

YEAR 1 — YEAR 5

PREPROJECT PLANNING
PROGRAMMING
SCHEMATIC DESIGN
DESIGN DEVELOPMENT
CONSTRUCTION DOCUMENTS
CONSTRUCTION
CASE STUDY ENDS

BACKGROUND

In an unusual move, Princeton University decided to make a marriage between two very different architectural firms to design a new building, a state-of-the-art facility for molecular biology research that would have a major design impact on the Neo-Gothic style campus. Although the union was referred to by university officials as a "shotgun wedding," the firms of Venturi, Rauch & Scott-Brown (VRSB), whose theories on content and image in architecture were among those that paved the way for Post-Modernism, and Payette Associates, experts on the workings of technical buildings, worked so well together that they have gone on to collaborate on several comparable projects. How did these firms integrate design of the building "from the outside in and inside out" so seamlessly? Part of the answer is that the key participants in the design process stressed teamwork over individual inspiration.

The Payette team designed a sophisticated, modular research facility that has a warm, inviting ambience. The Venturi team created a multicolored, richly patterned brick facade, that counterbalances the building's repetitive nature and adds a layer of historic meaning. Although the result was controversial—some critics have compared the design to the Purina Dog Chow package—the team of architects felt that the building was "absolutely the right thing to do," and for this they all credited the design process.

THE CLIENT

Princeton University's 240-year-old campus is steeped in tradition, as is the institution itself, often thought of as a bastion of conservatism. The university's well-known standards of excellence and humanistic values are reflected in its traditionally styled buildings and naturalistic landscapes—a microcosm of a harmonious environment for reflective endeavors. During the past decade, an expansion of the student body (including the admission of women) as well as of the range of activities at the school has led the University to undertake a series of construction projects. The result has been to introduce a variety of new architectural styles, which stand as evidence of the changes taking place within the institution.

In early 1983, Princeton was falling behind other universities in the field of molecular biology, an emerging discipline at the heart of major scientific advances. According to Jon Hlafter, Princeton's

director of physical planning, Princeton's plan was to assemble a "world class" molecular biology department around the research facility. When the president, provost, and academic officers convinced Dr. Arnold Levine to become the chairman and form the nucleus of the new department, part of the agreement was the guarantee of a new building and an "all-star" design team. The building under construction was to be an essential recruiting tool to entice researchers to join his faculty.

The creation of a new laboratory was not a typical project for Princeton. Not only would there be no user group to confer with, it would be the most expensive undertaking in Princeton's history and one of the largest new construction projects on campus. So when the trustees, members of the planning office, and Princeton president William G. Bowen met to discuss potential architects, they decided to shorten the usual selection process and handpick the best possible firm. (Usually the President's Advisory Committee on Architecture, along with representatives of the user department, interview firms on a short list and make a recommendation to the trustees.)

The firm of Princeton alumnus Robert Venturi, Venturi, Rauch & Scott-Brown, had just completed the much-admired dining and social center, Gordon Wu Hall, a short distance from the laboratory site. Hlafter recalls, "Most people were delighted with that building and what it did for the southern end of campus, and wanted him to continue to assist in planning the campus. Venturi had been able to articulate an interesting coming-together of styles at Wu Hall, and we felt he would do justice to the new and different site." But although the university would have liked Venturi to be the lead architect, his firm was not experienced with laboratory building types.

The search was extended to find a firm experienced with laboratories or similar installations with specialized features. At that time Payette Associates were completing the renovation of Princeton's chemistry building and had just finished a new molecular biology research facility for Harvard University and a similar building for Massachusetts General Hospital in Boston. Princeton recognized that Payette's experience could help them put together the program for their own lab. Payette, because of its special expertise, would develop the program and design the interior of the lab. VRSB, because of its design skills and sensitivity to the campus, would do the campus planning and design the exterior.

Left: Gordon Wu Hall, Princeton University, by Venturi, Rauch & Scott-Brown.

Below: Aerial view of the Princeton University campus.

THE SITE

Negotiations between Princeton and Dr. Levine set certain parameters for the building, including its size and site. Levine recalls, "Princeton had no plans or preconceived notions, and we were assured input on the design of the new facility starting with the site." For instance, the Princeton administration and Levine agreed that the department would have twenty faculty members. By averaging the amount of space required per faculty member, they could roughly determine the amount of space needed. They decided that there would be a teaching center and the kinds of facilities associated with the teaching function, including a large lecture hall and small lecture rooms. They knew that there would be both graduate and undergraduate majors, and they were able to estimate the number of students based on past enrollments.

They selected a site near the biology department building, which sits in a quadrangle with buildings that house the geology, physics, and mathematics departments. Proximity to these departments perfectly suited Dr. Levine's goal of building an intellectual community of scientists at Princeton.

SITE PLAN ANALYSIS

With construction of the lab building not far away, Princeton commissioned Venturi, Rauch & Scott-Brown to conduct a planning study of College Walk, the main pedestrian path through the campus. Part of this study was to provide a preliminary site plan analysis and a set of design guidelines for the lab. These guidelines included the following:

Assumptions:
- The new building will be located along the south side of College Walk and will face Guyot Hall.
- The building is to have a simple rectangular form and a loftlike interior, for flexibility of spaces and services.
- The expansion of the neighboring departments should be anticipated.

Design Guidelines:
- The building is to be parallel with College Walk, to reinforce the spatial continuity and identity of the Walk and to complement the form of Guyot Hall.
- The recommended setback is approximately fifty feet from the midpoint of the Walk, and is determined by the assumed height of the building, the position of the existing trees, and the general context of nearby buildings. Shadows are also to be considered.
- The building is to be a simple volume, with façade

elements providing architectural quality. Human-scale elements will modify the large story height needed to accommodate mechanical systems.
- Brick cladding is to be the material.
- An existing service road and parking area south of College Walk are to be maintained.
- Trees are to be maintained, as a foil to the scale of the building and as an element of continuity along the Walk.
- Future expansion toward the south is preferred, to leave the east side available for other building options.
- Tunnels are to be utilized, as connections across the Walk.

THE ARCHITECTS

Payette Associates is a 135-person firm based in Boston, with a specialty in medical research buildings. Originally established in 1932 by engineer Fred Markus and architect Paul Norka, the firm was taken over by Thomas Payette when the founding partners retired in 1974. The firm is organized around ten separate studios, each run by one of ten principals. Known for its systematic approach to complex problem solving, Payette is not expected to deliver signature design; the firm does not even have a design director. According to principal James Collins, Jr., "Everyone here is pulling for shared goals, or at least those beyond getting their name in lights; there are no stars."

The firm of Venturi, Rauch & Scott-Brown is housed in a converted factory on the outskirts of Philadelphia, which belies the firm's international reputation and its influence on a generation of designers. Robert Venturi and John Rauch established their practice in 1964; a few years later they were joined by Denise Scott-Brown, who became a partner in 1981. Robert Venturi has helped to define a Post-Modern vocabulary through ordinary building techniques. Venturi leads the sixty-member staff in all matters of design, encompassing architecture, urban design, exhibitions, and furniture design. At the time of the Princeton project, John Rauch was responsible for financial and technical issues, and Denise Scott-Brown led the planning portion of the practice.

Key members of the project team included: Payette vice-president David Rowan and John Rauch from VRSB, as the partners-in-charge; Jim Collins, Jr., of Payette as job captain; and Robert McCoy of VRSB as project manager. Project team meetings were held every two weeks.

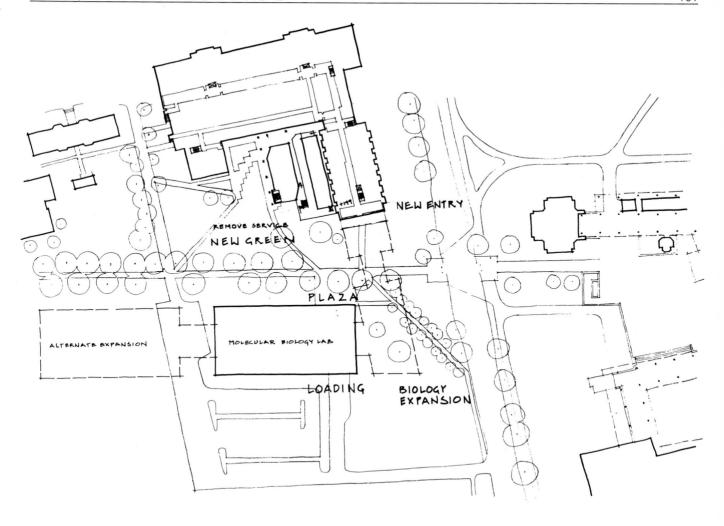

NEW ENTRY

REMOVE SERVICE

NEW GREEN

PLAZA

ALTERNATE EXPANSION

MOLECULAR BIOLOGY LAB

LOADING

BIOLOGY
EXPANSION

**Site plan analysis of the
proposed molecular biology
lab, part of VRSB's College
Walk study.**

DEVELOPMENT STUDIES for
PROPOSED MOLECULAR BIOLOGY LAB
PRINCETON UNIVERSITY

1

SCALE: 1'= 40'-0"   4-7-83   PAI/VRSB

PREPROJECT PLANNING
February 1983

The two principals establish management procedures to coordinate their work. A portion of the budget is allocated for the exterior and a projected project schedule is planned. The team becomes familiar with similar buildings and each other's work, strengthening the mutual respect and understanding that eventually made the collaboration a success.

SCOPE OF SERVICES

New Jersey law states that only one architect can be the architect of record, and the client wanted Payette to have legal responsibility for the job. A joint venture did not make sense under these conditions; therefore, the firms agreed that VRSB would design the exterior skin as a consultant to Payette. This arrangement, which allowed each firm to do what it was best at, was spelled out in an informal letter from VRSB to Payette defining the scope of services.

Dr. Levine and his assistant, Thomas Shank, formed a "building committee of two" to work with the architects in developing the program and planning the interior. The university administration was not concerned about the interior, as long as program needs were being met, but they did review the exterior design and the budget.

SCHEDULE

Once the project started to acquire momentum, director Hlafter says, "the University felt it was important to come to a realization of the end results as quickly as possible." A compressed schedule with overlapping phases, proposed in March 1983, aimed for occupancy in October 1985. The project generally stayed on this schedule, although occupancy was delayed until March 1986. The sequence of construction would be first the structure, then the skin, and finally the interior. Programming was to be refined during schematic design. VRSB's involvement would begin once the basic functional planning was complete. Schematics would continue into design development, allowing VRSB to devote more time to the elevations while Payette started detailing the interior. Construction would begin upon completion of design development.

ORIENTATION

The client and architects made studies of each other's work. Dr. Levine recalls that before he had moved to Princeton, Robert Venturi had visited him at the State University of New York's Stony Brook campus: "When I picked him up at the train station, he suggested that I drive him around to five or six buildings that I really liked. Then he pointed out what he liked. Later, he came to the lab and sat there for an afternoon, to observe us while we worked. He got to know what we did, why we did it, and what we liked."

Payette architects brought Dr. Levine and architect Venturi to look at the Fairchild Laboratory at Harvard. Payette architect Jim Collins says that Venturi became enthusiastic when he saw the red brick building with its wood-framed windows, railings, and sunshades. Venturi had thought the lab could not have windows, and so should perhaps be oriented perpendicularly to the College Walk. The team also visited buildings by Venturi. It became clear that fulfillment of the program requirements would not prescribe a certain building type or style. These visits helped the group to understand each other's work and develop a shared set of design goals.

Right: Fairchild Molecular Biology Laboratory at Harvard, by Payette Associates.

Below: Typical laboratory floor plan.

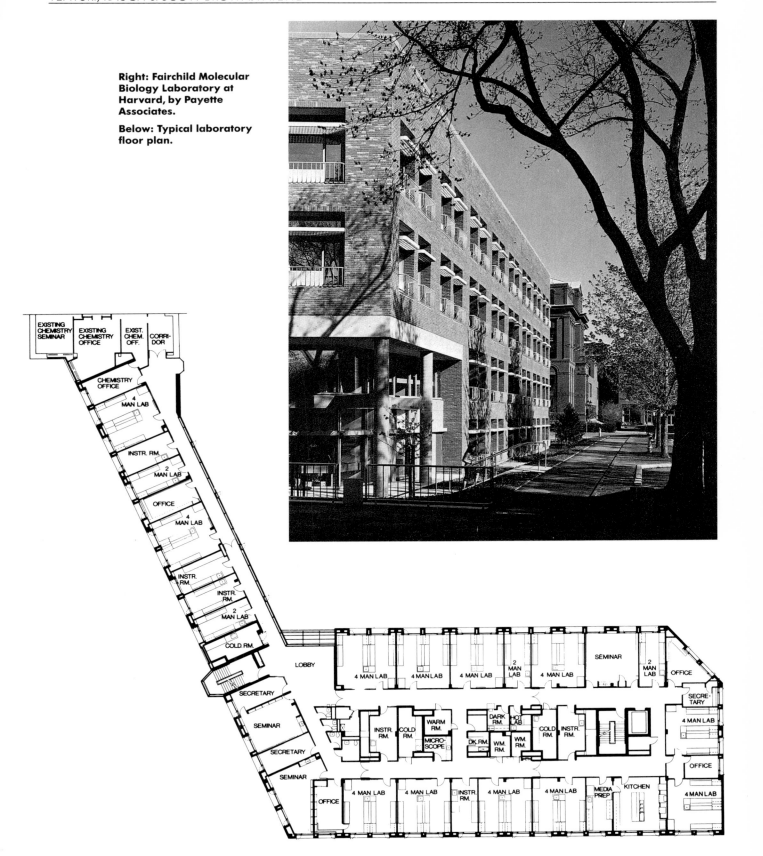

PROGRAMMING
March—May 1983

In the absence of a user group, the Payette team writes the program based on its members' past experience, with input from the Princeton chairman and his assistant. In addition to purely functional and technical needs, behavioral issues are also considered. A brief preliminary program sets overall size and scope. (Detailed requirements are refined during schematics.)

During the weekly program-development meetings, Payette architects and Princeton scientists planned the activities of the department vis-à-vis the characteristics of the space. In addition to identifying the building's functions and goals, the programming process also clarified its spirit. Architect Jim Collins learned that microbiologists are social people who feel strong ties to their scientific community; that they are deeply committed to their work, which is in the vanguard of today's science. The team's work was guided by this understanding of the users' communal spirit, as well as technical constraints.

BEHAVIORAL ISSUES

Dr. Levine has said that his highest priority in planning the building was "to force interaction between research groups and individuals." This goal set parameters for the size of the building. Based on the assumption that people interact better with those with whom they share floors, the twenty faculty offices were equally divided among three floors, approximately seven per floor. The height of the building was limited to three stories so that people could use the stairs and meet in the stairwell, rather than being forced to use the elevator.

To encourage interaction, lounges with kitchenettes were planned as places for informal gatherings. Blackboards were to

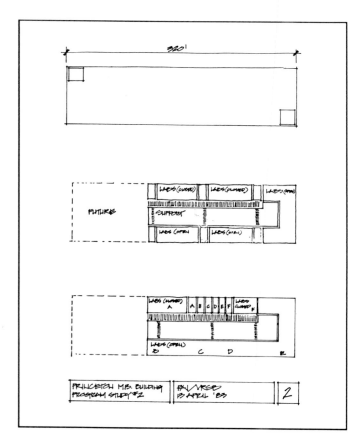

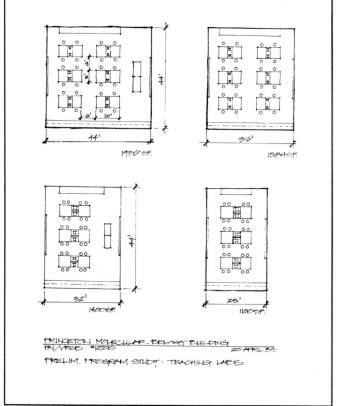

be provided in these lounges for impromptu work sessions. Offices were to be located where people would tend to cluster— in part to enhance competition by making it easy for users to see what others were working on.

Another behavioral goal was the creation of an environment in which no one would feel isolated, even in the corridors. Glass walls instead of solid ones were to be used, not just to bring light into the middle of the building, but also to allow people to see into labs and work areas. This feature would enhance safety as well. Corridors were to be wide enough to allow users to stand and talk

comfortably. The central stair was to be spacious enough to encourage conversation.

Special areas were programmed to allow the overlapping of social and academic activities. The chairman wanted to invite undergraduates to mingle with faculty and postdoctoral researchers over tea in the afternoon; therefore, 1,000 sf were planned for a central meeting room. Sitting areas were programmed for the lobby, as well as for an outdoor patio onto which classrooms could open. A large lecture hall was planned to include a kitchen so that snacks could be served at evening lectures. One classroom

was to have a large closet where chairs could be put away to make room for parties.

PROGRAM SUMMARY

The architects and the scientists each drew up their own lists of required spaces. Jim Collins reconciled the lists, and put together a two-page preliminary program summarizing square-footage requirements. (Payette believes that designers do not read voluminous programs.) Detailed analysis of relative sizes and adjacencies continued through schematic design. By July, the architects had a firm breakdown of space, furniture, and equipment needs.

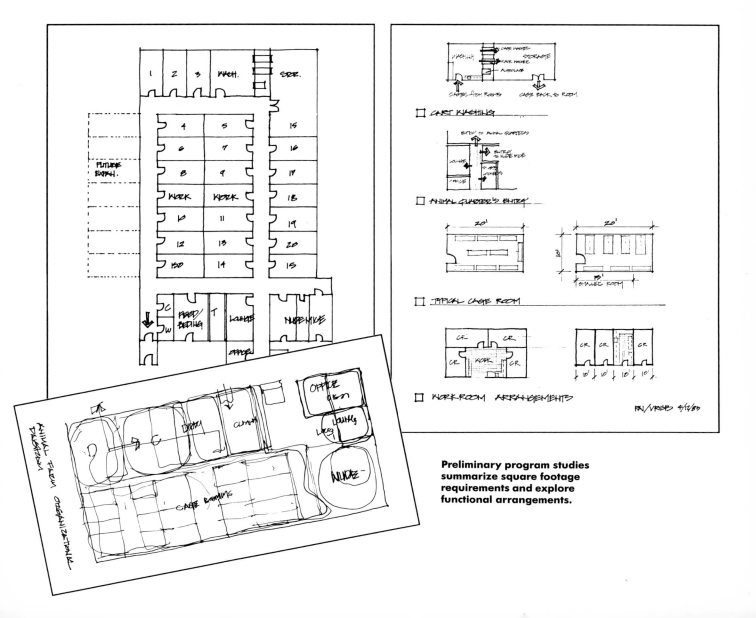

Preliminary program studies summarize square footage requirements and explore functional arrangements.

SCHEMATIC DESIGN
April—July 1983

Most design decisions are made during this phase. The program is refined through sketches diagramming relationships between and within nearly every room. Payette adapts their generic lab module to fit the requirements of this facility. Once the internal constraints are clear, Venturi shapes the external form and massing. Internal and external design decisions are integrated at the entry lobby and in the shape of the end walls.

DESIGN CONCEPT: A GENERIC, MODULAR LABORATORY

The use of the generic module that Payette Associates developed for Harvard's Fairchild Laboratory facilitated the process of planning the building's interior. In architect Jim Collins's words, "to have 'generated' the form would have been contrived." Approximately 80 percent of space in the Lewis Thomas Laboratory is made up of modules, used either as repetitive laboratories, offices, or support space, and concentrated in the core of the building. The

plan based on this modular grid was deliberately symmetrical and repetitive, not just for the sake of cost savings, but also because of what Dr. Levine has called the "egalitarian spirit" of the place: "We didn't want to make exceptions for faculty to take advantage of."

OVERALL ORGANIZATION

Based on the dimensions of the generic lab module, the architects determined that the building was to have a certain width. But how long was it to be? The module placed people near the windows, automatically requiring certain perimeter dimensions. A number of shapes potentially satisfied the program requirements.

The architects studied various forms in plan and section, skewing, thickening, and bending corners to vary the amount of perimeter. Some of the forms provided enough window wall and others did not. A rectangle was the simplest and most natural arrangement and had enough perimeter. Collins was concerned that Robert Venturi would want "to play with the shape," but his response was

positive. The box form was called for in the design guidelines and also suited Venturi's "decorated shed" style.

During meetings, work flow and adjacency requirements for nearly every room were studied by way of a series of sketches and diagrams, which were dated and filed and became part of the program documentation. The planning grid was divided into zones for seated work, standing work, and equipment. Then the characteristics of each area were detailed.

Each floor plan was designed with a single corridor, unlike the design of the Fairchild Laboratory, which has a racetrack corridor. This decision was based on the observation that people relate more to those who are nearby than to those at the far end of a hall. Collins says, "A single corridor functions like a Main Street and everybody's on it." Spur corridors led to labs on the far side of the central support zone. Each floor was to accommodate two major lab groups. Knowing the differing areas of research that would be pursued, the team was able to cluster laboratories in such a way as to complement researchers' intellectual interests, creating, in effect, neighborhoods along each Main Street/corridor.

The three floor plans were identical, yet each was organized around a special use area. For example, Dr. Levine explained, two to four researchers were going to be working with infectious agents, requiring a biological containment facility. This facility had to be at the core of the building, for safety reasons, so the rest of the building was planned around it. Other special areas included the administrative functions, on the first floor, and on the third floor, a chemical synthesis area and computer laboratory.

Right: The generic lab module developed by Payette for Harvard's Fairchild Laboratory.

Opposite page: Payette's rough sketches of interior layouts, top left; VRSB's rough sketches of exterior massings, top right. Program studies based on the modular lab, bottom left and right.

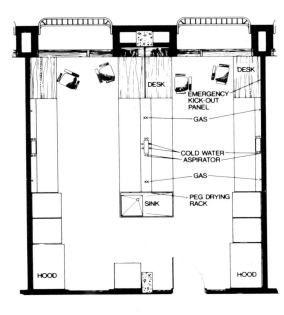

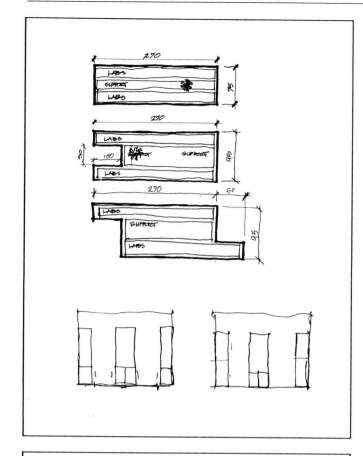

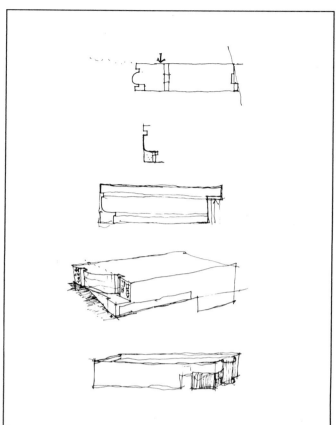

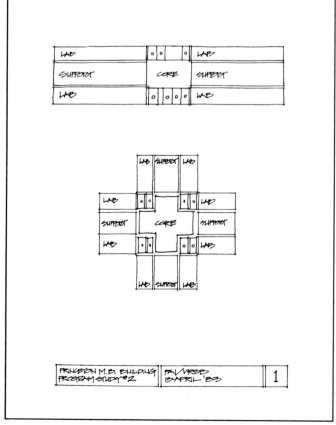

PRINCETON M.B. BUILDING PROGRAM STUDY #2 | PR/VRSB 13 APRIL '83 | 1

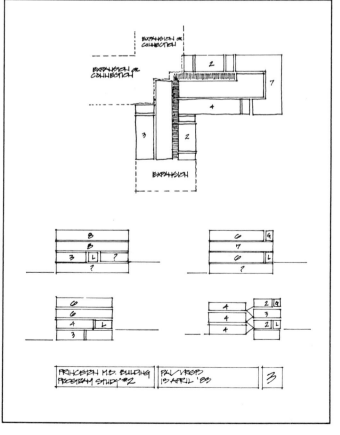

PRINCETON M.B. BUILDING PROGRAM STUDY #2 | PR/VRSB 13 APRIL '83 | 3

OFFICE LAYOUT AND WINDOW OPENINGS

Due to the construction schedule, elevations had to be designed before interior planning was complete. Although the architects could not predict at this point where the offices would be, decisions had to be made about windows. Not wanting to circumscribe the location of offices according to windows, they came up with a formula to cluster offices at the ends of the spur corridors, in zones of the building where people would tend to gather.

In between the office clusters a large research group would be combined with a small one in order to provoke competition. Each group was going to have to compete for its share of the unassigned lab space in between the offices. As the lab modules were easily customized to suit individual researchers, this design was flexible—there would be no need to move walls later. The ambiguity in the demarcation of space gave the administrator leeway in assigning space, not only for dealing with partitions but to respond to personality or "turf" problems.

Setting zones for office and lab modules established the general location of window openings and allowed the architects to plan a schematic layout of building systems, which, in turn, affected the elevations by circumscribing the minimum dimensions between window openings. The narrow widths between some paired windows were established by the size of the columns, while the ample widths between other paired windows were set by requirements for mechanical piping—air intake and all vertical risers are in the building's skin.

By the end of April 1983, the architects had figured out the essential elements of the building—the massing, the floor plans, and the repetitive window openings. Now they had to make the pieces work.

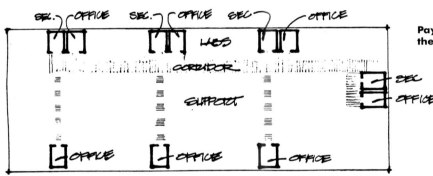

Payette's rough sketches of the building organization

EACH FLOOR SHALL CONTAIN SEVEN OFFICES FOUR OF THESE OFFICES SHALL HAVE SEC. AREA ADJACENT TO THEM

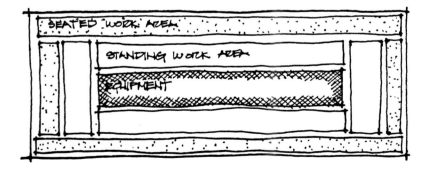

SHADED AREA

SUPPORT

OFFICE

LAB

Additional sketches by Payette, left; below: An early exterior elevation sketch by Venturi.

ENTRY LOBBY AND STAIR

As the Venturi team's design for the front façade composition evolved, it became clear that a decision about the placement of the main entry had to be reached. However, the location of the entry was going to affect the building's core and first-floor layout, which were still being studied by the Payette team. Here the design of the exterior and interior had to be integrated. Once the two teams had agreed on where to put the front door, it would be too late for one team to change its mind later.

In early April the architects met to evaluate the alternatives. There was little agreement except that entering the building at a point about a third of its overall length from the end felt most comfortable to both firms. The two firms postponed their decision. Payette architects felt they did not "understand" the building well enough at this point, and VRSB agreed that the decision should be driven by internal workings.

A sketch section made in mid-April suggested a direct connection between the front entry lobby and the lower level. Jim Collins stated, "I had a sort of loose train of thought and started drawing grand staircases, but totally missed the boat." Floor plans drawn in May showed no direct link from the lobby to the ground floor entry, but by early June the architects had finally solved the problem. Looking back to the first sketch they realized they had had the answer all along, but had not known it.

Their solution resolved both programmatic and design issues. Students would usually approach the building from College Walk, and faculty members would generally enter from the parking lot at the lower level. Because student activities were located at the lower level and the faculty's

activities were located upstairs, the staircase was to serve as a "classic mixing place," encouraging interaction outside of class. Aesthetically, the placement of the entry and stair at the third point was ideal, and it would have been virtually impossible to place them anywhere else.

Jim Collins points to this as an example of how the two firms' approaches complemented each other. From a programmatic

perspective, Payette Associates felt the entry should be "disarming, familiar, ordinary, comfortable. People coming into the building shouldn't feel psychologically intimidated by the nature of research taking place there." VRSB's philosophy is to glorify the ordinary. When Collins tried to rotate the upper portion of the stair, he received advice from Robert Venturi to "keep it as simple as possible as a foil for embellishments."

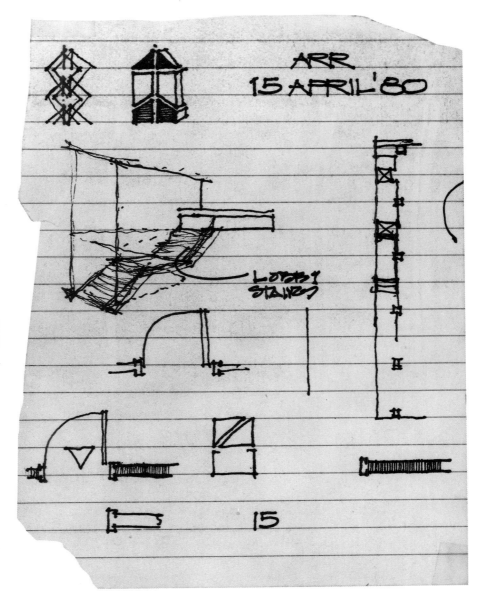

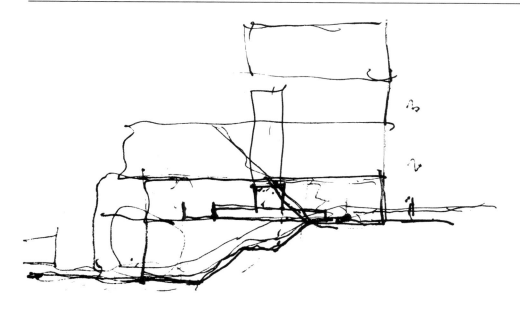

Stairway sketches, opposite and left, and floor organization diagram, below.

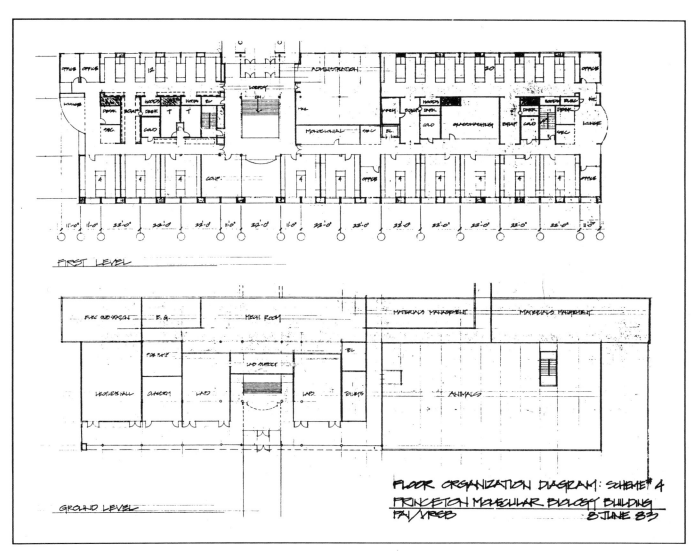

FIRST LEVEL

GROUND LEVEL

FLOOR ORGANIZATION DIAGRAM: SCHEME #4
PRINCETON MOLECULAR BIOLOGY BUILDING
PA/VRSB   8 JUNE 83

PUSHING OUT THE BOX

At this point the Venturi team began to manipulate the ends of the building. Collins recalls that planning the lounges at the ends of the corridors both satisfied the program and gave VRSB flexibility to shape the form. To do this, the architects juggled the building's efficiency ratio—the proportion of gross to net square feet. Each department was allotted a portion of the net space. The architects "played" with the gross square footage and counted the lounge areas as circulation space. Their aim was to carve out special areas that would be difficult for someone to claim later for different uses (i.e., for a secretarial station).

The design of these lounge areas went through many iterations. The lounges were to be open and inviting, but "noncommittal," so that someone using one would feel free not to join in an activity. Although the overall form began as a plain box, Dr. Levine recalls, "Once Venturi started to play with the ends, it became clear it was the right thing to do. We never reverted." Venturi's team studied subtle differences of form in plan and elevation—two grooves versus one, or varying curve shapes, for instance. In the final design, one end of the "boxy" building is bowed and the other is notched, each providing spatial relief from the repetitive interior and an unusual vantage point from which to view the campus.

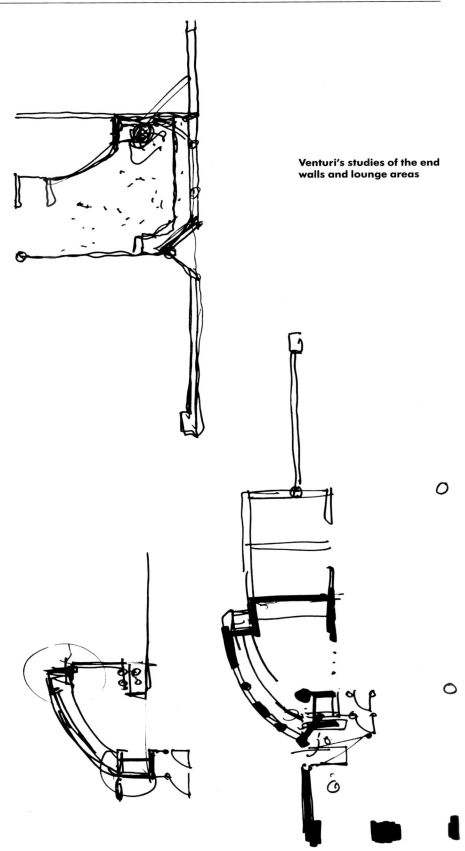

Venturi's studies of the end walls and lounge areas

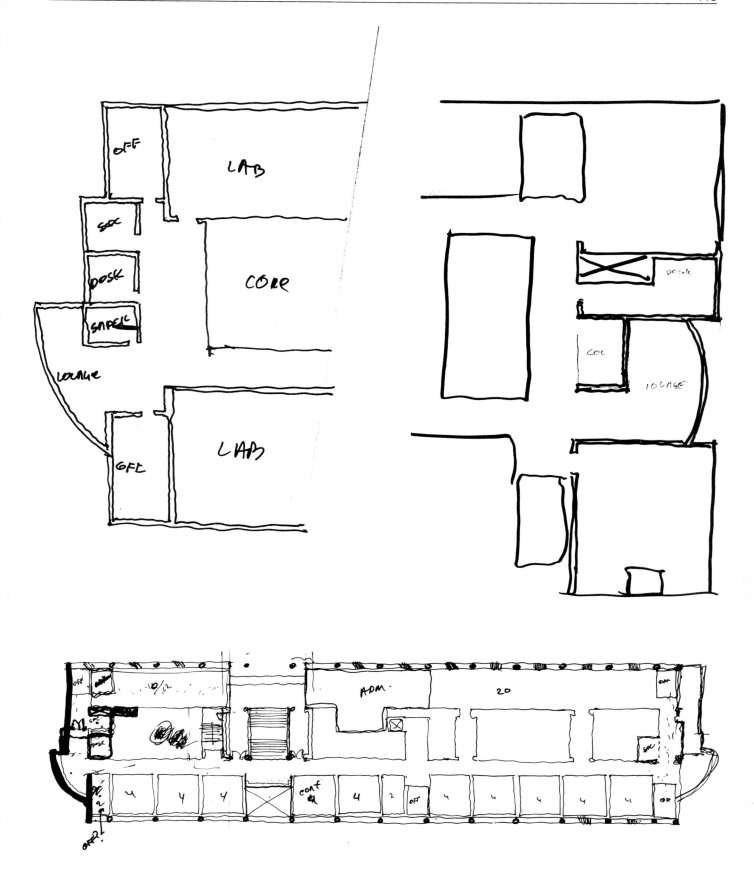

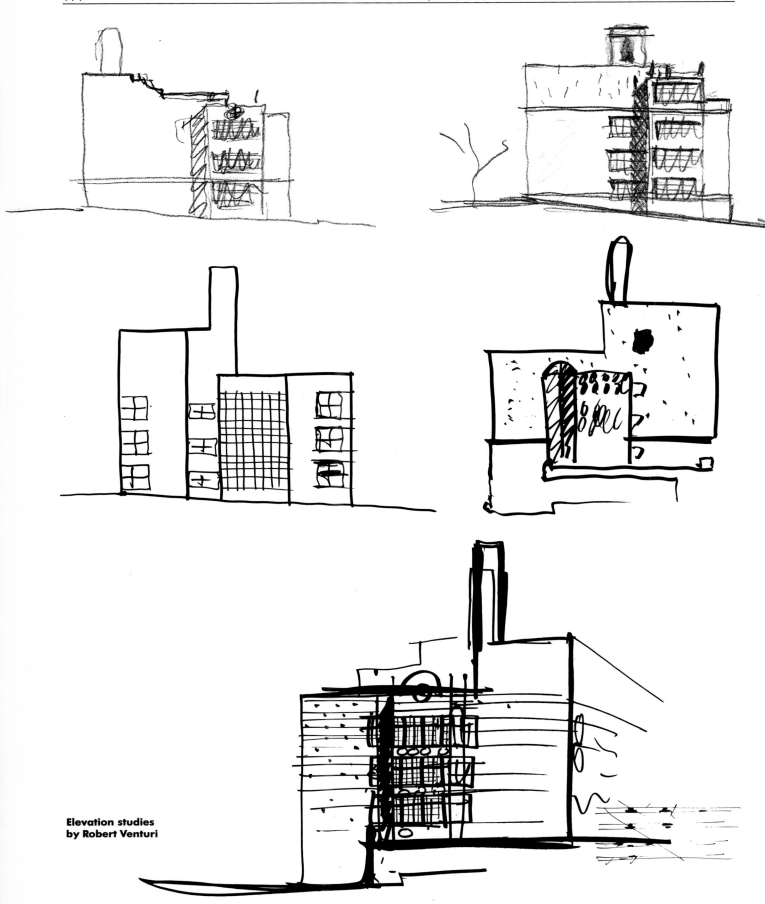

**Elevation studies
by Robert Venturi**

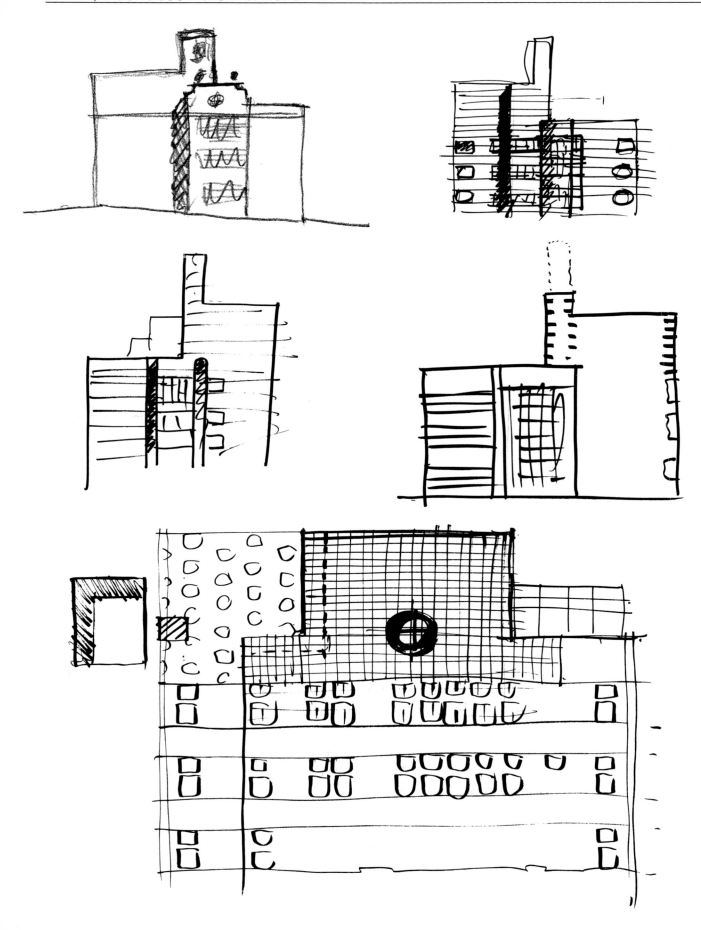

MECHANICAL SYSTEMS

Mechanical systems take up approximately 20 percent of the building's total square footage, but, to the extent possible, they were planned to give VRSB maximum flexibility in the design of the exterior. The planning of air-intake louvers and vertical risers located in the building's skin was coordinated with the development of window proportions, casework, and brick patterns. Ceiling plenums for overhead systems in the labs set vertical dimensions.

Payette Associates provided VRSB with schematic sections through windows for elevations studies, showing the relation of window to sill, the maximum window height, and floor-to-floor height. VRSB's details for stone window sills had to be assessed by Payette, the mechanical engineer, and the window fabricator, and so these sections were drawn repeatedly, as the design evolved.

For this type of facility, it is difficult to centralize exhaust air; and numerous stacks are usually required. The combination of exhaust stacks and air-intake louvers established a strong rhythm and scale for the front façade, which architect Venturi wanted control over. He also wanted to make the north façade higher—to give it more prominence, to match the height of the trees, and to improve the proportions of the building by making it less "square," as described in the design guidelines from the early site analysis.

Both of these aims could be achieved by transference of the mechanical room to the north side of the roof, rather than the middle (all exhaust air originates in the middle of the building). Payette decided to design its own proposal for this new scheme, so that the engineers could not later say it was impossible. (Although the system was not ultimately built according to their scheme, the architects felt that having had to go through the exercise improved their ability to leverage the decision in favor of Venturi's design.) Then, the scientists decided to put south-facing greenhouses on the roof, making the location of the mechanical room on the north side the only possibility. Once again, many factors converged to reinforce the "rightness" of a decision.

PRELIMINARY COST ESTIMATE

At the beginning of August 1983, a schematic set of drawings showing furniture and equipment, and including outline specifications, was issued to the construction manager, Barr & Barr, for pricing. Princeton usually works with construction managers, in lieu of bidding jobs, although technically they often hire a general contractor to provide that service. According to Gary Ireland, project manager for Princeton, "We prefer to involve the CM as early as possible—to assist in the design process by providing cost information and value engineering for the project as it develops. We get earlier insight on critical issues than with a project that goes out to bid."

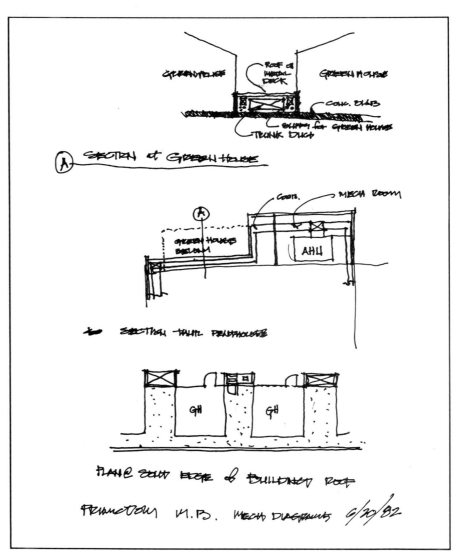

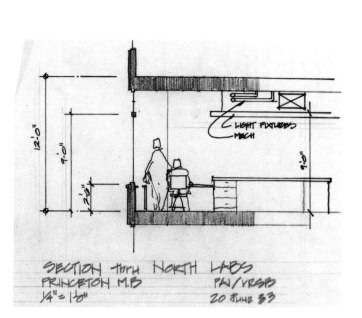

SECTION thru NORTH LABS
PRINCETON M.B PW/VRSB
¼" = 1'-0" 20 JUNE 83

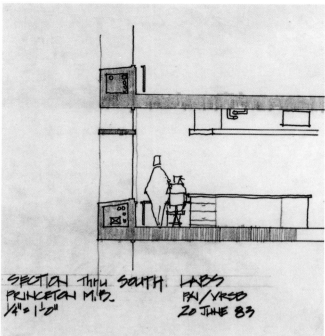

SECTION thru SOUTH LABS
PRINCETON M.B PW/VRSB
¼" = 1'-0" 20 JUNE 83

Opposite: Study for relocating mechanical equipment.

Above left and right: Payette's schematic sections through windows show clearances needed for mechanical equipment. Venturi's staff made full-scale mock-ups of the windows, left, to study the facade design.

DESIGN DEVELOPMENT
July—December 1983
CONSTRUCTION DOCUMENTS
October 1983—July 1984

Due to the compressed schedule and constraints imposed by the collaborative nature of the design process, during this phase the design is refined without major changes. VRSB continues to study the façade details, in particular the ornamental brick patterning. Payette sets up the drawing set so that the design development and documentation take place simultaneously.

FAÇADE DESIGN

According to architectural critic Karen Stein, Robert Venturi referred to both New England mills and Elizabethan manor houses, as a study in repetition and rhythm, for his design of the façade. The mills were appropriate models for the loftlike interior and modular lab spaces. The manor houses were chosen as models because of their resemblance to the surrounding campus architecture. Stein observed in *Architectural Record* (August 1986): "From these precedents came inspiration for the ornamental brick bands that add a layer of historical symbolism to the exterior. . . ."

Variations on the brick patterns were studied in exhaustive detail. The final design combines checkerboard and diaper patterns, which create several orders of scale and break down the building's bulk. At the main entry, the patterns are interrupted by a Gothic-inspired cutout in the cast stone, the shape of which also went through many iterations before finding its final form. The entrances were detailed to correlate with some of the materials found in the interior. VRSB architect John Schaff stated, "This level of intense and fine-grain material use seems tiny at the scale of the whole building, but Bob's [Venturi's] contribution

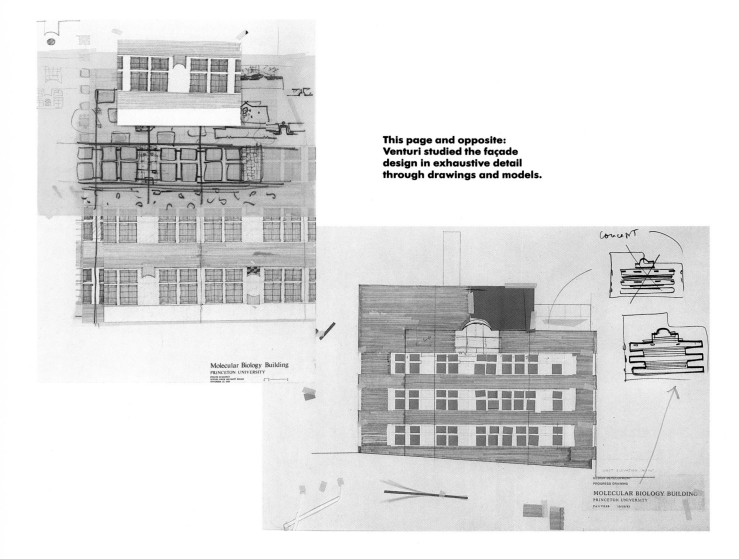

This page and opposite: Venturi studied the façade design in exhaustive detail through drawings and models.

Molecular Biology Building
PRINCETON UNIVERSITY

MOLECULAR BIOLOGY BUILDING
PRINCETON UNIVERSITY

was to make sure that those things happened."

The University imposed no directives or restraints on Venturi's design process. Princeton's Hlafter explains, "The number of patterns on the building is at least puzzling at first, but rarely does anyone say they've gotten bored by it. Some buildings are well designed and not controversial, but once you've seen them, there's nothing left to discover. With the Lewis Lab, I still discover things over time."

INTERIOR DESIGN

Having detailed the technical requirements for specific rooms and coordinated consultant work, the Payette team at this point developed the interior design. Stated architect Collins, "The lab is for people. A Ph.D. in biology doesn't want to work in a metal refrigerator." The goal of the Payette team was to create a traditional collegiate ambience, using red oak trim and paned glass partitions throughout, to add touches of warmth to the "high-tech" environment.

The entry lobby was to become one of the focal points of the interior, and an elaborate floor paving pattern in Italian marble was designed for that space. The continuity of materials used inside and out and the high level of detailing contributed to the seamlessness of the design of the building's public areas.

COST ESTIMATE

The preliminary construction cost estimate, based on the schematic drawings, came in at $2 million over budget. The University agreed to increase the construction budget by eliminating the need for contingency funds. After details for the skin and interior wood trim were estimated, the cost went up by another $1 million. Much of the effort during design development was a search for ways to cut costs without reduction of the size of the building or diminution of the design concept.

Molecular Biology Building
PRINCETON UNIVERSITY

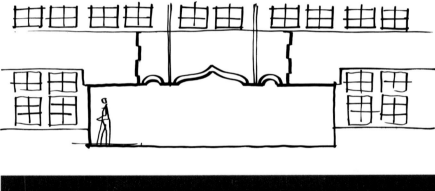

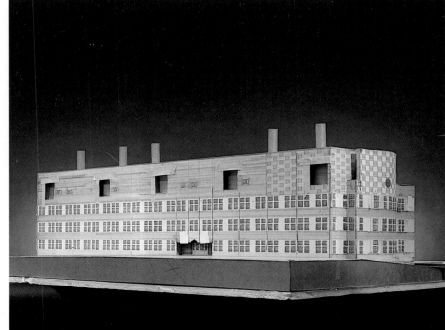

CONSTRUCTION ADMINISTRATION

The Venturi team provided Payette with sketch working drawings of the exterior skin (masonry, stone, and windows), to be redrawn for the final set. VRSB also oversaw this construction. In order to achieve the subtleties of the design, a high degree of control had to be maintained over the manufacture and installation of materials.

In December 1983, nine months after the architects first received the program, excavation began. Working drawings were not complete until the following July, compounding the possibilities for error in the construction of this highly complex facility. Despite the complexity of construction, or perhaps because of it, the collaborative spirit of the design process took over and inspired people to do whatever was in the best interest of the job.

Nearly everyone has a story to tell illustrating errors made at this stage. Jon Hlafter says: "Colored brick was ordered from a manufacturer in Utah. When thirty freight cars full of brick arrived, they were the wrong color. Apparently they had been fired in a new kiln which didn't provide exactly the right temperature. In some designs, if the color is too light or too dark, it can be easy to adjust, but not when the media is brick. It was a clear mistake by the company."

Venturi said that he preferred not to use that brick, but that he did not want to compromise the schedule and would go along with the client's decision. Princeton president William Bowen managed to arrange for a train to go to Utah to get the correct material. Recalls Princeton's Jon Hlafter, "We had the choice of building the building in a way that would not carry out the architects' idea, or take the steps to expedite the replacement of the bricks, and that's what we chose to do."

Hlafter advises that working with patterned brick is not easy: "Different colors of brick are made of clays with different densities, which absorb moisture from the mortar around them at varying rates. If you want to play with subtleties, there are lots of technical controls you have to be prepared to do." But, difficulties aside, according to VRSB architect John Schaff, "The masons loved putting up the brick patterns. They also made mistakes, since the pattern was so complicated, and we had to inspect the work carefully. But Bob decided to leave some of the mistakes in. The fact that it wasn't perfect expressed the homemade, quiltlike quality that he had in mind for the building."

The final design: Ground and first floor plans, right; north elevation, opposite page.

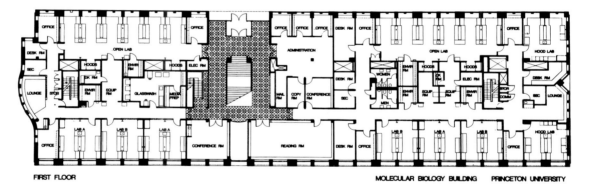

FIRST FLOOR

MOLECULAR BIOLOGY BUILDING   PRINCETON UNIVERSITY

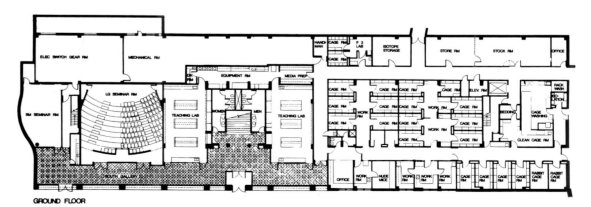

GROUND FLOOR

OBSERVATIONS

"At the start of design there's a process of exploration. When something feels right, you know it."—Jim Collins, Jr.

- "The design of the Lewis Lab represents the ultimate rightness. Something happened," says architect Jim Collins. "Venturi was ready, and when the right building came along, he knew what to do." However, throughout the process, the convergence of multiple factors—programmatic, formal, or technical—reaffirmed the architects' sense of the "rightness" of their choices.

- One reason the relationship between VRSB and Payette was so successful is that it was grounded in the firms' mutual respect for what each other brought to the design process and in their recognition of the opportunity to learn from each other. According to Princeton's Jon Hlafter, "You try to put together the best components in a process, whether in designing a building or anything else. If the two architects don't get along, it would be a disaster. This was one of those times when people felt good about bringing their expertise into a forum where they had to work with others who knew more about something than they did."

- A strong organizational framework enabled design team members to do what they did best. "Day to day, people didn't worry about where they were in the organization chart. The attitude was to go in a room and do the best job possible, not let other people down—the ultimate teamwork approach. We knew no one could do it alone," says Collins.

- Collins continues: "The reason Princeton has great buildings is not just that they hire great architects, but they are a great client. They didn't interfere, but everyone knew they expected great things.

They created an environment. They had a pulse on what was going on and had the courage to allow more experimental work, which might possibly expose them to criticism."

- Director Jon Hlafter explains Princeton's philosophy: "There is a need to allow consultant architects and engineers to do what they can do best. If I felt that I could do a better job than the architect I hired, then I shouldn't have hired him in the first place. If it turns out that what they are doing doesn't have logical, coherent thinking behind it, then you have to put an end to it. At Princeton we don't invest in architectural speculation or theory. Buildings must meet stated goals of program and budget. In this case we wanted the architects to produce a topflight, world-class molecular biology building and we succeeded."

- In many ways, this building type lent itself to teamwork. Payette's generic laboratory, a highly symmetrical and repetitive form with a loftlike spatial system, is ideally suited for VRSB's "decorated shed" approach. While VRSB was "painting the facade," Payette was engaged in a very different process; programming and design were integrated. The linking of programming information to design ideas along the way defined what was possible and shaped the program itself.

- One aspect of this parallel process was that it yielded two very different experiences for the client. In the words of Princeton's Dr. Levine: "Working with Venturi was fantastic, but, while we felt like equal partners with Payette in determining the shape of things, with Venturi it was more like watching him change his mind as the idea evolved. It was hard to grasp what he had in mind. I thought I knew what the building would be like, but when it went up, I was surprised."

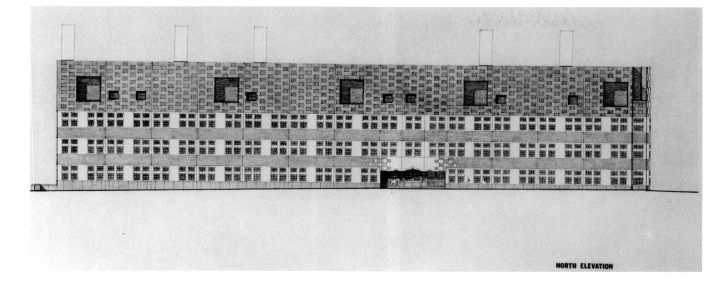

NORTH ELEVATION

The finished building, this page and opposite, clockwise from top left: The main entrance; a lounge area; an end wall; a laboratory; and an auxiliary entrance.

ADDITION TO ASU COLLEGE OF ARCHITECTURE AND ENVIRONMENTAL DESIGN

DOES A BUILDING TEACH?

Using a limited-entry competition, Arizona State University in Tempe commissioned a nationally recognized architect to design a complex addition to its College of Architecture and Environmental Design. Because of its location on the city edge of ASU's urban campus, the building's appearance was a key issue; it represented a public face of the University. Architect Alan Chimacoff's approach to the limitations of site and a tight budget was to design a box (and use limited resources to embellish the façade), and to ingeniously explore internal spatial qualities. Much of the success of the project was due to the role played by the construction manager, also an outside consultant, to evaluate the project program, budget, and competition submissions as well as to monitor the building's size and cost throughout the process. This is a case study of the use of the competition process to get more services and better design for less money.

PROJECT OVERVIEW

Project 100,000 sf addition to ASU's College of Architecture and Environmental Design.

Architect The Hillier Group, Alan Chimacoff, Director of Design, Princeton, New Jersey; Architecture One, Ltd., Phoenix, Arizona, associated architects.

Client Arizona State University, Tempe, Arizona; 3D/International, Inc., Phoenix, Arizona, construction manager.

Charge To create a state-of-the-art facility with architectural distinction to help achieve the school's goals and enhance its national reputation.

Issues ✔ Using a competition to commission a significant design and more services for less money.

✔ Design of an addition to be compatible with the architectural character of the original building, the rest of the campus, and the regional vernacular—while making a strong independent statement.

✔ Development of a design concept without benefit of a dialogue between architect and client.

✔ Benefits of working with the construction manager in order to maximize a tight program and budget and to interface with University procedures.

✔ Working with architects as clients.

Duration Seventeen months from planning through completion of working drawings (April 1986–August 1987).

Budget $11.5 million for the total project; $8.64 million for construction.

TIMELINE

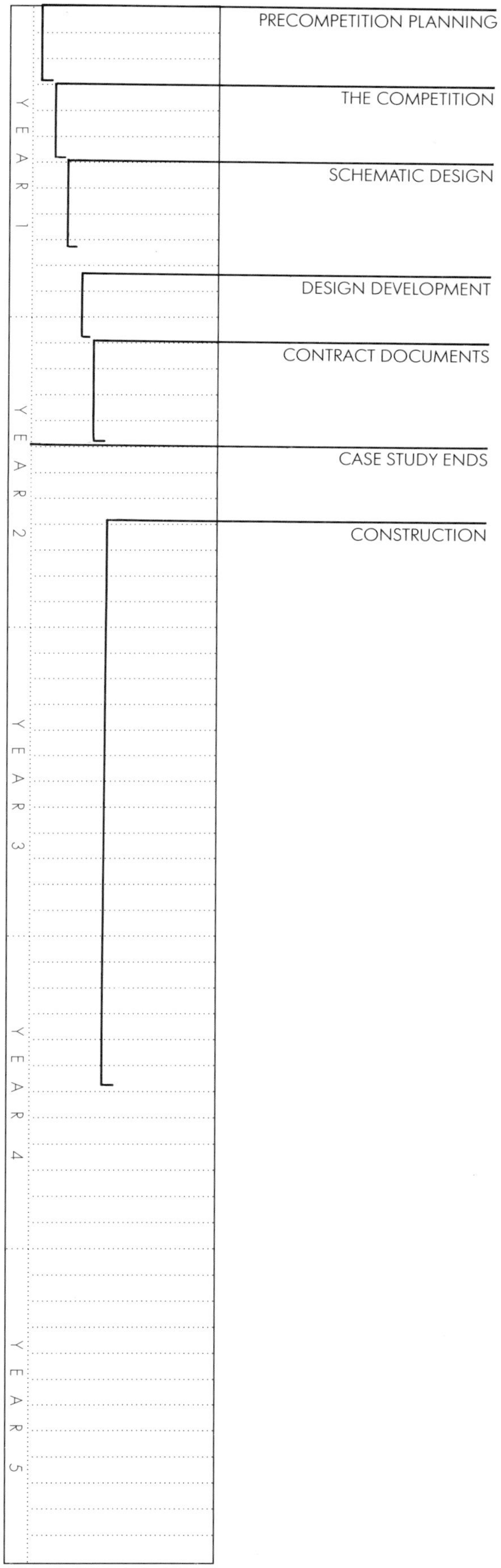

YEAR 1

YEAR 2

YEAR 3

YEAR 4

YEAR 5

PRECOMPETITION PLANNING

THE COMPETITION

SCHEMATIC DESIGN

DESIGN DEVELOPMENT

CONTRACT DOCUMENTS

CASE STUDY ENDS

CONSTRUCTION

BACKGROUND

Like many schools in the Sunbelt, Arizona State University is growing rapidly. In the last few years, ASU has undertaken a major capital expansion program, involving up to $100 million of work a year, perhaps encouraged by University president Russell Nelson's belief that the school "needed first-class buildings to be a first-class institution." After years of small, scattered projects, suddenly the equivalent of ten $10 million buildings were going up, making the board of regents one of the most active developers in the state. At the Tempe campus, the regents had commissioned buildings such as libraries, laboratories, computer education facilities, and a fine arts center.

After all this, the University's Office of Planning and Construction was not equipped to oversee such a high volume of complex construction. Some of the new buildings were dysfunctional upon completion or ran over budget. Consequently, in 1984 the board of regents adopted new regulations to control the building procurement process, including a policy that a construction manager must be hired for all state school projects.

Development plans for the College of Architecture and Environmental Design projected a 20 percent increase in the current student population of 1,000 over the following ten years, leading to the need to expand the college's 50,000 sf building. According to ASU's associate dean Timothy McGinty, "Some of the faculty, particularly the younger faculty [who had been hired from Princeton and Cornell, he pointed out] were terrified that the expansion wouldn't be of a high enough level, but would result in a competent but bland architectural statement," like the existing building, designed twenty-five years earlier by a local architect in a "softened brutalism" style.

DECISION FOR A COMPETITION

There had been five competitions in The Valley (as the Phoenix area is known) in the previous year-and-a-half. Roger Schluntz, director of ASU's Department of Architecture, had organized several, among them one for The Fine Arts Center, won by architect Antoine Predock. Schluntz convinced the dean of the College of Architecture and Environmental Design, Gerald McSheffrey, and ASU's president, Russell Nelson, to sponsor a competition for the new architecture building as well. McSheffrey was appointed professional advisor and chair of the building committee, which included representatives from the school's three programs (architecture, planning, and design) and from the administration. Tim McGinty would chair the Building Program Committee.

Although the Fine Arts Center competition process had been considered a success in many ways, it had created some problems when the winning entry turned out to be 40 percent too big, and over budget. The construction manager had not been brought in on that job until the schematic design phase. To avoid repetition of this problem, ASU brought the construction management team on board before the competition for the School of Architecture addition began—to help evaluate the project program, the budget, and the submissions.

The Houston-based firm, 3D/International (3D/I) was paid a lump sum to serve as an advisor about the project to the client, in service to the client, the architect, and the contractor. In other words, the construction manager acted as an extension of ASU's Office of Planning and Construction, because the university's own staff was so overworked by the extensive building program.

Architect Ward Simpson handled this project for 3D/I. His role was to serve basically as an overall project manager—to monitor the building's size and cost, help price options, evaluate bids, and prevent errors. He expedited the whole process by running biweekly job meetings for which he set the agendas ahead of time and arranged for the participation of appropriate people. Trained as an architect, Simpson had just completed working as the construction manager on the Fine Arts Center at the time this project began.

PRECOMPETITION PLANNING
April–June 1986

The program and budget are developed by the faculty committee and construction manager and then negotiated with the University administration. Once the size and cost of the project are set, it will be hard to make changes, so a lot of planning is required at this stage. The building committee organizes the competition.

PROGRAMMING

Associate Dean McGinty began work on the program by researching the experience of other schools of architecture with recent buildings and writing for copies of their programs. He also looked at schools that had held competitions for other types of buildings and spoke with the people involved.

McGinty says that one issue he confronted was that "a university is an institution based in change. Deans and department heads, along with their agendas, come and go." Therefore the building needed to provide flexibility for future organizational change. Another issue, points out 3D/I's Ward Simpson, was that "A university is an institution in conflict with itself. The business people want to control expenses while the academics will want as much as possible." According to McGinty, "Finding a balance between what people thought they deserved and what the University felt was appropriate was a real challenge."

McGinty enlisted the members of an architectural class in programming, to help "do it the right way." Guided by the motto, "Don't ask people what they need, ask them what's the best they've ever seen," the class interviewed staff, faculty, and students and surveyed opinions. McGinty analyzed these polls along with the information gathered from other schools and wrote a detailed program that justified a need for 140,000 gross square feet (gsf). The board of regents would only approve 100,000 gsf, however. Part of the disagreement lay in the fact that the regents used an efficiency ratio (net/gross square feet) of 75 percent, even though the construction manager advised that a ratio of 65% would be more appropriate for this type of building. "This led to some strategic thinking about the investment. Where were we going to grow? We had to winnow out what was unimportant," recalls McGinty.

The final program included a library, shop facilities, computer laboratories, exhibit galleries, research facilities, and project archives—in addition to classrooms, lecture halls, studios, and offices. The technology research laboratory, which requires twenty-two-foot ceilings for building mock-ups, simulations, and testing, was one element that the building committee refused to cut from the program. This laboratory also required direct access to an outdoor work area as well as to a loading dock.

Another program objective was to "take full advantage of the microcomputer revolution" and so become a model for other schools. A local area network (LAN) was to be provided, so that in future, computers could be installed in every room. Nearly all students and faculty members use personal computers, and the design of the building was to allow for flexibility in the location of hardware.

Fostering a sense of community among the three divisions of the College—architecture, urban planning, and design—was another stated goal of the building program. To promote interaction among the faculty, the program called for clusters of faculty offices, to be associated with different research or studio spaces. A mailroom was envisioned as a faculty lounge, as it was a place where everyone had to go every day. Opportunities for outdoor activities were also to be provided.

BUDGET

The construction manager reviewed both the program and the budget by modeling the projected construction costs, based on past experience with similar building types. His conclusion was that the budget was inadequate. Specifically, the allocation for extension of the existing building's utilities was unrealistic, because the level of service was insufficient. The regents chose to ignore this advice and approved $11.5 million for a 100,000 sf building. The construction budget was reduced by $80,000, to pay for the competition.

SCOPE OF SERVICES

The full fee (the state caps fees at 6 percent of construction costs) would be paid according to the design contract, although as a result of the competition it would be reduced in scope. To accelerate the process, the construction manager and the ASU facilities group developed a contract that was more complete than typical, listing a package of deliverables for each phase of work. The schedule called for the building to be ready for the start of classes in the fall of 1989, which would coincide with the twenty-fifth anniversary of the school.

The faculty and building committee organized a competition and prepared a program to achieve school goals and satisfy functional requirements.

THE SITE

Arizona State University is located in Tempe, eleven miles from downtown Phoenix. With eleven colleges and an enrollment of 40,000, ASU is a small city in itself. The College of Architecture and Environmental Design lies on the edge of campus that borders the City of Tempe.

By virtue of its site, the new building had an important role to play—as an intermediary between the University and the urban environment. The site for the expansion was a 90,000 sf parcel immediately to the north of the existing building. It was bordered on three sides by public streets. University Drive, along the north edge of the site, is a heavily used, four-lane street. Along the eastern edge is a dead-end public way into the campus. On the south side is a service alley, separating the site from the existing College of Architecture.

The faculty originally wanted a site at least twice as large as this one. They feared the small site would not only be hard to build on, but would also force the design of a tall building, in order to leave ground space available for the outdoor courts. To prove that the building would not fit on the site, ASU's Tim McGinty drew up a schematic layout. His arguments did not convince Dean McSheffrey, however, who thought the site was fine.

The new building had to be appropriate to the region, the campus setting, and the existing College of Architecture. However, the original building, with its exposed-aggregate, poured-in-place concrete façade, was quite different from the prevailing style of the campus architecture and from vernacular Southwestern style.

ARCHITECT SELECTION

As part of ASU's standard architect selection process, the college building committee advertises the job in local papers; the Office of Planning and Construction reviews the credentials submitted and gives a ranked list of architects to the ASU Design

Review Board; and the board along with the user committee interview the firms and recommend three to the president, who then makes a selection.

The only difference between this selection process and the competition was that, in the competition, the three firms recommended by the Design Review Board were asked to submit designs, and the jury review took the place of the interview. In addition, the younger faculty, acting on their own initiative, invited fifty architects, including Alan Chimacoff, to submit qualifications. Twenty-six firms responded.

According to McGinty, in addition to demonstrated design competence and professional recognition, the building committee looked for firms whose experience included:

1. a completed building similar in scope, complexity, and quality, designed for a public institution or state bureaucracy;
2. "one or more good, dumb boxes," as the

committee felt that the program and site constraints dictated that the building would have to assume this form, and that its character would be determined by developing the skin; and
3. energy conservation and life-cycle cost techniques.

The three firms invited to compete were: The Hillier Group, Hammond Beeby & Babka, and Coover Saemish Anderson in association with Hoover Burg Desmond. (Alan Chimacoff had just joined The Hillier Group as director of design, so he and the firm decided to submit joint qualifications.) Each firm received a $20,000 honorarium.

At a precompetition orientation meeting, the three firms visited the site and neighboring area, and were shown what the building committee liked about the campus, including "hidden" courts that give the campus its unique character. Each firm had to submit a signed contract before submitting its entry, and name a local associate architect. At this time, the firms could submit in writing any questions regarding the program. The building committee's response in writing would be the only client involvement allowed during the competition.

THE ARCHITECTS

The Hillier Group is a multidisciplinary firm with a staff of 250 and offices in Princeton and Philadelphia. In addition to architecture, interior design, construction management, and real estate development, the firm offers services in landscape architecture, land planning, and graphics. Alan Chimacoff, a professor of architecture at Princeton University for fifteen years, joined The Hillier Group as director of design in 1986.

The project team, which also produced the competition entry, included: Alan Chimacoff, in charge of design; Gerard F. X. Geier II, project manager; Douglas Harvey, project coordinator; and designers Eric Baker and Keat Tan. The team's major responsibility was to refine the scheme through design development, after which they were to turn it over to a local associate architect, Architecture One.

The Hillier Group selected Architecture One after interviewing a number of firms, discovered through referrals and the local AIA. At Architecture One, Will Craig was the project manager and Frank Roberts the principal in charge. They were responsible for producing the contract documents, construction administration, and generally handling local issues.

The site

THE COMPETITION
July–September 1986

The firms have twelve weeks to develop their submissions. The competition requirements are focused on size and budget. To address these constraints, The Hillier Group's approach is to start with the simplest form possible—a box—and develop the design by embellishing its surface and exploring interior spatial qualities.

PROGRAM CONSTRAINTS

Chimacoff described the image of the school conjured up by the program as a "rambling two-story structure surrounding various kinds of courts." Yet, the accommodation of both a large bicycle storage court and outdoor work court on the ground level would have taken up most of the site area. The team's first step, then, was to test the volume according to some tentative goals:

- To maintain the existing building's three-story height.
- To bridge the addition over the street.
- To carve out the two smallest courts possible.

The team used a computerized stacking program to determine how much of the program area would fit into a volume defined by these parameters. The answer surprised them: The entire program took up only 2.5 stories.

DESIGN CONCEPT

The shell had to be built for $76 per square foot. Chimacoff comments, "Even in Arizona you couldn't afford to build a complex building at that price. So we decided to build the simplest form possible. If your basic design is simple and pragmatic, you'll have much more money left for embellishment and details." (Chimacoff says he learned this from Gordon Wu Hall, designed by Robert Venturi for Princeton University when he served on

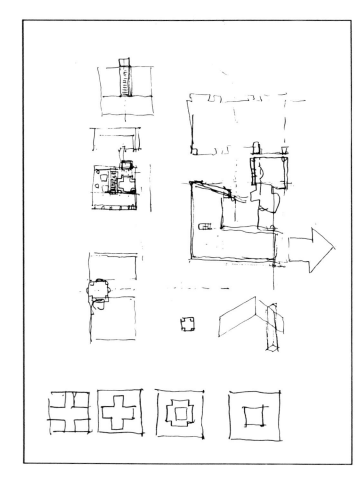

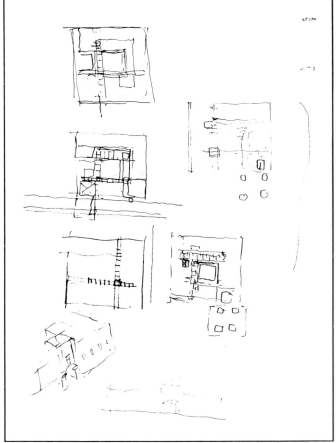

the architectural advisory board there.) This approach disciplined the designer's thought processes. "We chose to explore the surface and what we could do spatially within the box."

A preliminary sketch in the architect's notebook contained the kernel of the design concept—"stacked donuts." Two interior courts organized the building spatially. Chimacoff quotes an adage of Colin Rowe: "Free plan, paralyzed section; free section, paralyzed plan," comparing the tradeoff between the open-plan quality of a loft-type space with the particular nature of a more classical design. Frank Lloyd Wright's Johnson Wax

building was a source for the formal entry passageway. The campus visit inspired ideas for a hidden court and a "column court," to commemorate a concrete annex building scheduled for demolition.

Chimacoff proposed a three-and-a-half-story structure that would take up most of the site and create a plaza out of the street in between the two buildings. A tower housing research activities would bridge the mall and symbolically link the old and new. Because the existing building is symmetrical, the architects thought of having two bridges, for balance. This idea was soon abandoned.

Chimacoff's early notebook sketches show the kernel of the design concept.

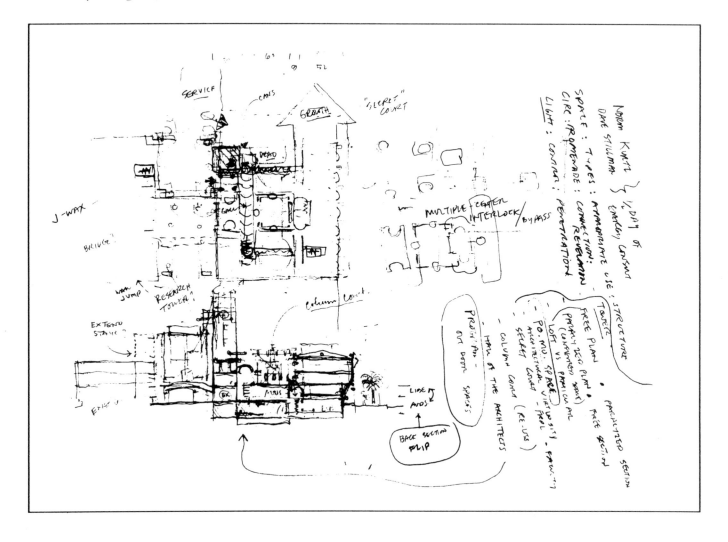

THE SUBMISSION

In their narrative, the architects wrote that the purpose of the building was to promote "learning" and "community," and so the building was designed with two "centers," of importance and of the form. The "center of learning" consisted of the building entry, which faced the library entrance, and the ceremonial stairway. The "center of community" was established by a set of stacked courts in the middle of the building, an outdoor court above an indoor one.

"These courts reveal the organization of the building— concentric and multilayered," wrote the architects. The lower court served as a lobby for lecture rooms, providing a focus for the student community. The outdoor court above was to be the heart of a concentric layout of studios, research spaces, and faculty offices. Faculty offices would encircle it on two levels. The court was intended primarily for faculty use.

Seven skylights in the form of kiosks—six of them designed in the style of influential architects—would connect the two courts and symbolically represent "seven lanterns of architecture." The seventh skylight, made up of columns salvaged from the concrete annex (the column court), "beyond representing nostalgia and local context . . . stands for all other worthy architects. . . ."

Building Systems. The structural system proposed was a poured-in-place reinforced concrete frame. For the exterior wall, the architects chose a simple, inexpensive system: stucco, concrete block, aluminum windows and doors, glass block, glazed ceramic tile, and redwood sunshades. The tower wall would consist of exposed steel framing and an aluminum curtain wall with clear and translucent glazing. For energy considerations, walls would have heavier-than-normal mass; glazing on the south façade was to be shaded, and glazing on the north and east façades was to be minimized. The mechanical system would distribute conditioned air via vertical ducts located at each corner of the interior courtyard.

Cost. Since the size and cost of the proposal totalled at slightly over the program estimate, it appeared that the program would have to be revised.

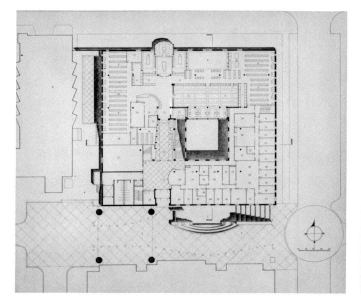

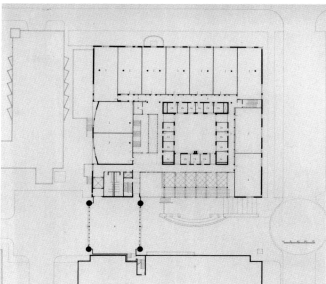

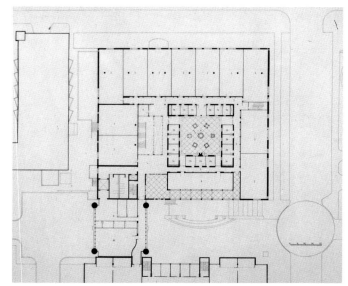

From the competition submission. This page, clockwise from upper left: First, second, and third floor plans. Opposite page: Three of the "Seven Lanterns of Architecture."

From the competition submission: Drawings illustrate the exterior of the building, opposite page, and the interior commons, above.

JUDGING THE ENTRIES

Prior to the public presentation of the submissions, members of the building committee critiqued each design with respect to the program, analyzing how each responded to the project goals and building and site issues. The construction manager analyzed the entries in terms of "cost and constructability issues." Nearly 300 students and faculty attended the presentations in early October. The jury was led by Joseph Esherick, former chairman of the Department of Architecture at the University of California at Berkeley, and included former ASU faculty and representatives of the building committee and the administration.

The Hillier team was informally notified the following day that they had won. Chimacoff's design was particularly praised "for its use of circulation spaces to encourage interaction among students and faculty." Associate Dean McGinty explains, "One reason we selected Alan's proposal was that the building was very elastic, not tied to a rigid system. . . . We knew it would be resilient enough to respond to the kinds of changes we'd have to make." 3D/I architect Ward Simpson recalls that the jurors were impressed with Chimacoff's skill in dealing with materials and textures. Students were enthusiastic about the design's Post-Modern—what they called "Northeastern"—influence.

SCHEMATIC DESIGN
October 1986–January 1987

The architects start a standard five-phase contract in schematics with a high-speed head start. Program and design revisions are discussed during the first real meetings with the client. The basic concept remains intact, and the plans are refined through a team effort between the architect, client, and construction manager.

CRITIQUE OF SUBMISSION

The architects began the actual job by reviewing their design with the building committee. Associate Dean McGinty posted the drawings in the architecture department and invited students and faculty members to write down their comments.

"Many of the faculty and local residents didn't approve of the character of the building. Rather than cladding the frame with a cosmetic skin, they would have preferred a building which integrated structure with appearance more," according to McGinty. One of the main concerns was with the choice of materials. "Many people felt the aesthetic of stucco had connotations inappropriate for a university," says project manager Gerard Geier. ASU wanted a material more like stone and asked to see other options.

Geier suggested using a type of concrete masonry unit he was familiar with because of his work on a Texas project. The block was sandblasted to expose the aggregate, creating a colorful, rich texture. Chimacoff liked this idea, as it could be used to interpret the wall surface of the local Biltmore Hotel, which featured patterned concrete block in the California style of Frank Lloyd Wright. ASU approved the use of this material

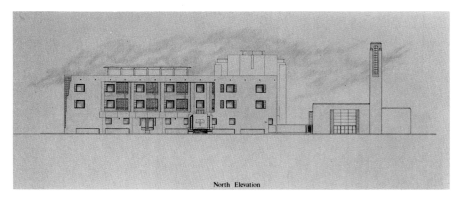

North Elevation

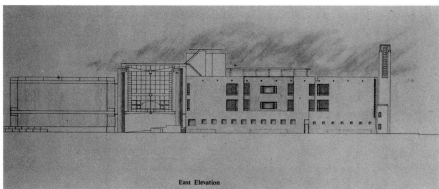

East Elevation

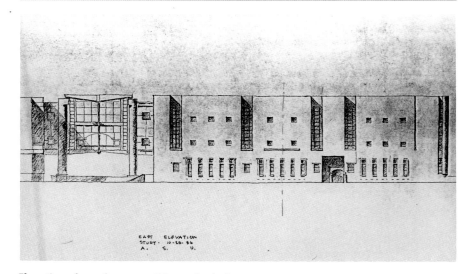

EAST ELEVATION
STUDY · 10-28-86
A. S. U.

Elevations from the competition submission

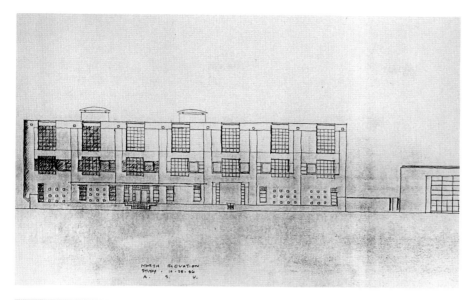

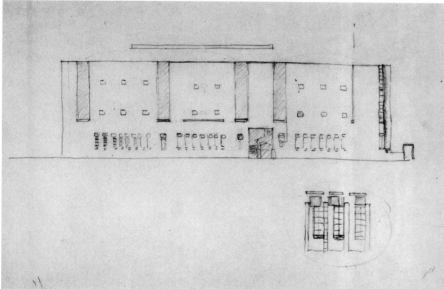

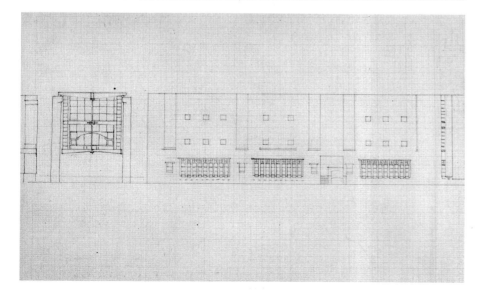

in concept, and the architects asked Architecture One to research fabrication methods and costs.

The design called for "peeling back" one corner of the masonry wall with glass to mark the entry to the campus. The faculty felt that this gesture would be unbecoming for an institutional building. In the revised design, the corner was articulated with a round bullnose shape, which, in Chimacoff's words, "served the same expressive function."

Another criticism was that the design was not responsive enough to climate. "There was no real attempt to resolve problems with the sun, such as vertical shades or deep-set windows. The relatively small amount of trellis was not enough, so that people questioned why it wasn't done all over," says McGinty. In response, the architects designed sunscreens for the windows, a solution McGinty felt was symbolic. "But the building, being compact and square, is relatively energy efficient by virtue of form, if not design."

Above: The Arizona Biltmore served as a reference for Chimacoff's design of the wall surface.

Left: Elevations revised in response to faculty comments.

PROGRAM REVISIONS

There had been a six-month gap between the time the program had been written and the time when the client was able to see how the design interpreted the program. Referring to the latter, McGinty recalls, "Now we could take a look and say 'Is that what you think we meant? If we'd known, we'd never have stated that requirement so strongly.' A lot came out and a lot needed to be revised." Primarily written to identify space requirements and justify budget needs, the program did not include an analysis of the working relationships between spaces. The architects now sat down with each group leader to reevaluate the design in terms of functional issues and to address questions raised by the competition.

The competition design was 10 percent too large. Together, the architects and client committee searched for ways to "shrink" the building, but the 75 percent net/gross allowable simply did not include enough circulation space. For example, the lower floor included three lecture rooms, to accommodate a total of 350 people, but not enough queuing space for the times when all three rooms would be used simultaneously. Part of the construction manager's evolving role was to convince the administration on behalf of the faculty to adjust the efficiency ratio.

The building committee decided that the research tower worked symbolically but not programmatically, and that it was more important that the link between the buildings be a student commons. The bridge structure was reduced in size by one-half, and research functions were relocated to the basement.

Space for the research activity was created by filling in an area that had been only partially excavated. This change improved the organization of the basement level, generally felt to have been the only real weak part of the competition design. Some reductions were made simply by "removing the fat" and "packing" the vertical circulation and toilet core more efficiently.

COST

Chimacoff credits construction management project manager Ward Simpson for being "firm and forceful about reducing both the area and cost. This effort, established during schematics, was diligently in force throughout the project." Simpson says that there were some causes he had to champion. One was the "smart" building feature to accommodate computers in

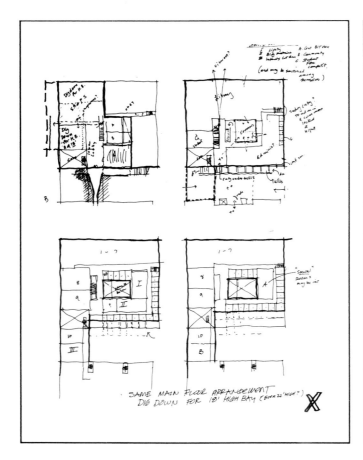

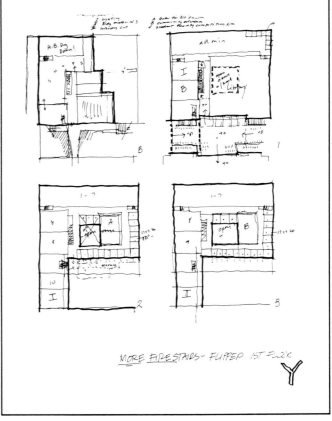

every room, for which the board of regents had given more construction dollars per square foot than usual. "If the choice was between skylights and having a big enough conduit, I made sure the 'smart' building features weren't lost or diminished, since it was important to the users and to the intent of the board of regents."

The construction manager's cost-estimating efforts helped the architects to achieve their desired effects—for example, in the selection of building systems. Over half of the building would have exposed structure; architect Chimacoff wanted to use a waffle slab system for aesthetic reasons. "Many people," recalls Simpson, "thought this method was expensive and old-fashioned." After evaluating four alternative systems, Simpson found the waffle slab was effective.

UTILITIES

It soon became apparent that, as the construction manager had warned, existing utilities could not be extended, and that the amount budgeted was not enough to bring in new service from outside the project area. Although the architects were not at fault, according to University procedures a project cannot proceed unless it is on budget. The process was in danger of being stalled. A special consultant was called in and, in the midst of evaluating the campus infrastructure in general, reviewed ASU's options. The university chose to build a new tunnel at a cost of $1.5 million. This caused a delay of three months. Luckily, enough time had been built into the construction schedule, although the documentation phase had to be compressed.

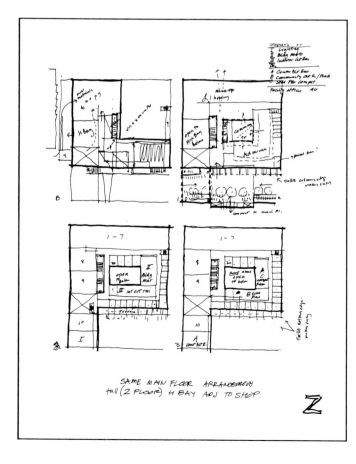

The architecture faculty refined their understanding of the program in response to Chimacoff's interpretation of their requirements in his competition submission.

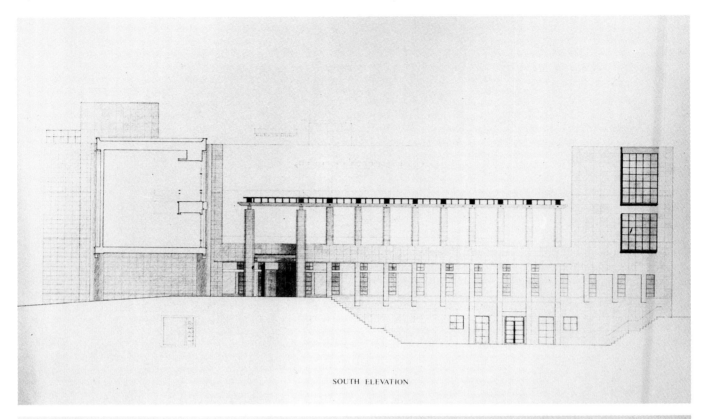

SOUTH ELEVATION

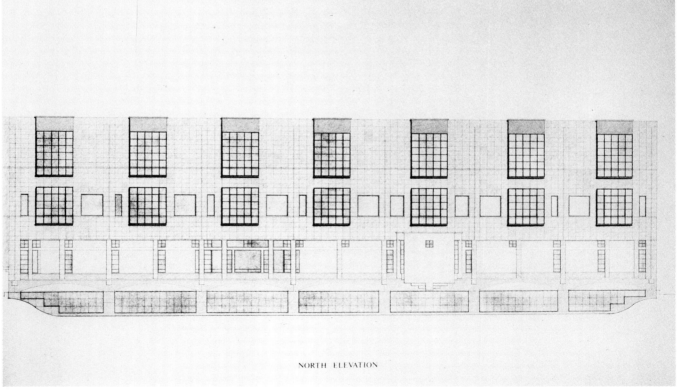

NORTH ELEVATION

**Revised elevations created a greater
sense of openness on the ground floor
and introduced an "artist window"
motif symbolic of the design studios
behind them.**

DESIGN DEVELOPMENT
February—April 1987

During this phase the architects detail an exterior wall system they know works and is affordable, develop the floor plan so that all program requirements are met, refine the elevations, and determine what materials and finishes will be used to construct the building. The package of design development drawings is planned to be as efficient and accurate as possible, since they are to be used both for a presentation set and as the basis of working drawings.

EXTERIOR WALL SYSTEM

The architects were not able to find three suppliers, as required on public jobs, to make the kind of concrete masonry units they wanted. Instead, they worked with local manufacturers to develop a precast concrete block veneer system. The wall system consisted of 3″ × 16″ × 24″ blocks tied onto backup construction of standard concrete block walls and poured-in-place columns.

The precast blocks had beveled edges and created a gridded surface, similar in appearance to cut limestone. Although the pattern of blocks varied, the wall was designed to look like one continuous surface. As the most prevalent material on the campus is brick, the architects wanted the scale of the block to provide a transition from the "monolithic" concrete façade of the existing building to the small-scaled texture of bricks on the other buildings on campus. They chose a pink-orange sandstone to complement the existing orangish brick. Problems related to the wall surface were also studied, such as how to make the transition between the various scales, and how the building materials, old versus new, would meet at the bridge.

WINDOWS

Chimacoff has stated that the competition design's "smooth wall surfaces with small window openings cut into them, like adobe" expressed "an Easterner's notion of traditional Southwestern architecture." The building committee asked him to rethink this, to come up with something "more appropriate," and to create a ground floor that was more open—"so that people on the outside could look in and have a sense of lively activities taking place inside." These concerns "engendered a need for more windows," Chimacoff recalls.

Another consideration that led to revision of the facade was Chimacoff's "personal preference for implicit movement in a façade." He set up an overall pattern that allowed variation in the amounts of window to be found around the building. This approach also addressed the practical difficulty that there were so many different kinds of rooms and conditions for daylighting. The upper two floors were outfitted with large, gridded, "artist studio" windows, symbolic of the design studios behind them. Small punched windows remained "as a punctuation mark, a memory of the original idea."

A full-size mock-up was built to study the wall system.

INTERIOR PLANNING

As architects, the faculty members could choose to be fully involved in the process of interior planning. "Since they knew how they wanted areas to work, they could arrange the parts better than I could have," says Chimacoff. This give-and-take principle worked out well within the framework of Chimacoff's design concept, as the faculty members/architects developed rough sketches for the administrative offices and the shop, and Hillier architects incorporated their ideas in the design development drawings.

Library. "As originally developed, the Special Collections Room was the keystone of the plan. It was seen as a focal point, directly opposite the main entry. There were a series of spaces and events along a processional corridor leading up to the library door, with the Special Collections Room right in front," describes project manager Geier. "Once the librarians and faculty were able to give their feedback, it turned out they didn't want it to be so highly honorific. The meaning wasn't as precious to them as it was to us." In terms of function and control of access, it made more sense to locate the collection within the library's enclosed support area. In the final scheme, the front part of the library still had a reading room and was "special," but not "ceremonial," as originally designed.

Rough sketches by the faculty helped The Hillier Group refine the functional organization of the interior.

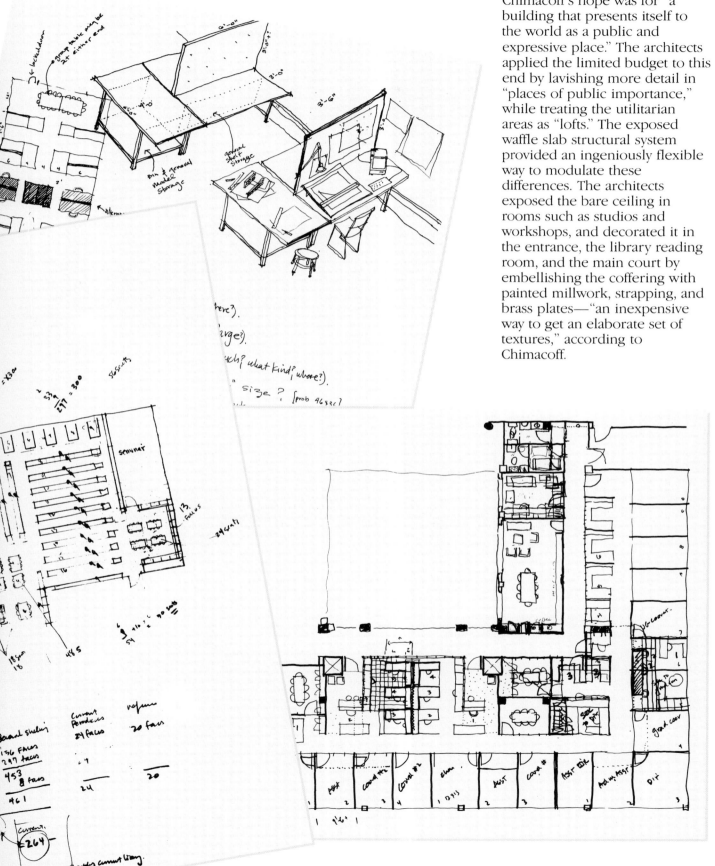

DECORATIVE DETAILS

Chimacoff's hope was for "a building that presents itself to the world as a public and expressive place." The architects applied the limited budget to this end by lavishing more detail in "places of public importance," while treating the utilitarian areas as "lofts." The exposed waffle slab structural system provided an ingeniously flexible way to modulate these differences. The architects exposed the bare ceiling in rooms such as studios and workshops, and decorated it in the entrance, the library reading room, and the main court by embellishing the coffering with painted millwork, strapping, and brass plates—"an inexpensive way to get an elaborate set of textures," according to Chimacoff.

CONTRACT DOCUMENTS
May—August 1987

The major responsibility for the work during these phases shifts to the local architects, who produce the working drawings and specifications. Largely due to the construction manager's efforts early on, the building ends up on target for both budget and size.

The Hillier team's role during this phase was to serve as advisor to Architecture One, reviewing samples related to design issues, and changes that had impact on the design intent. During this time, Architecture One began a separate contract to specify the interior finishes, furniture, and equipment (FF&E). To review their selections with the team in Princeton, the members of the Architecture One team sent a videotape of the presentation. This worked so well that they continued the practice during construction, videotaping their site inspections.

Thanks to the construction manager's efforts in monitoring cost throughout, bids were only $90,000 over budget, including the additional expense for the utilities tunnel. (Another reason for this may have been the "soft" construction market at the time.) The schedule also remained essentially the same, despite the delays caused by the utilities tunnel and the University reviews, which took longer than planned. During construction, the construction manager's role continued, Simpson says, as "a neutral party concerned with the owner's interests, as well as overseeing the architect's monitoring of the contractor's change-order additions and credits."

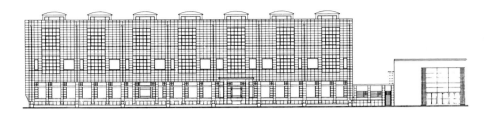

NORTH ELEVATION　0 2　8　16

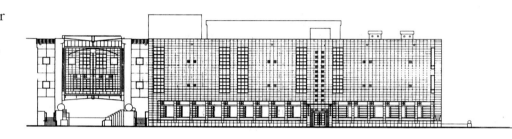

EAST ELEVATION　0 2　8　16

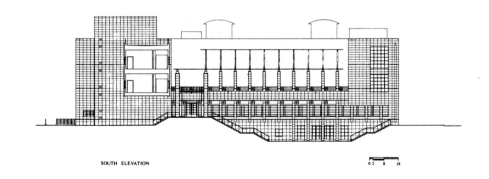

SOUTH ELEVATION　0 2　8　16

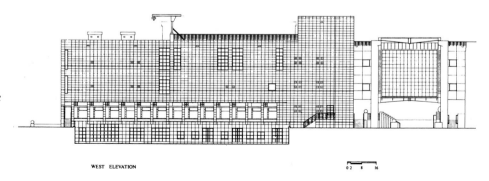

WEST ELEVATION　0 2　8　16

LAST-MINUTE CHANGES

During the spring a new dean, John Meunier, joined the architecture faculty and invigorated the design process with fresh insights, even though it was in the working drawing stage. In late May, Dean Meunier and Associate Dean Tim McGinty spent a day with the Hillier architects at their Princeton offices, reiterating their concern that some parts of the scheme were not fully resolved.

Meunier felt that the bridge was "the most powerful rhetorical element in the project," but that it did not have a strong enough relation with the main court. He suggested enclosing a terrace outside the court and connecting it with the commons—a change that Chimacoff believes "really activates those spaces." Furnished as a café and used as a student lounge, the bridge was to become the major review space for the school. "The function of criticism and review of student work is most appropriate for such a strong physical link and symbolic location," says Meunier.

The dean also encouraged the architects to rethink the rhythm and scale of window openings on the north elevation. Chimacoff agreed that the design needed more work. The final elevation, which centered the studio windows in the bays and replaced the large square windows with vertical openings on either side of the columns, expressed what the dean describes as a "syncopation of rhythm and richness of ordering, which make this a truly modern building."

"Everyone felt the changes were an improvement and well worth the investment of design time," says 3D/I's Ward Simpson. But after having agreed to the new utilities tunnel, the administration was reluctant to approve any changes, no matter how simple. Simpson played a crucial role in reassuring ASU that addressing the dean's concerns would not force the project over budget or break the schedule.

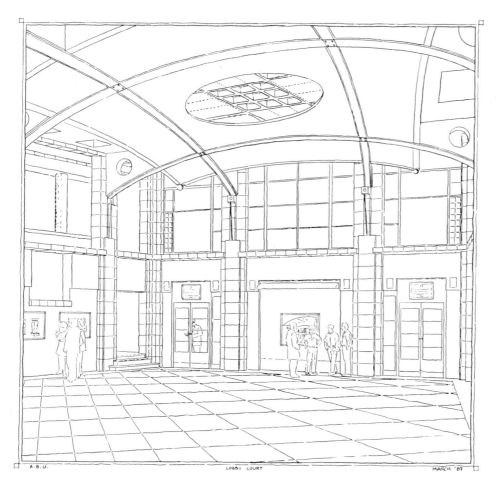

Opposite page, top to bottom: North, east, south, and west elevations from the design development submission.

Left: Interior perspective showing coffered ceiling treatment.

OBSERVATIONS

This building was designed to enhance teaching, and the evolution of its design shows that a building, too, can learn.

- In architect Chimacoff's opinion, "The competition enabled ASU to develop a complex project to the crude schematic stage on a small budget. Each firm spent an enormous amount of uncompensated time." A large firm such as The Hillier Group could afford the financial risk involved in competing, and also wanted the opportunity for national exposure. While the purpose of a competition is to encourage creative ideas, often what ultimately gets built does not resemble the original submission. In projects with fixed schedule and fees, competitions are most successful when used to select a design and not just an architect.

- Architect Chimacoff feels that "having had no dialogue with the client during the competition was a major drawback. It means you have to interpret the client's intent and then hope they will like the decisions you made on their behalf." Dean Meunier agrees that competitions "artificially separate the major protagonists in a building," yet he points out that Chimacoff's design—"a superbly robust solution to the program"—benefitted by being unencumbered by the client's preconceived ideas, in particular about how to organize departmental functions to encourage interaction and interdisciplinary work.

- Having architects as clients can be frustrating, as they may be more critical, but in this case the client's expertise enabled them to have a creative interaction with the design architect, which strengthened the process. Associate Dean McGinty explains, "The geometry of the scheme wouldn't fall apart if we challenged any of his assumptions. Chimacoff had a strong conceptual image and he kept developing and refining it in the process of handling what we threw at him."

- A drawback of the competition process, points out Dean Meunier, is that it reinforces the trend to team up "outside" design architects with local technical architects. "This removes the design architect from the process of design through all

Above: A model of the final building. Right: The building under construction.

the details, which robs the building of the creative energy of the design architect as it gets developed though contract documents. . . . What you get is a few set pieces where the design is sustained and an awful lot of the building where it isn't."

- Construction manager Ward Simpson feels this fragmented approach resulted in a lack of attention to the interior design of the building. "The architects should have planned the furniture layouts at the end of schematics and again at the end of design development, but there was no fee budgeted for this work. If you don't start interiors at the end of schematics at the very latest, it is too late to make changes based on what you will learn, about such things as outlets and phone plugs." One way for clients to avoid this problem is to include interior design in the contract earlier in the process.

- According to Chimacoff, "A lot of the success of the project is on account of the construction manager's careful, thoughtful, crafty management of the architects and associated consultants. He made sure everyone stayed on schedule, had the right information, and that the information produced

was in line with the budget." This discipline was not onerous, but provided a stimulus that motivated the entire team.

- But as Simpson observes, "The hardest part of the process to control is the owner." The construction manager had warned the ASU administration about the problem with the utilities, for example. Simpson adds, "Within a project like this, some occurrences have no rational explanation. But what is really interesting is how the building becomes what it is by way of the personalities involved and just the process of making decisions."

- In this case, the decision-making process was characterized by close cooperation, communication, and fun. "I really enjoyed responding to Alan," McGinty commented afterward. Chimacoff adds, "The reason people enjoyed working on this project is because just about everyone on the team had a level of mutual respect for each other. This creates an environment where there is a willingness to share ideas and pull together for the best interest of the project."

The renovation of the Aetna Life & Casualty home office is an example of how large-scale, complex corporate projects are demanding more teamwork between architects and clients, new computer skills, and additional services such as facility management. Aetna's facility management staff had developed a master plan for the renovation of 1.6 million sf over five years, based on a standardized workstation. They used a competition to test their ideas and to select an architect who could work well as part of their team. Aetna also stipulated that the architect use CAD to produce the contract documents. Jung/Brannen customized their own drafting software to be able to encode the drawings with alphanumeric information, creating a facility management tool called "Aetna 2000."

PROJECT OVERVIEW

Project 1.6 million sf renovation of corporate headquarters.

Architect Jung/Brannen Associates, Inc., Boston, Massachusetts, with the Aetna Facility Management Home Office Renovation Team.

Client Aetna Life & Casualty, Hartford, Connecticut.

Charge To provide a dignified, comfortable facility that can accommodate a dynamic and changing staff and meet the company's needs for the next two decades.

Issues ✔ Implementation of a system of standardized workstations to accommodate constantly changing business needs affecting a staff of 5,000; provide a shared identity to unify two different buildings, and coordinate with the installation of all new mechanical and electric systems.

✔ Organizing the process so that construction could be phased over five years (during "business as usual") within a fixed budget.

✔ At the beginning of the project, building a mock-up to evaluate the design concept and estimate costs.

✔ Role of the client facility management team as key decision makers in the process.

✔ Use of computers to organize the complex process and to support facility management.

Duration Competition: four months; renovation: six years (May 1985–1991).

Budget Withheld at client's request.

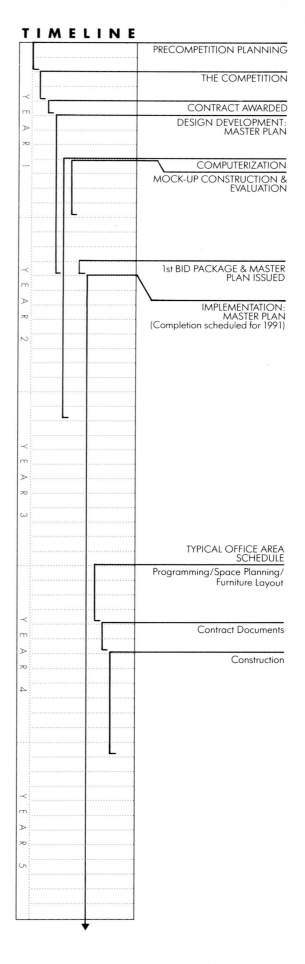

TIMELINE

YEAR 1
PRECOMPETITION PLANNING
THE COMPETITION
CONTRACT AWARDED
DESIGN DEVELOPMENT: MASTER PLAN
COMPUTERIZATION
MOCK-UP CONSTRUCTION & EVALUATION

YEAR 2
1st BID PACKAGE & MASTER PLAN ISSUED
IMPLEMENTATION: MASTER PLAN
(Completion scheduled for 1991)

YEAR 3

TYPICAL OFFICE AREA SCHEDULE
Programming/Space Planning/ Furniture Layout

YEAR 4
Contract Documents
Construction

YEAR 5

BACKGROUND

In the course of a ten-year period of major construction, the Aetna Life & Casualty assembled a facility management staff that had a sophisticated understanding of the building design and construction processes. This case study of the renovation of Aetna's home office building complex describes how the facility management group planned the project and set up a framework for working with an architect to take their ideas further than they could have done alone.

Aetna's team spent nearly two years developing a master plan for the renovation of the 2.02 million sf home office. The team then held a competition to select an architect, with the outcome based on the competitors' responses to the master plan and abilities to work as part of Aetna's team. The competition requirements included the submission of working drawings for two substantial mock-ups, an inversion of the standard sequence of steps in the design process (which generally concludes with working drawings). The winning architects began work after having studied the project from both a "macro" and a "micro" perspective.

To simplify its work as well as postoccupancy tasks, the facility management group wanted documentation of the project to be computerized. As the design process evolved, so did the team's understanding of how to automate the process. The client's commitment, coupled with the architect's expertise, led to the development of innovative facility management software tailored to Aetna's particular needs.

THE CLIENT

Aetna Life & Casualty had been studying the need to renovate its 2.02 million sf headquarters complex in Hartford, Connecticut, for some time. In 1979 the home office was housed in the headquarters building and thirteen leased sites in Hartford. Business was in a prolonged growth cycle, and the company needed more space. In the preceding fifty years, the work force had grown from 2,600 people to 6,000. The company wanted to decentralize and give each division its "own turf," according to architect Jack Dollard, a consultant to the corporation. But by 1980 the office market had become very tight, and the company no longer had the option to lease space; they had to build.

As a result, during the late 1970s and early 1980s, Aetna undertook major investment in new facilities

to house each of its major divisions. Employee Benefits went into a new 1 million sf building and computer center in Middletown, Connecticut; the Financial division took 350,000 sf in City Place, a new tower in Hartford developed by the Urban Investment Corporation, then a subsidiary of Aetna; Corporate Administration and Corporate Human Resources moved to a 400,000 sf renovated factory; the Commercial Insurance and Personal Financial Security divisions remained in the 2.02 million sf "home office"; and the Aetna Institute, a new educational facility, was planned for a site across the street from the home office. In this process, Aetna built a sophisticated facility management (FM) organization.

Aetna Facility Management has three functional divisions:

1. The Field Lease Department, which takes care of field office planning, design, and leasing, and is responsible for field offices nationwide.
2. Home Office Properties, which is responsible for operations and maintenance of facilities in Hartford. This division operates the buildings on a day-to-day basis.
3. The Facility Planning Department, which manages major construction and renovation projects in the greater Hartford area. Facility Planning includes three units: Workplace Consulting, which provides research and development and postoccupancy evaluations on new technology, furniture systems, and building interiors; Office Planning and Design (OPD), which handles general space planning; and the Renovation Team.

Aetna Life & Casualty's Home Office complex in Hartford, Connecticut.

THE SITE/FACILITY

Aetna's home office is actually five contiguous buildings, although the largest two give the place its architectural character. The main structure is the so-called "Colonial" building, designed by James Gamble Rogers in a monumentally scaled Georgian style. Built in the 1920s, the interior was considered very modern for an office building, with under-floor wiring, large windows, and substantial, quality materials.

The "Tower" building, constructed in 1974, was designed by the firm Kevin Roche, John Dinkeloo and Associates in the "brutalist" style. Aetna was then a major buyer of IBM products, and this building was one of the first to be planned around the requirements of computers. Made of cast-in-place concrete with granite cladding, an exposed concrete interior, few exterior windows, and an interior light well, the Tower reflects in its design the perceived need to protect and guard the mainframe computer. The Tower was conceived of as an addition to the Colonial building and did not even have its own front door.

To provide future flexibility, the Tower has a seventeen-foot clear ceiling height and fifty-two-foot-long span bays. "No one knew what the future might be, and at one time they thought the space might be filled with mainframes. They didn't anticipate the PC environment," says architect Jack Dollard. Although the Tower building reflects some of the most progressive design thinking of its time, the monumental and intimidating space is not an ideal work environment and was not well accepted by Aetna staff.

PREPROJECT PLANNING
1982–1984

The need to renovate the headquarters became apparent in early 1982. As divisions were being relocated to their new facilities, Aetna reorganized and all the planning changed. The company was growing so fast that five-year personnel projections were being exceeded in one year. As a result of such growth and change, the home office needed more space. And planners were concerned that the headquarters would not be up to par with the company's other new buildings in terms of technology and quality of the environment.

"The interior of the home office was getting very shabby," says Arlis Bobb, project manager for the renovation. "The carpet was patched, the walls needed painting, lighting was poor, furniture was old-fashioned and just sort of jumbled in. Workstations consisted of movable partitions of varying heights, haphazardly arranged. You could tell somebody's rank by the overhang on the desk."

But planners could not have put another employee in the home office even if there had been space. The introduction of personal computers (PCs) into the workplace had put new demands on the existing mechanical and electrical systems. The heat load generated from the PCs had overloaded the capacity of the air-conditioning equipment, and there wasn't room for one more cable in the trench.

A six-member committee, including corporate division heads, business planners, and architect Jack Dollard, was organized to study the renovation of the home office. Although $300 million of construction was underway, by this time, early 1982, the business had entered a down cycle. However, a commitment for the renovation had already been made and "in a half-hearted way they said 'OK, let's get that going with a preliminary study,'" Dollard recalls.

Prerenovation conditions in the Colonial (Rogers) building, this page, and in the Tower building, opposite page.

PRELIMINARY STUDY: 1982

Dollard and one designer from the facility management staff did that preliminary study. They looked at both functional and aesthetic issues, based on their recent experience with new construction and an evaluation of the two different building types. They drew up preliminary plans and models and then built 1,000 sf mock-ups in both buildings. Aetna frequently uses mock-ups. "With mock-ups, clients always know what they're buying," says Dollard. They let users preview what the space will be like and give their feedback. "It's much better to do this early in the process, because at the end it's too late to change anything," he feels. At that time certain basic decisions were made, among them, to have interior offices with glass walls, perimeter open work areas, a low ambient light level, carpet tiles, and a bright color scheme.

Working with an estimator, the team came up with a budget of $100 million for the project, or a third of the cost for an all-new facility. "When we presented this proposal to Aetna's Financial Planning and Corporate Administration groups," tells Dollard, "the hierarchy wasn't really interested. Actually, they were stalling for time, so they authorized funding for further study."

HOME OFFICE RENOVATION TEAM

Aetna's Office Planning and Design unit then formed the Home Office Renovation Team, with Arlis Bobb as project manager. Rod Midford of Industrial Construction Corporation (ICC) was hired as construction manager to provide cost estimates and technical advice and the Workplace Consulting Unit provided interior consulting. Eventually, the staff grew to nine designers, but in the beginning members of the team included interior designer Pamela Visco, CAD manager Douglas Kuzmicki, and administrator Rose Miles. Jack Dollard advised the team on design issues.

SECOND STUDY: 1983

The team now took the opportunity to design what the members "really wanted to see happen." They put together a detailed presentation, including an analysis of the differences and similarities of the two buildings and how to unify them. Their approach was to develop a master plan, which, Dollard points out, was an innovative decision at that time for interior renovation. The team had learned the importance of starting out with a master plan from previous experience in building the facility at Middletown. In Middletown, the team's first major new construction project, the facility planners had not had a good handle on the organization of the process. "We were behind the eight ball," recalls Arlis Bobb.

"The objective," Dollard says, "was to develop a floor plan not for specific departments but for the highest density of people." This concept, which they called "dense pack planning," addresses the "high churn rate" associated with the way insurance companies work. Typically, the facility management group moves 16,000 employees per year, or 50 to 60 percent of the workforce. In the Colonial and Tower buildings alone, 2,500 to 3,000 people usually move every year. "People would physically move everything, desks and all. It was expensive, complicated, and time-consuming."

Since it was easier to move people than to move workstations, the team's solution was to standardize the workstation to fit within a common footprint. They decided to limit the number of choices people could have that would require physical changes and instead offer people accessory and equipment options. Although the workstation itself became smaller, the amount of square footage per person actually increased, since more support facilities and shared facilities, such as conference rooms, had to be taken into consideration.

PLANS FOR A COMPETITION

Aetna top executives approved this second proposal in concept. But when a new chairman came on board, according to Dollard, he wanted the team "to test its ideas against the best firms in the field." This led to the idea of a competition. Aetna would invite architects to critique the Home Office Renovation Team's master plan and either suggest how to embellish its ideas or come up with an alternative approach. Part of the competition would be to produce working drawings for a 6,000 and 12,000 sf mock-up in each building. In this way the competition would simulate an actual work situation. "In selecting the architect, teamwork was a prime consideration," says Arlis Bobb. "We wanted to know who we'd be working with and what the

relationship would be like."

The Home Office Renovation Team decided to limit the selection of firms to the New York/Boston corridor because they had had difficulty working long distance with a Texas-based firm in the design of the Middletown facility. This time they decided to require the firm chosen to open a site office. Another requirement was that the firm be able to work with a personal-computer system. The team invited twelve firms to submit qualifications and ten accepted. Each went to Hartford for a half-day visit to inspect Aetna's facilities and the preliminary plans.

After the visit, there was a two-hour interview, in which the firm was asked to take one hour to respond to Aetna's master plan and one hour to talk about itself. The jury consisted of Jack Dollard; Arlis Bobb; Richard Coughlin, head of the Facility Management Department; and construction manager Rod Mitford. Each juror rated the firm, based on its past work, willingness to work as part of Aetna's team, and other factors. The jurors invited Jung/Brannen Associates (J/BA), Kohn Pedersen Fox Conway (KPFC), and Gensler and Associates/Architects to compete.

"Jung/Brannen was unknown to us, but partner Bob Hsiung really impressed us with his thoughtful sensibility about both buildings and the opportunity to bring the two together. KPFC made an excellent presentation. Gensler represented one of the top nationally known firms," explains Dollard.

THE ARCHITECTS

Jung/Brannen Associates was founded in 1968 and has since become one of Boston's largest architecture and interior design firms, with a staff of over 200. J/BA now specializes in buildings for high-technology industries. This technical bent is reflected in their own practice: The firm uses seven different CAD systems. Jung/Brannen's Research and Development Corporation was set up to customize these systems for all phases of design, as well as to provide support and training services.

J/BA handled the Aetna assignment on an architectural basis with interior designers on the team as required. This decision was based on Jung/Brannen's assessment of the type of management skills required for a complex project of Aetna's scale; J/BA had its strongest concentration of management expertise in its architectural group. The project team consisted of Robert Brannen, principal in charge; Robert Hsiung, design principal; Norman Adams, project director; Lindsay Boutros Ghali, project manager; Phil Koeniger, project architect; Steve Courtney, project associate; and Bruce Forbes, director of CAD services.

HOSP / AETNA 85
PFSD

NORTH CENTER

SOUTH CENTER

18 / 33

CONF
DIR/MGR
DIR/MGR
CONF
AVP
DIR/MGR
AVP
DIR/MGR
CONF
DIR/MGR
AVP
34
34

18 / 33

WEST WING

WEST OF CENTER
ROGERS BUILDING

Early planning studies by Aetna's Home Office Renovation Team, clockwise from top left: Rendering of a typical office area in the Colonial building; typical office area in the Tower building; master plan portion as applied in the Colonial building.

THE COMPETITION
June–September 1985
The actual five-week competition is planned to take place during the summer, to test the firms under pressure. Aetna wants to simulate the strains of the actual working relationship.

In June the firms were briefed on the client's intent, the program, the concept of the workspace, and the project budget, which was based on the construction manager's detailed cost estimate. Designer Robert Hsiung recalls that one of the "givens" was that Aetna wanted to project a strong corporate culture. The challenge was how to give this form. During July, the Aetna team met weekly with the firms as they developed their initial concepts. The final weeks of August were used as a charrette to draw up the master plan and produce working drawings for the two mock-ups.

JUNG/BRANNEN'S DESIGN CONCEPT
Designer Robert Hsiung's objective was "to use the best qualities of each building and generate synergy." Hsiung says he wanted to create "an additional layer to the corporate culture, apply it to both buildings, and provide a commonality." He conducted the meetings with Aetna's team as if they were work sessions during a real job. His approach to the master plan was to "take what they had and enhance it."

The J/BA concept was an interior landscape system inspired by the architects' own office and incorporating Aetna's planning ideas. A trellis was used to form a circulation spine. It also provided a ceiling for and defined the central closed office zone, leaving the perimeter open for workstations. The architects diagrammed how to adapt the trellis to different conditions. For example, there were closed offices, the trellis became a dropped ceiling with acoustic tile, lighting and ventilation provided above. Where the existing ceiling was high enough, the trellis became a mezzanine. Finishes and lighting varied for each building—in the Tower the

Preliminary diagrams for applying the master plan in the Colonial building, left, and the Tower building, right.

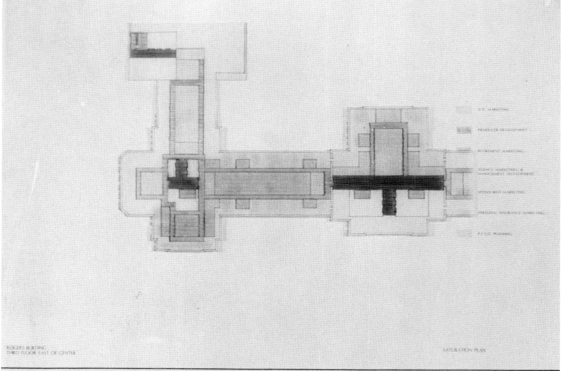

trellis was wood; in the Colonial building, it was painted white.

Although the master plan included design only of the permanent features, it provided a guideline for the overall development of the project, organizing a system of elements that included open workspaces, closed workspaces/conference rooms, the trellis/fixed circulation spine, and informal meeting areas, which Aetna dubbed "oases." The special areas in the plan, such as the new entry to the Tower, the Tower atrium, a company store, and the executive office area, were handled separately.

"We made the point that in this way we were not imposing our will on the corporation. The plan was to be used as a start and a way of working, which could evolve with additional input from Aetna," says Robert Hsiung. "Aetna saw its own idea in it, and about halfway through, we were pretty confident we had won."

AWARDING THE CONTRACT

In September Aetna named Jung/Brannen as the winners. Dollard recalls, "J/BA did a sincere job, not unique, just well done. And they were very pleased about opening a site office. Aetna is not trying to be outrageous, but it does want to treat its employees well, wants them to be comfortable. The culture is based on a high level of appropriateness, not uniqueness."

SCOPE OF SERVICES

The contract included developing the master plan, design of the sixteen special areas, production of the drawings, and coordination with the other consultants. Also stipulated was that J/BA would help Aetna set up its computer system and train its staff on CAD.

J/BA opened its site office a floor below the Aetna team's offices. Robert Hsiung oversaw all design issues from Boston and ran weekly design review meetings in Hartford with the facility management team and Jack Dollard. ICC's Rod Mitford, now also the general contractor, sat in on these meetings to give pricing or technical information.

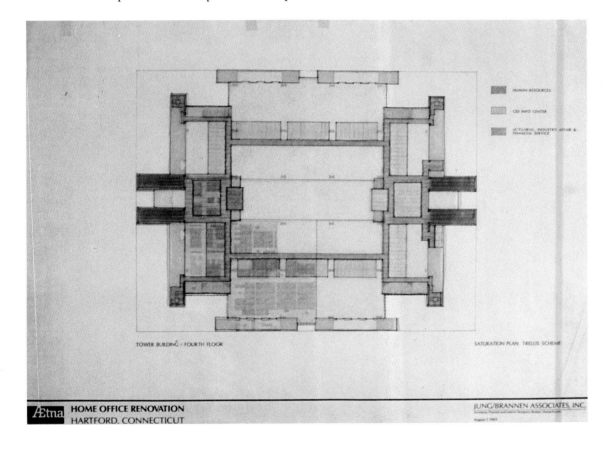

TOWER BUILDING - FOURTH FLOOR   SATURATION PLAN: TRELLIS SCHEME

HUMAN RESOURCES
CIO INFO CENTER
ACTUARIAL, INDUSTRY AFFAIR & FINANCIAL SERVICE

Ætna HOME OFFICE RENOVATION
HARTFORD, CONNECTICUT

JUNG/BRANNEN ASSOCIATES, INC.

From the competition submission: Working drawing for the Colonial building mock-up at right; master plan, Colonial building, bottom.

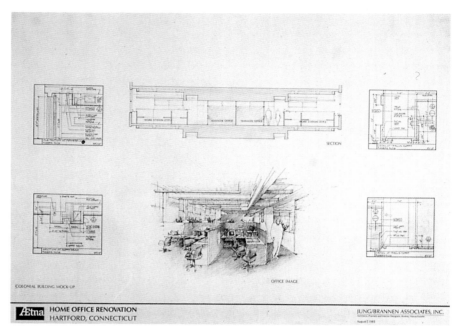

COLONIAL BUILDING MOCK-UP

OFFICE IMAGE

SECTION

Ætna HOME OFFICE RENOVATION
HARTFORD, CONNECTICUT

JUNG/BRANNEN ASSOCIATES, INC.
August 7, 1985

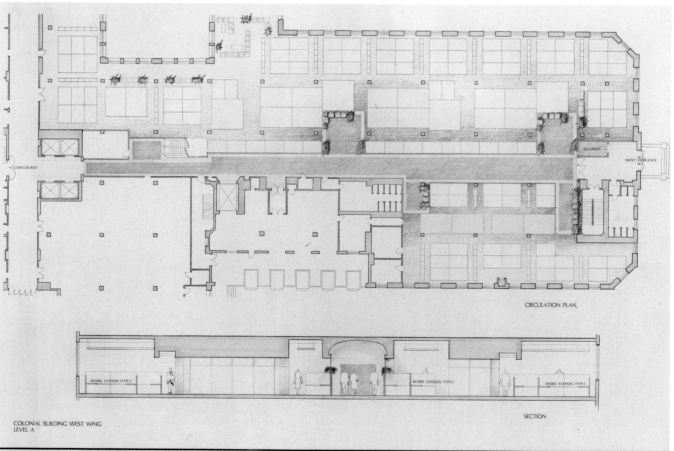

CONCOURSE

SECURITY

WEST ENTRANCE

CIRCULATION PLAN,

WORK STATION (TYP.)

WORK STATION (TYP.)

WORK STATION (TYP.)

SECTION

COLONIAL BUILDING WEST WING
LEVEL A

Ætna HOME OFFICE RENOVATION
HARTFORD, CONNECTICUT

JUNG/BRANNEN ASSOCIATES, INC.
Architects, Planners and Interior Designers, Boston, Massachusetts
August 7, 1985

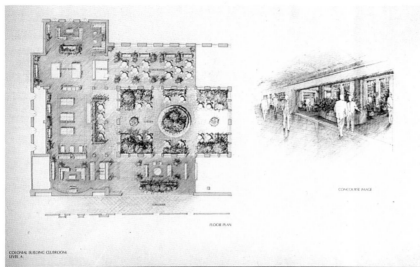

FLOOR PLAN

CONCOURSE IMAGE

COLONIAL BUILDING CLUBROOM
LEVEL A

Atna **HOME OFFICE RENOVATION**
HARTFORD, CONNECTICUT

JUNG/BRANNEN ASSOCIATES, INC.

Special areas include, top to
bottom: The Club Room; the
Colonial building entry; and
the Tower building entry.

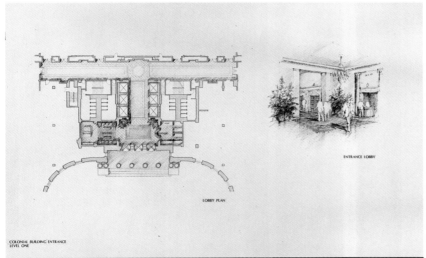

LOBBY PLAN

ENTRANCE LOBBY

COLONIAL BUILDING ENTRANCE
LEVEL ONE

Atna **HOME OFFICE RENOVATION**
HARTFORD, CONNECTICUT

JUNG/BRANNEN ASSOCIATES, INC.

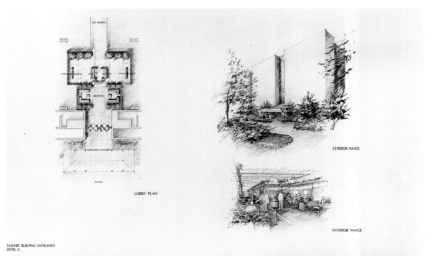

LOBBY PLAN

EXTERIOR IMAGE

INTERIOR IMAGE

TOWER BUILDING ENTRANCE
LEVEL A

Atna **HOME OFFICE RENOVATION**
HARTFORD, CONNECTICUT

JUNG/BRANNEN ASSOCIATES, INC.

DESIGN DEVELOPMENT: MASTER PLAN
October 1985–August 1986

The first task is to finalize the master plan and revise working drawings for the mock-up, as per Aetna's comments. The mock-up is then built and evaluated. Construction is broken down into twenty-four "bid packages," each a job in itself, to be phased over five years. Bidding on the first package is to include a firm price for all typical office areas (70 percent of the overall project), based on the mock-up and master plan.

This page: The developed master plan of the Tower building, right, and Colonial building, below.

Opposite page: Perspective views of a typical Tower building office area, top, and Colonial building office area, bottom.

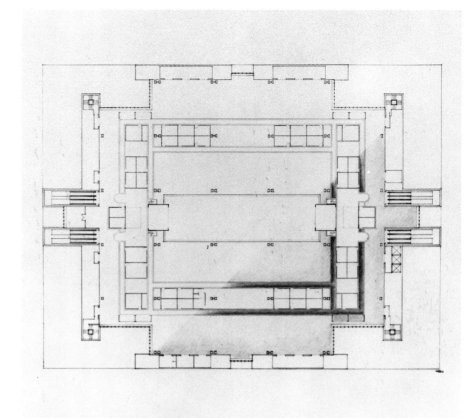

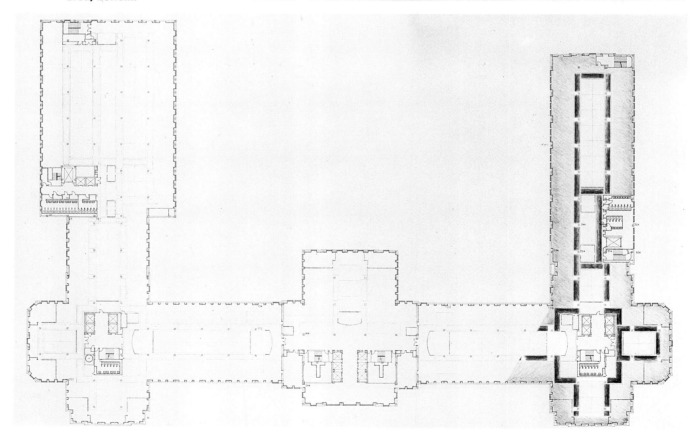

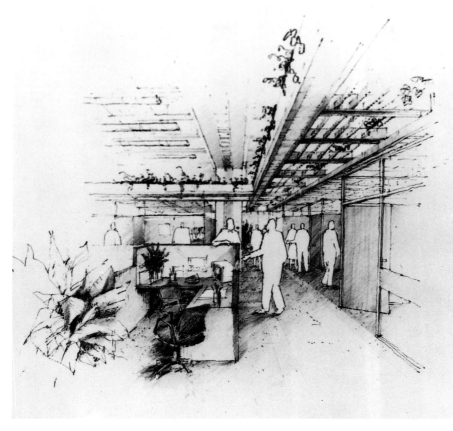

REFINING THE MASTER PLAN

The first step in design development was to refine the master plan and apply it to the entire 1.5 million sf. Architect Philip Koeniger recalls, "We took a hard look at the building and what was best for Aetna's business and, on a floor-by-floor basis, how each area interfaced with the surrounding areas. Aetna's Renovation Team and ICC developed the construction phasing. We helped them with that plan and the scheduling for the bid packages. Some departments weren't ready or didn't have a good idea about what their identity should be. The master plan brought each floor up to the level of design development."

The master plan set of drawings were done at ¹⁄₁₆" scale and mostly relied on reflected ceiling plans. The ceiling plan had a very strong relation to the floor plan—the trellis/circulation spine was mirrored in the carpet pattern; low ceilings were enclosed office areas; and high ceilings were open office areas. The areas where ceilings dropped coordinated with the mechanical and electrical systems.

The renovation included a revamped HVAC system, new power, and new lighting. Coordinating with the engineers was a major part of the architects' job. Aetna's in-house staff along with consulting engineers conducted a major study of the building systems, which evaluated life safety issues as well. An entirely new sprinkler system was needed to bring the facility up to code. To help coordinate this work, all consultants worked with the same computer system.

MOCK-UP CONSTRUCTION AND EVALUATION

Although the mock-up was to have been built immediately following the competition, Aetna wanted to make some changes first. Construction began in January and took four months. The evaluation period lasted an unexpectedly long three months.

The focus of the evaluation was to analyze how the workstation, oasis, and office worked together as an integrated whole. The evaluation process took place in three phases, based on input from three sources: experts (i.e., planners and designers); users; and observers. All components of the mock-up were studied, from floor to ceiling. Aetna discovered, for example, that executive secretaries needed a roomier module than the standard footprint. Another observation was that some means of removing equipment from worksurfaces needed to be provided to better accommodate personal computers.

Two versions of the mock-up were built for the Colonial building, reflecting alternative approaches to ceiling treatment and colors. One mock-up was built for the Tower building, and it had to be redesigned when the cost estimates came in over budget. Doug Kuzmicki recalls, "Our reaction was, if we have to cut costs, let's first reevaluate where monies should be spent: Certain areas needed more attention and others had probably been overemphasized." J/BA evaluated lighting fixtures, ceiling systems, and construction details for the trellis system. Aetna staff had researched carpets, furniture systems, wall treatments, signage, graphics, and plant programs. The J/BA team then wrote up a master finish schedule as part of the first bid package.

Hsiung compared the process to designing a car: "First you design one model, then you customize it. First we designed the system, them we spent a lot of time selecting the details, testing specifics, and estimating costs. Once everyone agreed on what was to be done, Aetna wanted everything to be the same. Then we started 'mass producing' the rest of the project."

FIRST BID PACKAGE

In August, the team issued the first bid package and master plan. Also included were detailed plans for a typical floor in each building, with information on materials, finishes, partition types, and typical construction conditions keyed in. For this first set, only the base drawings were produced with CAD.

The bidding process was handled by the construction manager/general contractor. Contractors had to commit to their prices for the next six years. The various subcontractors bid on all typical office space at once—based on the master plan—plus the two specific areas of the first bid package. The basis for pricing included the mock-ups, the master plan, written specifications, and field verification. Field conditions were fairly consistent due to the buildings' repetitive floor plans and single owner. Subsequent bid packages were issued with more detail, and contractors could adjust their bid at the time of issue based on the initially submitted unit prices.

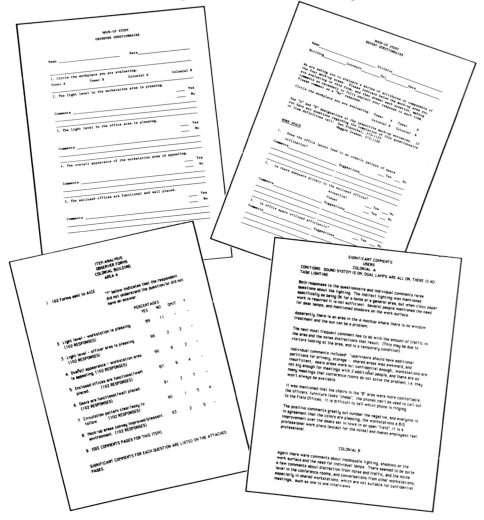

IMPLEMENTATION: MASTER PLAN
September 1986– Early 1991

Renovation takes place during Aetna's routine workweeks. As each project area comes up in the schedule, Aetna's team does the programming, space planning, and furniture layouts, according to the master plan. J/BA incorporates this information in the contract documents and coordinates with the engineering consultants.

SCHEDULING

All client groups were given up to two years' notice prior to the renovation of their area, so they could include the move in their business planning. Explains the Home Office Renovation Team's administrator, Rose Miles: "If the group's organization changes, we may not find out until a month before we move them, but we work with them to accommodate those changes. We also have to provide appropriate swing space. If a group does a kind of work that can't be moved around, like systems people, we try and move them only once." The entire project was scheduled in advance, and staying on target meant keeping clients well informed so they could make their decisions on time.

Opposite page: Aetna's facility managers developed a set of forms to elicit users' and experts' evaluations of the mock-ups.

Below: A sample schedule. Phasing the renovation into thirty-one separate bid packages was planned well in advance.

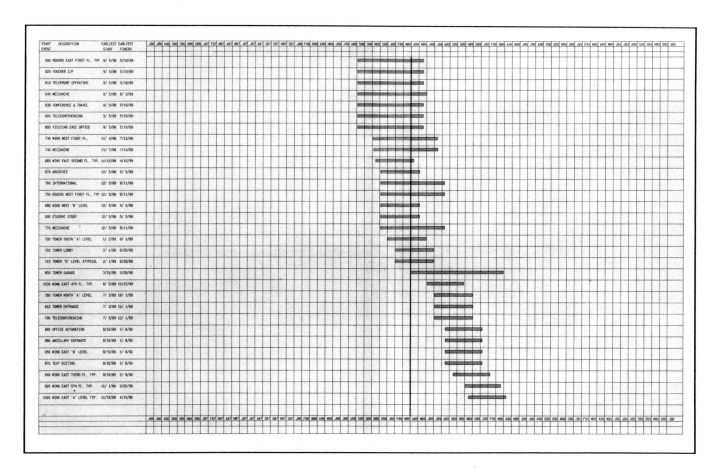

**Above: The Tower building
mock-up of an oasis area.**

**Right: Study to refine the
Colonial building mock-up.**

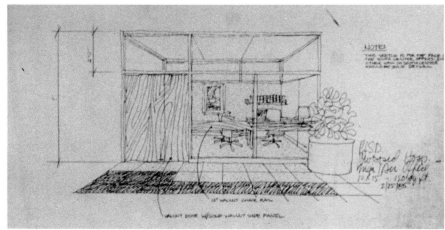

PROGRAMMING

Aetna's designers began the programming of typical office areas over a year before the move-in date with an orientation meeting for each department. In those meetings they explained the background of the renovation, what changes had been made, and what to expect in the coming months—such as the unavoidable loud noises and dust of the construction site. Some Aetna departments reorganized again during the renovation, and the facility planners had to counter a certain amount of anxiety about the renovation, which to some people seemed to mirror feelings of uncertainty about the future.

Aetna's staff handled all programming and space planning. In the beginning of the project they put together a handbook that explained the master plan and its parts, included all the forms used, codified furniture standards and listed finish options, described the design process, and explained all procedures, such as how to fill out a purchase order. Initially this book was given to new designers to use as a training manual and to the division heads as part of the orientation. It also laid the groundwork for computerization of the process.

Early on, Aetna CAD manager Doug Kuzmicki saw the need to automate the furniture specification process: "Due to the volume of furniture needed, we couldn't ask someone to sit down and count every component." Once codified, the data was easily put into a spreadsheet format with Lotus software. This document could be used both to track inventory and to create purchase orders directly from the program's furniture specifications.

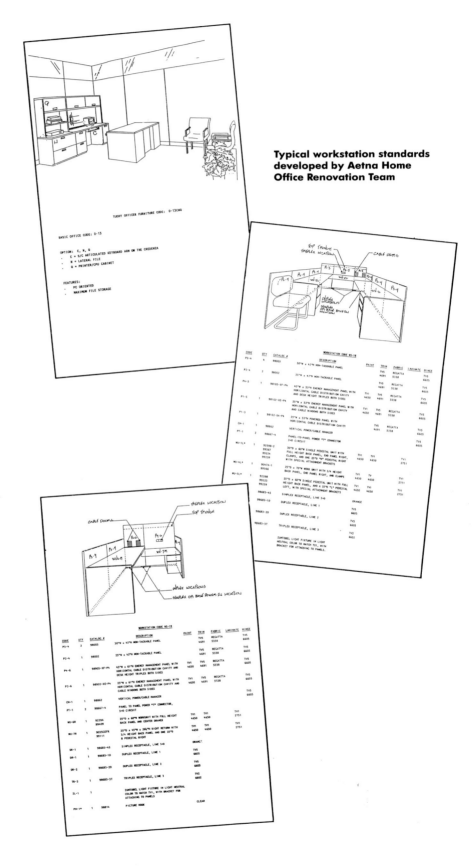

Typical workstation standards developed by Aetna Home Office Renovation Team

Aetna staff selected the carpet, fabrics, and finishes in all typical office areas. However, their choices were not made in a vacuum: All decisions were later shared and discussed with the J/BA team during the design review meetings.

CONTRACT DOCUMENTS

Once the Renovation Team designers got a sign-off from the department heads, they submitted their drawings to J/BA, as Dollard says, "to put into the contract documents Mix-Master." The J/BA team evaluated the furniture layout for code violations or conflicts with the master plan. "We also started to work with the consultants to coordinate electrical and mechanical systems, looking for problems such as equipment rooms with overly large heat loads or cooling systems, and making sure that all equipment was keyed in and all information was provided for circuiting."

Aetna designers and engineers reviewed the documents as they were developed to make sure the plans were compatible with the furniture layouts and any additional engineering changes. After Aetna signed off on the plans, J/BA sent them to the general contractor. The subcontractors reviewed them and adjusted the pricing, if there had been any changes to the typical offices, or bid on them if they were new areas.

FIVE-MONTH REVIEWS

It took nearly one year between the end of programming and the move-in date: one or two months to produce construction documents and send them out for bids, and another six to eight months for construction. During this time there was much possibility for change. Halfway through the process the departments had an opportunity to review the documents and make changes, if necessary. Past that point, the departments had to wait until after move-in. Thirty days after move-in punchlist items were completed. Ninety days later, the renovation team turned over the finished space— along with a set of as-built drawings including all the trades and furniture layouts—to the group handling day-to-day facility management.

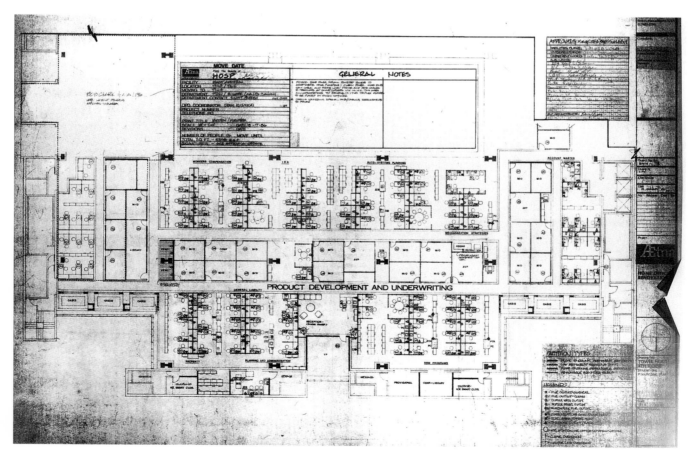

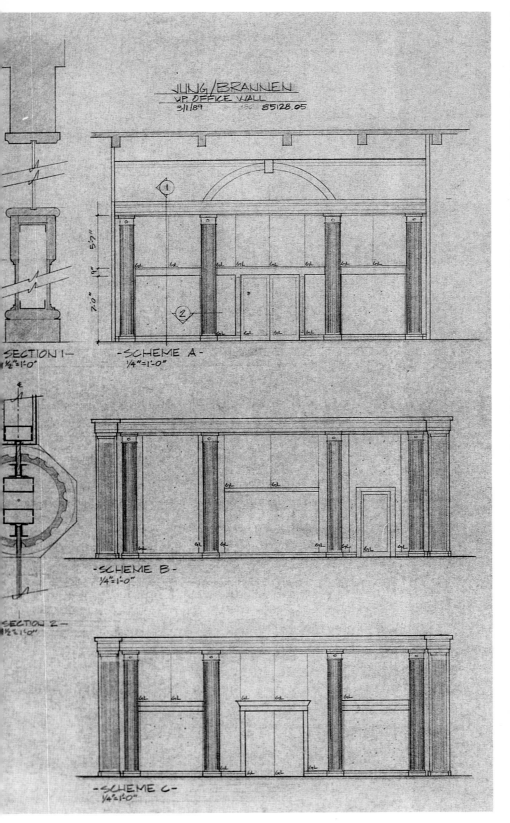

SPECIAL AREAS

The sixteen special areas—including a shopping arcade, a new entry, an atrium, a corporate communications center, an employee health center, and executive suites—had been brought up to the schematic design level as part of the competition. As they came up in the schedule, the process was the same as with the typical office area, only J/BA was more involved, starting earlier in the cycle. Aetna staff did the programming with the appropriate client group, and Robert Hsiung led J/BA staff in developing the design of some areas while Aetna designers detailed others, such as the executive offices.

Opposite page: Early working drawings were produced by hand with all furniture specifications in a separate spreadsheet format.

This page: Schematic designs for special areas and executive offices.

COMPUTERIZATION
January 1986–June 1987

Implementing the computerized system takes a long time. Aetna decides to work with J/BA's drafting/design program, but discovers it does not handle furniture or space planning operations easily. They ask the architects to adapt their software. Jung/Brannen's Research and Development Corporation takes Aetna's request one step further and writes a new program, called "Aetna 2000," to integrate the furniture data base with the drawings.

Aetna knew computerization would be essential on a project of this size. Arlis Bobb recalls: "It was overwhelming, at first, so many things needed to happen— drawings, scheduling, planning swing space, tracking furniture, placing orders. If we weren't well organized we'd drown. We began by looking at what had to happen in a given year (just about 500,000 sf space per year for five years) and how to organize that. Then we considered what would be needed later for someone to take over and manage the space. . . . In Middletown we didn't have these systems in place. When we handed the drawings over to OPD, they weren't accurate as-builts."

"The corporation had been evaluating CAD since 1981 but kept holding off for better prices and improvements," says Jack Dollard. "Finally they decided they couldn't postpone any longer, and they decided to go with a PC-based system." However, J/BA used a mainframe system for the competition and then later switched to a more economical PC system for the actual work.

At the start of the renovation project Aetna was just setting up its own computer system. It took time for the company to get up to speed with the new technology, train their staff, and organize the drawings. At first only the base plans were drawn with CAD; the rest were drawn manually. Aetna had agreed to use J/BA's own software, ARCHIBUS, but they soon discovered that this program,

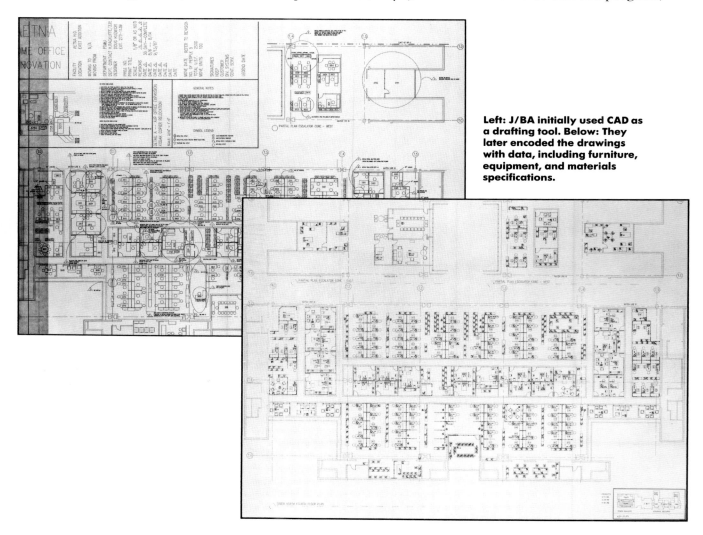

Left: J/BA initially used CAD as a drafting tool. Below: They later encoded the drawings with data, including furniture, equipment, and materials specifications.

intended for architectural drafting, did not handle furniture planning well. The facility managers asked the architects to modify the program to better suit Aetna's particular needs. This request led, eventually, to the computerization of the overall process.

At that time Aetna's furniture data base was provided as a "legend" accompanying the CAD drawings. The computer operator had to compare the Lotus-based spread-sheet with the floor plans to check for accuracy. The architects saw an opportunity to merge the two documents into one. They decided to use Aetna as a pilot and worked closely with Aetna's staff and the CAD vendor,

Autodesk, to customize ARCHIBUS to integrate alphanumeric information, such as furniture specifications, with the drawings. The new program, called "Aetna 2000," provides a means for encoding graphic symbols with information, so that not only can the designers easily develop furniture layouts directly on the plans, they can also generate quantity take-offs or call up reports on a variety of designators, including cost centers, power requirements, telephone lists, and the like.

Writing the program took a year-and-a-half, during which time the concept evolved as the team developed a better understanding of the master

plan, the design process, and the computer system. Later they went back to automate the earlier phases. "Automating the master plan helped keep it accurate and flexible," says Doug Kuzmicki. "Since the information is fully integrated, it's easy to make changes and update the program data without having to redo the whole thing."

Now, Aetna's Office Planning and Design unit is taking the whole concept even further. It is gathering corporate information from diverse sources—e.g., the company telephone directory— and interfacing it with the "intelligent" building plans to create a truly comprehensive facility management information system.

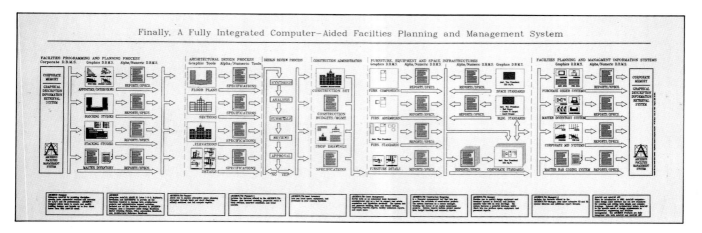

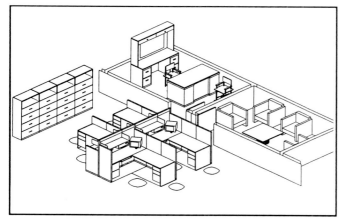

Above: J/BA's diagram illustrates the use of computers in facility planning, design, and management process.

Left: A sample "intelligent" workstation.

OBSERVATIONS

"The basic planning principle, the common footprint, really works well. When a dream like that turns into a reality, it makes the people working on it feel very good."—Arlis Bobb

- The master plan approach, based on a system of standardized components, was an excellent solution to the problem of how to plan a highly complex environment in a way that would accommodate growth and change over time. The system did not constrain design creativity, and it allowed for flexibility and individualized solutions within a consistent framework. This both addressed the intrinsic challenge of renovating the enormous facility and the specific desire of the client for a shared corporate identity.
- Building a mock-up is a good decision-making method—what you see is what you get. Going from two to three dimensions is a real leap for many people, no matter how clear the drawings may be to the designers. Using the mock-up to get user input generated both support and enthusiasm at a time when many people felt anxious about the

changes taking place in the company. By being involved in the decision-making process early on, people become more accepting of the concept of the single workstation standard.
- Computerizing the process ended up shaping it as well. Aetna CAD manager Doug Kuzmicki explains, "When the ideas for the renovation were first presented, no one had any idea of the extent of the role the computer would play. When we started work, this type of automation wasn't possible; then the technology developed in such a way that allowed it to happen. The timing was right." The computer provided the facility managers with both an accurate set of as-built drawings and a "living data base" that could be easily updated. The computer also offered the architects the opportunity to provide additional services, such as to develop software, to maintain the facility management data base, and to train and consult with the facility management staff.
- Standardizing the system of workstations, furniture components, and circulation spine made computerization relatively easy. Preparing for facility management during programming is more

A finished space in the Tower building

complicated. "You have to keep track of more information. If you move something, you have to move all the designators attached to it too," says Doug Kuzmicki. "It takes a large up-front commitment to make a project like this work," adds Arlis Bobb. "There is a long lead time getting people trained, getting the drawings set up. It's much faster to start out in a normal way. We were pleased the corporation agreed to go along with it."

- "A lot of the success is because of what we learned on the past projects—about staff needs, client relationships, the design of work facilities, and most of all, about streamlining decision making," observes administrator Rose Miles. "You've got to keep the client [department] involved enough, informed enough, every step of the way so key divisional people understand the need to make decisions fast. Timing was essential. It's like aiming at a moving target."

- "The project was set up in the spirit of team work," says Arlis Bobb. "When we selected the architect, we wanted to know who we'd be working with and what the relationship would be like. Our attitude was, there's a job to be done and let's help each other to do it. We didn't want a situation where people were pointing fingers." The role of the architect on such a team is not to be the "master builder" but, instead, is more service-oriented. "The team effort was the way to get the best job for the money," says architect Robert Hsiung. And it was quite a team. At the completion of the first bid package over 300 people were involved, including 17 from Aetna Facility Planning, 15 from J/BA, 12 engineers, and over 200 tradespeople from seventeen different building trades.

- "All business is cyclical. Most companies are planning on the up cycles, when they're enthusiastic; when they start building they are on the down cycle and the budget gets clipped. It can be demoralizing. We were reversed, but the commitment was there because the company had a long-range perspective," points out consulting architect Jack Dollard. This underscores the need for corporations to base facility-planning decisions on a broader set of criteria than short-term economic considerations.

A finished space in the Colonial building

CAMBRIDGESIDE

A MIXED-USE CENTER

To encourage revitalization of a blighted riverfront industrial district, the City of Cambridge initiated the East Cambridge Riverfront Plan. Thanks to the city's strict enforcement of the urban design guidelines incorporated in the Plan, ten years later it had successfully created a thriving, urbane community. The Plan enabled the city to leverage public design improvements: a new waterfront canal and private park to achieve large-scale private revitalization of the area. CambridgeSide, a mixed-used complex by Arrowstreet Incorporated, was the largest and most critical project in the overall scheme—when it fell into place so did everything else. The process of how a master plan for CambridgeSide evolved over the course of four years until it satisfied the complex criteria of the developer, the anchor tenants, and the city, is a model for public/private partnerships to rebuild deteriorated older cities.

PROJECT OVERVIEW

Project Master plan for a 940,000 sf mixed-use complex combining a regional shopping center with offices, housing, and a parking garage.

Architect Arrowstreet Incorporated, Architects and Planners, Cambridge, Massachusetts.

Client New England Development, Newton, Massachusetts.

Charge To satisfy the developer's commercial formula as well as the anchor tenant, and to meet the city's urban design guidelines.

Issues ✔ Relocation of the site's anchor store into its new building without disruption of its business or parking.

✔ Integration of a traditional retail center with a festival marketplace in such a way that both urban design and retail formulas "work."

✔ Accommodation for parking of 2,750 cars, truck access, a new through street, open space requirements, and excavation below a high water table in a dense urban area.

✔ Evolving project parameters and shifting site boundaries.

✔ Revitalization of urban areas through a realistic mix of uses and high standards of design quality in a public/private partnership.

Duration Master plan: four years; building design: one year (January 1984–October 1988).

Budget Withheld at client's request.

TIMELINE

YEAR 1 | YEAR 2 | YEAR 3 | YEAR 4 | YEAR 5

- PRELIMINARY PLANNING STUDIES
- SCHEMATIC MASTER PLAN
- ONGOING CRA REVIEW
- DESIGN DEVELOPMENT
- PUD PROCESS
- BUILDING DESIGN DEVELOPMENT
- CONSTRUCTION (Completion scheduled for Fall 1990)
- CASE STUDY ENDS

BACKGROUND

East Cambridge, Massachusetts, which sits
across the Charles River from Boston, is fairly typical
of communities in the so-called Rust Belt of the
northeastern United States. A thriving manufacturing
district through the end of World War II, its economy
faltered beginning in the 1950s. By the 1970s,
East Cambridge was forty acres of abandoned
warehouses and weedy parking lots. Companies that
wanted to stay in the area could not get bank loans
to improve their facilities, and many moved away,
selling their property to developers.

The decay and abandonment in turn provided an
opportunity for renewal, which the City of
Cambridge took advantage of (with the help of a
booming regional economy). In only ten years,
starting in 1978, the blighted waterfront was on its
way to becoming a lively community of shops,
housing, offices, and parks. The key to this
transformation was a municipally developed urban
design plan—the East Cambridge Riverfront Plan
(the Plan)—and the city's strict enforcement of its
guidelines. By providing public improvements such
as a waterfront canal and park system, the city was
able to leverage large-scale private investment for
the revitalization of the area within a framework that
benefits many interest groups.

The heart of the Plan was the transformation of
the dilapidated Lechmere Canal into the focal point
of a mix of retail activity and housing. When the Plan
first came out, few people were aware of the canal's
existence, whereas the Lechmere department store
nearby was a popular destination. Wanting to secure
its future on the site, the store teamed up with a
developer to acquire the land next to the canal and
build a mall (CambridgeSide), in which it would be
an anchor store.

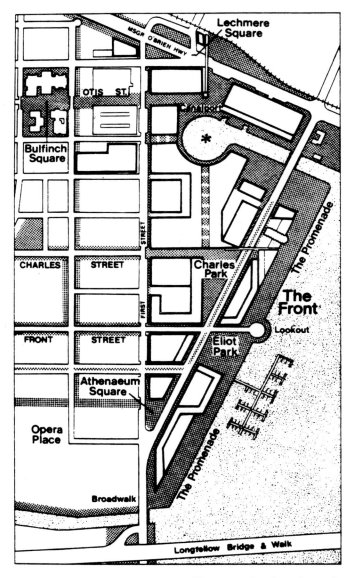

**Diagrams showing planned
open space and major neighborhood landmarks from the
East Cambridge Riverfront
Plan, 1978.**

THE EAST CAMBRIDGE RIVERFRONT PLAN: 1978

The City of Cambridge Community Development Department began a study to determine the future of the East Cambridge neighborhood in 1976. The Plan—produced by the department's head of urban design, Roger Boothe, and architect Dennis Carlone—was published in 1978. Key planning issues addressed included:

- Making the riverfront an active, people-oriented place.
- Protecting the scale and historic character of the community.
- Linking the residential neighborhood to the river.
- Reducing the role of the automobile.
- Providing a framework for development to benefit a broad range of interests.

The Plan targeted the riverfront area as most vulnerable to development pressure and divided it into four districts, including the area around the canal, which was known as the Lechmere Triangle, or simply, the Triangle. A set of development policies was proposed for each district, to set up a framework of clearly defined objectives for evaluating both private proposals and public actions, such as roadway improvements. Guidelines were provided for each district, specifying preferred land use; scale of development; location, arrangement, and massing of buildings; traffic patterns; circulation within and among buildings; and design details.

To enforce the Plan, Cambridge adopted a planned unit development (PUD) zoning district to replace the neighborhood's industrial zoning— which had allowed building density with a floor area ratio (FAR) up to four times the site area (FAR = 4:1)—with a basic allowable level of development equal to the site area (FAR = 1:1). However, the city planning board agreed that it might allow additional area up to FAR = 2:1 if a developer respected the Plan's design guidelines and environmental findings. This bonus offered developers a powerful incentive to comply.

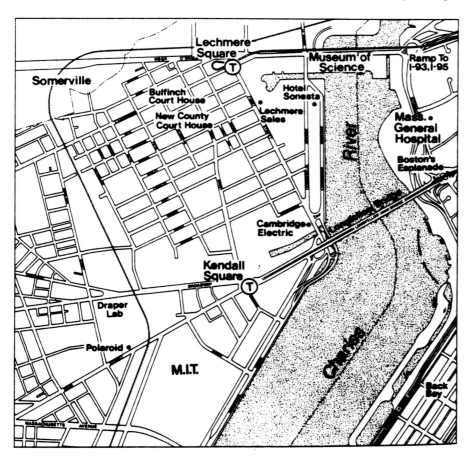

THE URBAN DESIGN CONCEPT

The Plan was structured around a sixteen-acre open space system that tied together the four districts. The city's urban designers, Roger Boothe and Dennis Carlone, envisioned a wide variety of architecture and uses fitting into this network over time, an idea loosely inspired by the "Emerald Necklace" linear park system designed for Boston by Frederick Law Olmsted. The interconnected components of this open space system were:

- Canal Park, the hub of the system, which would be the renovated Lechmere Canal with a fountain at its center.
- A crescent of buildings with active ground-floor uses ringing Canal Park.
- A retail mall leading from Canal Park to a triangular park—Triangle Park—on an extension of local Charles Street.
- Triangle Park, leading to Front Park—directly on the Charles River.
- Riverfront Esplanade, leading back to Canal Park.

By 1980 Cambridge had been awarded two Urban Development Action Grants (UDAGs) that had enabled the city to build the roadway improvements, a parking garage, and the Canal Park, which together were the focal point of the urban design for the riverfront area. This gave the effort enormous credibility in the eyes of developers. But despite this early momentum, it was not easy to implement the urban design guidelines, and by 1985 a large portion of the Lechmere Triangle district remained undeveloped. Architect Dennis Carlone recalls that "in almost every case, developers and their architects would 'pooh pooh' the process. They didn't take the guidelines seriously."

DESIGN GUIDELINES: 1985

It had became clear that the Plan's urban design review process needed to be clarified for everyone concerned. In 1985 a second document was issued to spell out how the goals of the Plan were to be implemented. It defined specific design guidelines ranging from general principles for open space and circulation design; to the mix of land uses (retail, housing, office, parking); to elements of architectural form including height, scale, massing, streetwalls, and setbacks; to details such as balconies, canopies, and signage. This document also focused attention on the ability of the area to absorb additional traffic and impacts to the infrastructure system. An environmental impact study (EIS) had concluded that new development should not include more than 2,000 parking spaces.

THE CLIENT/THE SITE

Lechmere's store occupied a converted bus depot on First Street, within the Lechmere Triangle development district. The company would probably have continued to operate out of this facility for many more years if the site had not suddenly become so desirable as a result of the pressure for growth from the region's booming economy. The Riverfront Plan stipulated that the ten-acre Triangle district was to be a 24-hour, pedestrian-oriented, 800,000 sf mixed-use development incorporating a major regional shopping center, offices, residential spaces, and parking.

Public improvements to attract private investment were to include upgrading the mass transit facilities nearby and rehabilitating the Lechmere Canal. Canal Park, with its 100-foot-high-fountain, would be the focal point of the development. The urban design guidelines called for a covered arcade on axis with the fountain leading to Triangle Park. The guidelines further stated that the site's development should reinforce existing retail activity on First Street; respect the local street grid; and strengthen pedestrian linkages through the commercial area to the residential neighborhood, riverfront park, and mass transit.

Lechmere's flagship East Cambridge store was the original and most profitable in the chain, which had been founded by a Russian immigrant who had moved to the area in the 1910s. The company has had a strong sense of commitment to the neighborhood, and, although it did not own this store, it possessed first right of refusal when the owner, the Cohen Brothers, decided to sell the land. In this way the store could indirectly control the property by teaming up with a developer and exercising its option to purchase.

THE DEVELOPER

By the early 1980s, sensing that the Cohens were ready to sell their property, the Lechmere Company turned for planning advice to Steven Karp, president of New England Development Corporation (NED), the developer of most of the malls where Lechmere's stores were located. The developer had been interested in the site since the late 1970s, but at that time interest rates had been going up and the Riverfront Plan had not made sense to him financially. Five years later, an improved economy and other development made the urban design concept more believable, but NED felt it needed to study the economic feasibility of the project further.

When the city announced in late 1983 that it would build, by eminent domain, a five-story public parking garage on First Street, Lechmere became concerned about the impact of the changes on its store. Karp referred the company to Arrowstreet Incorporated, an architectural firm that had prepared master plans for some of NED's large-scale retail projects.

THE ARCHITECTS

Arrowstreet Incorporated is a 75-member firm based in Cambridge, Massachusetts. Founded in 1973, the multidisciplinary firm has specialized in large-scale environmental design, an approach that integrates methods of architecture and planning to produce buildings that respond to the public interest as well as to the political, economic, and social issues that affect the success of a project. Arrowstreet's design philosophy is that buildings should not be isolated architectural statements, but ought to make a positive contribution to the surrounding environment.

Key members of the team for CambridgeSide consisted of partner Robert Slattery as project director, associate Brad Edgerly as project designer, and partner James Batchelor as project architect.

The site

PRELIMINARY PLANNING STUDIES
January–February 1984

Opportunities for developing the site are explored, including assembling various land packages through purchase or swap agreements with abutting owners.

Lechmere principals asked Arrowstreet partner Robert Slattery to sit in on the Cambridge Planning Board hearings for the proposed garage and then to look at how the changes in the area would affect the store's receiving area. The architects were also asked to suggest better uses for the land than surface parking. At the time, the Lechmere store had 700 parking spots, and the company could not imagine doing business with fewer. As project director, Slattery studied the range of alternatives from the practical (just fixing up the receiving area), to the radical (involving a total reorganization of the store on the site).

One option was to adapt a prototype store being developed by Lechmere at another location for the East Cambridge site. This idea evolved into a small mall, with a pedestrian concourse leading to the riverfront park. The architects built a wood model of this scheme and presented it to the city.

The Cambridge Community Development Department staff rejected this proposal for not being in compliance with the Plan, which they cited, point by point, on major issues. They insisted that the proposal include an extension of Charles Street through the site; that it align a

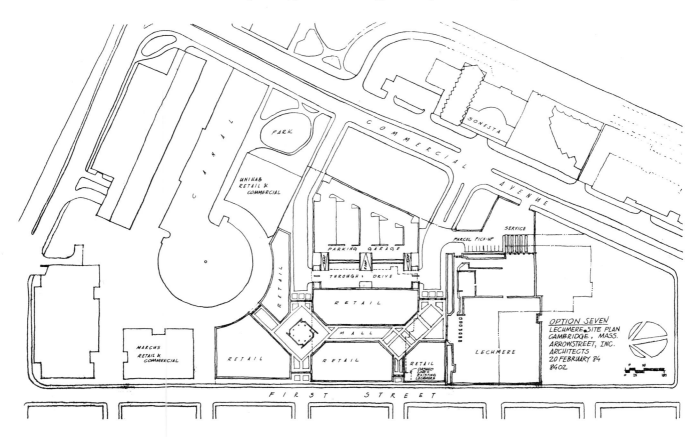

pedestrian arcade on axis with the fountain; and that it provide the specified amount of open space, which would include Triangle Park.

LAND PURCHASE FEASIBILITY STUDIES

Following this study, NED asked Arrowstreet to analyze the site's potential for development, given Lechmere's conditions for exercising their option to purchase the land and turn it over to him to develop: Throughout the transition to a new building, the store must remain open for business and adequate parking must be provided.

During the summer of 1984, the architects explored options for developing the site with and without land exchanges from the neighboring property owners. Three parcels of land were involved:

- The land on which the Lechmere store and parking lot were located (the largest parcel).
- The Sonesta Hotel, the second largest parcel, with land on both sides of Commercial Avenue, the major through street.
- A parcel at the apex of the triangle owned by the Lotus Company. Lotus had hired architect Moshe Safdie and developer Cabot Cabot & Forbes (CC&F) to develop a high-profile corporate headquarters.

Four development scenarios were considered, with the assumption that NED would be able to purchase the Cohen parcel:

- Developing the owned land, which was an odd shape and had limited access from Commercial Avenue.
- Developing the owned land plus the Sonesta land, which was not for sale but whose owner was neither for nor against the idea.
- Developing all the land in the triangle.
- Arranging a land swap with Lotus involving a "finger" of NED-owned land abutting their property.

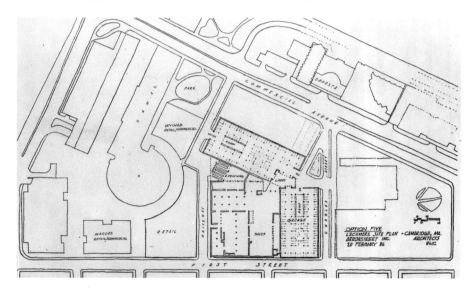

Left: Option Seven shows the possibility of a new store based on a prototype being developed by Lechmere at another location.

Above: Option Five shows a less radical approach that did not require major land exchanges with abutting owners.

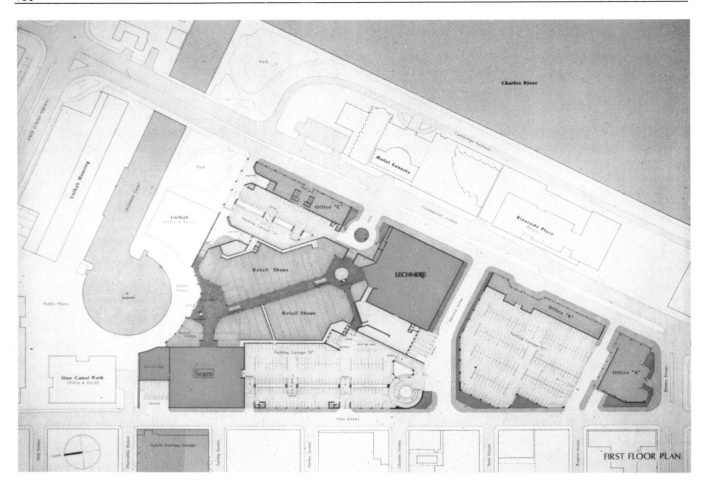

FIRST FLOOR PLAN

The charette scheme. Above: The project is developed on the owned parcel alone. Opposite page: Another early scheme for the whole site, without a triangular park.

CHARRETTE: February 1984

Legal agreements developed that set in motion the fourteen-day period Lechmere had to exercise its land purchase option. All of a sudden, a two-step process had to take place:

1. Lechmere had to buy the land, which would not involve a simple decision, since the company was owned by a larger corporation.
2. NED then had to immediately buy the land back from Lechmere. This meant Karp had to decide on the feasibility of the project based on the Cohen parcel alone, in the event that

none of the other landowners would sell or swap parcels (even though there was a good chance that some sort of deal would be possible).

Arrowstreet architects had one week to help Karp decide. They went through the earlier studies and put together a proposal that included a mall on axis with the fountain, a park off the Charles Street extension on axis with the mall, and an animated First Street edge. The scheme attempted to comply with the city's Plan and stayed within the available property lines. The developer decided to purchase the land.

SCHEMATIC MASTER PLAN
March 1984– December 1985

This phase reflects a lack of basic agreement between the developer and the city, since the developer's ideas are not fully compatible with the urban design concept of the Plan. Numerous schemes are explored, primarily aimed at resolving the proposed character of the project's retail component: whether it would be an enclosed suburban shopping mall or an open-air "festival" marketplace.

The city's planners became more involved in discussions with NED and Arrowstreet. NED preferred to build on the site an enclosed mall based on a formula that the developer knew worked: a mall anchored with a major department store at either end. This suburban-type mall is "introverted"; it does not relate to its surroundings and can theoretically be built anywhere.

However, the city wanted a mall anchored by open space— one in which "extroverted" stores define the public spaces. It wanted active ground-floor uses throughout and a building that could be seen into and out of easily.

The architects and the developer agreed that the festival-marketplace model (such as Boston's Quincy Market) was not appropriate for CambridgeSide. Architect Edgerly points out, "Quincy Market doesn't have either on-site parking or an anchor store, and it has multiple points of access. CambridgeSide is on the edge of the city; it's really neither urban nor suburban, it's a hybrid." Also, they knew that many festival markets have not been successful; the so-called "magical formula" does not always work.

Project Scale and Parking. Karp felt strongly that a certain scale of development was necessary, believing that the mass of a project has a direct relation to its success. Based on a maximum allowable building area for the site of approximately 900,000 sf (FAR = 2:1), the maximum amount of parking permitted would be 2,000 cars. But the parking requirement for that scale of retail development is around 2,500 cars, which alone could take up 900,000 sf.

Truck Access. NED felt that the city underestimated the problem of accommodating service and deliveries for 150 stores while complying with the guidelines' requirement for active project edges. Arrowstreet developed various schemes to address this issue, including a huge underground staging area devoted to trucks alone, a costly engineering solution due to the long structural spans required for trucks and the high water table of the site.

Context. The developer was not yet convinced that Canal Park would be a good neighbor for CambridgeSide, and so was reluctant to build the pedestrian arcade on axis with the fountain that was specified in the development guidelines. At that time, the park only existed as a drawing, and, as Cambridge's urban design head Roger Boothe acknowledged later, not many people understood the city's idea to reconstruct the canal, let alone that the canal was even there.

New Public Street. The city felt very strongly about providing the community with access to the retail center and the river. Yet at the same time, a right-of-way through the site for a future intersection with Commercial Avenue had not been reconciled with the Charles Street extension, and curb cuts were about to be built along with the improvements to Commercial Avenue.

Public Open Space. Triangle Park was an essential component of the urban design concept. The city felt that the park needed a recognizable form to be perceived as part of the open-space network.

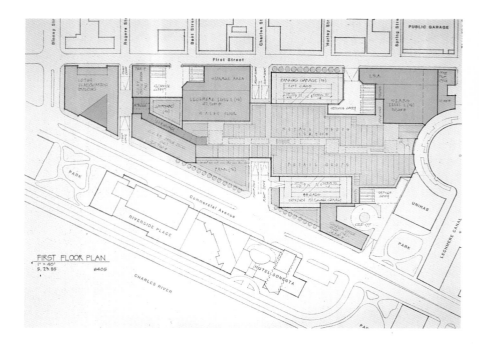

PROPOSAL FOR A TWO-LEVEL MALL: June 1985

The architects submitted a proposal for a two-story mall to the city for design review. Even though the site had an 85-foot-height limit, NED did not consider a multilevel retail space feasible. This scheme included the following elements:

- The mall led to the fountain but was not really on axis with it; the fountain could not be seen from the mall.
- First Street was used for truck access. Charles Street was included as a pedestrian connection only.
- The mall was situated 22 feet above grade because it was partly over a garage, which in turn had to be above the water table.
- There was a large office component and no housing.
- The plan did not include Triangle Park.

The city found parts of this proposal interesting, but rejected it. The city planners wanted tighter compliance with their design guidelines.

PROPOSAL FOR A THREE-LEVEL MALL: September 1985

In the meantime, vertical malls were being built elsewhere. NED conducted its own market studies of multilevel retail spaces and came up with optimistic reports. The developer and architects decided to try out a three-level scheme.

The developer also made a major concession: The whole mall would be on grade. NED decided to spend extra money on the engineering required for deep excavation below the water level to build an underground parking structure. Not only did this choice make the cost of parking expensive, it also meant that the parking would not be visible. At that time there were not too many underground parking garages associated with retail space, as they were considered to be unsafe and disorienting. Earlier schemes had avoided underground parking by locating parking on the roof of the project, a solution that had been totally unacceptable to the city.

In this proposal:

- The mall was on axis with the fountain.
- There was a park on Charles Street.
- Parking on First Street was set back behind the retail shops.
- The mall had three anchor stores.

SECOND PROPOSAL FOR A TWO-LEVEL MALL: December 1985

NED's confidence in the leasability of three levels of retail space wavered, however, and the scheme reverted to being two floors with two anchor stores. Three-level centers elsewhere were having a tough time leasing the top floor, as vertical transportation of shoppers was not yet well understood. Lechmere had a very precise approach to merchandising: At that time their operations were tailored for one level, and the company could hardly imagine the store expanding to two, let alone three, selling floors.

The developer's attitude toward the project at this stage was still noncommittal; NED had not yet formally entered the PUD process, feeling that the city was not understanding such specific retail project concerns as variety of locations within a mall, sight lines, traffic flow, the depth of stores, the number of wrap-around stores there would be, and the selection of which stores would get exterior entries.

Through repeated meetings, the city's planners were willing to listen and learn about retail requirements, but then asked Arrowstreet to refine their proposals to make them conform more closely to the urban design concept. NED acted as the intermediary with the stores. In this way the plan evolved slowly, week by week, month by month.

Still, the city had been giving mixed signals. Early in the implementation of the Riverfront Plan, the planning board had been willing to bend the rules to accommodate developers in order to get plans underway. Cabot Cabot & Forbes had received permission for an office building that was a third larger than that allowed by the guidelines. As a result, the riverfront park had become three acres smaller and had lost its direct link to the residential community. These exceptions had given NED good reason to believe that everything was negotiable.

But as the momentum of development had picked up, the planning board had become firmer in its commitment to stick by the guidelines. By late 1985, the area was booming and Canal Park was under construction. The message from the city to the developer, through the architect, was to cooperate.

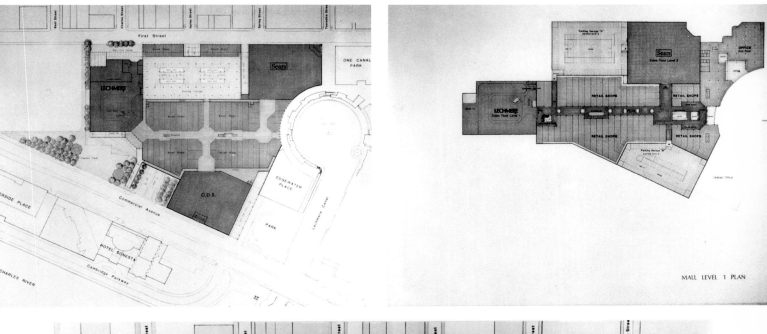

MALL LEVEL 1 PLAN

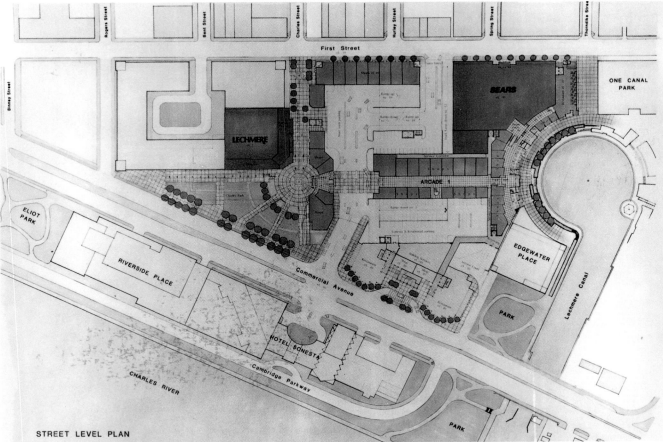

STREET LEVEL PLAN

Top: The first plan with a three-level mall, left; a two-level mall with two anchor stores within the strict parcel boundaries and an office building beside the canal, right. Bottom: A three-level mall, with the arcade for the first time on axis with the fountain, and a new Charles Park. Housing and office space is built above and along the edge of the retail crescent.

DESIGN DEVELOPMENT
January 1986–June 1987

Once the developer recognizes the need to reach an agreement with the city, as well as the benefits of the urban design concept, things begin to fall in place. A master plan that works without complex land swaps is developed and refined.

Gradually, as mutual respect grew, the developer, Arrowstreet, and the city planners became a team. By this time, NED's perception of the market for the project had changed. The developer was now determined to work out a plan that was mutually beneficial for NED, the stores, and the city. NED hired a consultant to help expedite the development process with city agencies.

The developer, architects, and contractor made a series of trips around the country to study the elements that worked in other malls. The team had been looking for precedent, measuring dimensions, noting construction details and materials, and studying vertical transportation, access, and circulation through malls of every variety.

Karp had found California's collection of malls interesting and had especially liked the West Side Pavilion in Los Angeles, a multilevel mall in a location that shared some of the idiosyncrasies of East Cambridge. At Laguna Beach he had admired the vertical transportation in a former J. C. Penney's department store that had been converted to a three-level mall and atrium.

In Washington, D.C., the team had liked Georgetown Park, and had studied why the Mazza Galleria did not seem to work. Although Galleria II in Baltimore had given them some ideas, it

had also confirmed their conclusion that as a type, festival marketplaces did not suit this project. The problems of urban projects such as Herald Square and Trump Tower in New York City had also been analyzed.

The team had been particularly impressed with the then-brand-new St. Louis Center, an urban project that bridged streets and tied into two old department stores, despite the fact that it had not yet done well in terms of sales. Karp remembers: "We liked so many things about it that we ran out and bought a video camera to record the way people moved through the space, colors, level changes—a general sense of excitement. We felt this method would recall certain concerns once we were back at the office better than a slide show would. While we were there, someone recalled a mall they'd heard about in Minneapolis. We flew up there that night and came away with some new ideas that were so good the architects made changes to the plan as soon as they got back."

On some occasions the developer would also take the city's planners to malls to explain why he had made certain choices. As the developer's reasons became clear to the planners, Karp found them becoming more reasonable. This mutual education process taking place in the course of design reviews and negotiations led to major advances in how both sides viewed the project.

Snapshots of malls visited by the team included Westside Pavilion in Hollywood, upper left and right; Owings Mills, Baltimore, lower left and center; and St. Louis Center, St. Louis, lower right.

PROPOSAL FOR AN L-SHAPED MALL: February 1986

Lechmere and Sears were confirmed at this point as prime tenants in CambridgeSide. If a third anchor could not be found, the developer would be left with a very deep and odd-shaped site. NED asked Arrowstreet to replan the mall with only two anchors. The developer was concerned about the size of parking bays, the size of shops generated by that structure, and what the leasing patterns would be.

The architects designed an L-shaped mall, which made the remote corners of the site more valuable from a leasing perspective, since it allowed for more standard floor plans. Housing was included on Commercial Avenue. Although earlier schemes had included housing above the retail crescent, Karp had felt that the cost of housing there would have been too high for the market. However, during the lengthy planning process, two luxury housing projects had been approved and were under construction. If they established the market for high-priced housing, the CambridgeSide housing would be in the ideal location. Allocating the edge for housing also helped create a smaller, easier shape to plan for the retail activities. But despite these advantages, the city was holding out for a scheme that included an arcade on axis with the fountain.

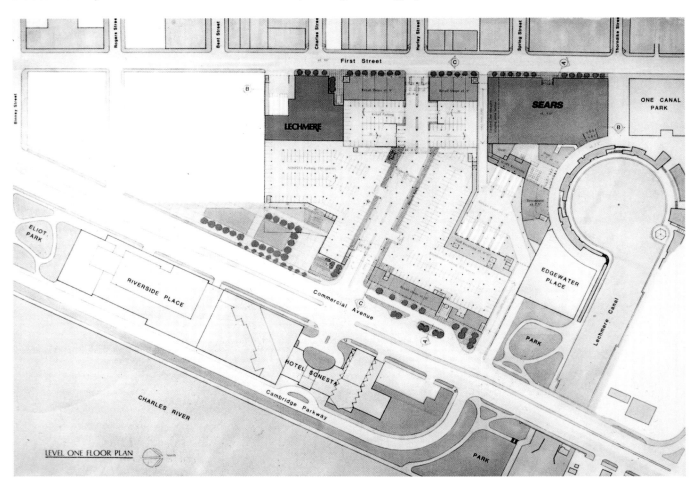

LEVEL ONE FLOOR PLAN

Above: L-shaped arcade plan with the major entry on Commercial Avenue and a pedestrian link to First Street.

Right: "Breakthrough" scheme with a street-level arcade on axis with the fountain and housing on its own land overlooking the canal.

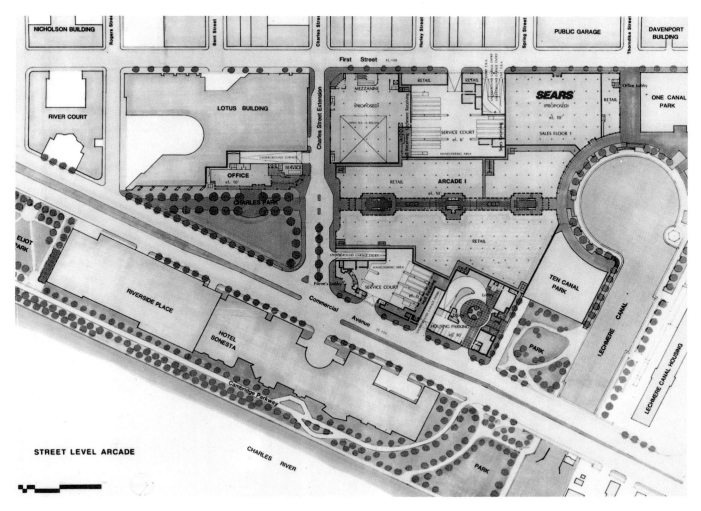

(map labels)

NICHOLSON BUILDING

PUBLIC GARAGE

DAVENPORT BUILDING

Rogers Street

Gent Street

Charles Street

Hurley Street

Spring Street

Thorndike Street

First Street FL 10

RIVER COURT

LOTUS BUILDING

Charles Street Extension

MEZZANINE

(PROPOSED)

OPEN TO +6 BELOW

SEARS
(PROPOSED)
el. 10'

RETAIL

RETAIL

One Canal Park

ONE CANAL PARK

RETAIL

SERVICE COURT
el. 6'

SALES FLOOR 1

UNDERGROUND GARAGE

SERVICE

OFFICE
el. 10'

RETAIL

ARCADE I
el. 10'

MANEUVERING AREA

CHARLES PARK

RETAIL

ELIOT PARK

RIVERSIDE PLACE

UNDERGROUND GARAGE ENTRY

Filene's Lobby

MANEUVERING AREA

SERVICE COURT
el. 6'

TEN CANAL PARK

LECHMERE CANAL

Commercial

HOUSING PARKING
el. 10'

PARK

HOTEL
SONESTA

Avenue FL 10

LECHMERE CANAL HOUSING

Cambridge Parkway

PARK

STREET LEVEL ARCADE

CHARLES RIVER

PARK

A BREAKTHROUGH:
May 1986

The architects next developed a scheme that they really liked. It included a minor arcade, with shallow stalls, at street level, and featured a food court on the side of the mall facing the water. A pedestrian street and park were also added. The drawback was that the plan relied on a land exchange.

Lechmere needed at least a 40,000 sf footprint for its store. Although the land owned by NED was big enough to accommodate this, it could not also include a triangular park on axis with the arcade as specified in the urban design guidelines. In order to comply with the city's mandate, NED needed to swap a

"finger" of land with Lotus, who did not want to trade. Because neither Lotus nor the city were flexible, this plan could not work. Surprisingly, the team was still confident that a solution was at hand.

Shortly after this last proposal had been rejected, Filene's, an upscale clothing store, decided to lease 80,000 sf, to become the third anchor. With this commitment, the team developed the master plan so that it could work without major land deals. After having gone through all of the possible iterations, the pieces of this jigsaw puzzle began to fall into place.

The architects now knew the plan would have to include three

anchor stores as well as an arcade on axis with the fountain. The city wanted the food court on the arcade, not off to one side. While the idea of including housing made sense to everyone, the architects felt it should be on the planners' own site. Another consideration was that since the project would be built in phases, there would have to be an area for materials storage. The solution was to flip the housing component to where the food court had been, off to the side overlooking the canal. This location would also serve to store materials during construction of the mall. The food court was put into the crescent. In September the team presented this plan to the city.

PUD PROCESS
January–June 1987

The city's urban design staff feels the concept is now reasonably in compliance with the urban design guidelines. The PUD process starts as Arrowstreet begins to produce the set of special permit drawings.

FIRST SUBMISSION: January 1987

With slight differences, the first plan submitted ended up being very close to the final approved scheme. Features included the following:

- A grade-level arcade is on axis with the fountain on one end and Triangle Park on the other.
- The mall has three levels and three anchor stores. A festival-type marketplace at street level opens onto the parks, but the upper two levels are built just like a regional shopping center, with access limited to the three anchor stores.
- Lechmere is located to the north side of Charles Street, where in the early planning stages it had seemed not to fit.
- There are shops as well as entries to the department stores along the streets extending from the neighborhood grid: First and Charles.
- Charles Street extends through the site.
- A narrow office building is located on the "finger" of land, within NED's property lines.
- There is three-level underground parking and two truck service courts, with direct vertical access to the shopping levels.

In this submission, Lechmere's new store was practically touching its existing building. The architects had resisted this plan because of the incredible difficulty in building so close. Although they were eventually able to fit the new building in, it took every inch of space. The foundation had to be built around the existing transformer vaults and mechanical space between the old and new structures.

Architect Edgerly points out that "In the end, the city dictated these building lines. The scheme was the only way to make the puzzle fit, but no one wanted to do it. Going through the process made everyone comfortable with it."

The next problem was how to get the project "whole" through the permit process. There was still concern that other interest groups in the city would be opposed to the project's scale, which now exceeded the maximum amount of building square footage and parking initially specified in the Plan.

Over the next few months, many meetings took place with neighborhood groups and the planning board. Karp served as spokesperson for the stores and negotiated various minor changes in the Plan and concessions on parking.

SECOND SUBMISSION: April 1987

By April, a concept had been developed that satisfied nearly everyone. Steven Karp continued to successfully negotiate on the stores' behalf. The space between Sears and Lechmere, which was a Sears automotive department, became a small garage instead. Subtle aspects of the urban design still had to be refined, but the building footprint was now fixed.

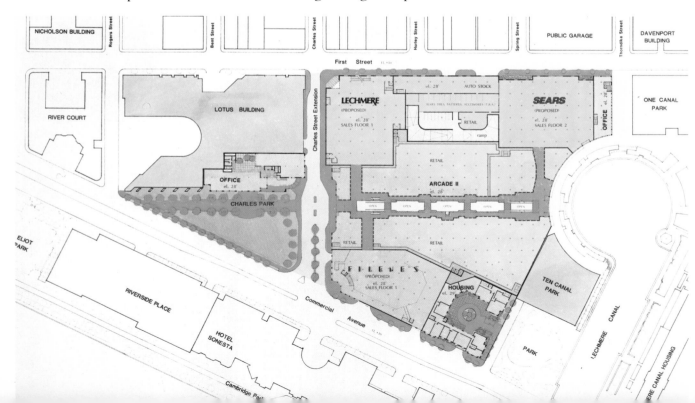

FINAL APPROVAL:
June 1987

The key issue affecting final approval was parking. The first plan submitted to the city had included three levels of rooftop parking in addition to a below-grade lot, for a total of 3,200 cars. The approved plan, eliminating the garage between Lechmere and Sears, had parking for only 2,750 cars. The anchor stores were not happy with this concession.

NED commissioned a marketing study to analyze the parking factor. The study revealed that neighborhood residents were concerned that if not enough parking were provided at CambridgeSide, people would park on the local streets. With this information, the developer was able to convince the planning board that the stores needed more parking. The approved PUD master plan was subsequently revised to include a six-story garage with retail space on the ground floor.

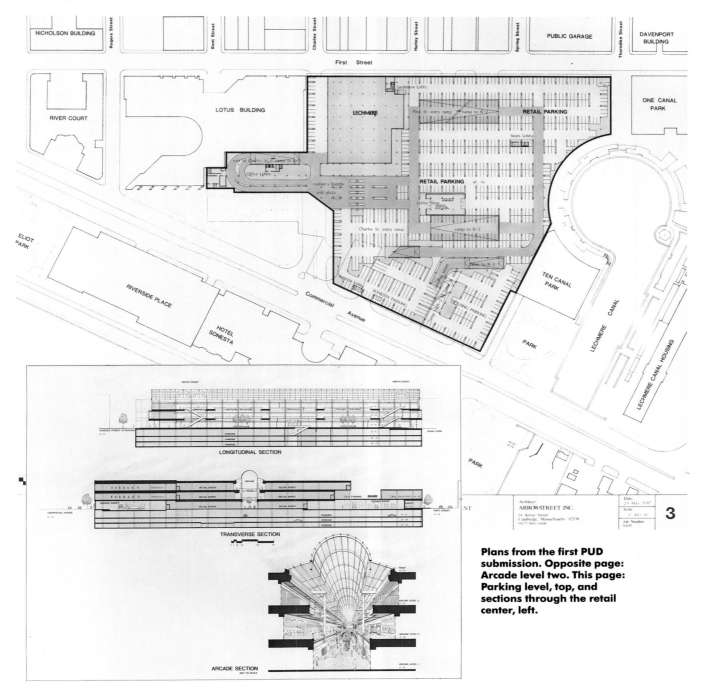

Plans from the first PUD submission. Opposite page: Arcade level two. This page: Parking level, top, and sections through the retail center, left.

BUILDING DESIGN DEVELOPMENT
February 1987–October 1988

The design for CambridgeSide progresses parallel with the development of the master plan. In fact, the master plan can be seen as an extended schematic design phase for the building. Upon final approval of the PUD set of plans, detailed design of the building progresses rapidly.

As part of the PUD agreement with the developer, the city had the right to review the design throughout the working drawing phase and even during construction. Critical design submissions were held at 90 percent completion of schematics; 50 percent and 90 percent completion of design development; and 50 percent, 90 percent, and 100 percent of construction documentation.

"The aim of the reviews," says urban design consultant Dennis Carlone, "is so that the buildings will be as 'humanistic' as possible, not just with active retail on the ground floor, but actually friendly." To achieve this, the planning staff evaluates elements such as materials, shadows, awnings, windows, balconies, colors, and signage. In the case of CambridgeSide, the city's design review encompassed the entire ground-floor arcade, since it is open to the public.

The city wanted the mall to hang together but not be monolithic. The use of smaller-scale elements, streetwalls with shop windows, and entries that are built out to meet the sidewalk and announce the

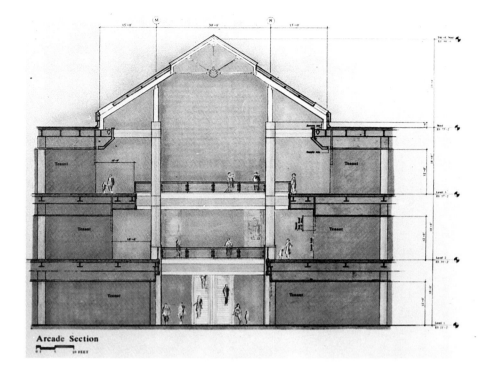

Arcade Section

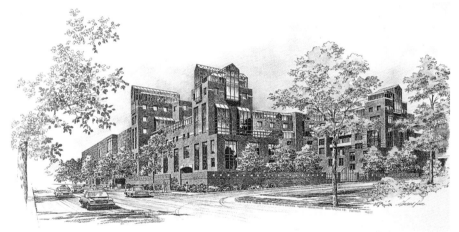

Section through the building, top. Rendering of the housing portion of the development, bottom.

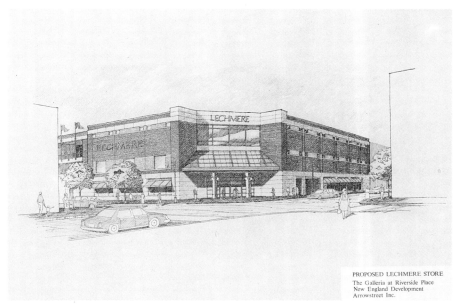

PROPOSED LECHMERE STORE
The Galleria at Riverside Place
New England Development
Arrowstreet Inc.

presence of more than one store help make the building part of the urban fabric, not just a box. Each store has its own identity.

One example of how multiple considerations came together to determine the final form of the building is the roof. For a long time the mall was to have an all-glass barrel-vault roof over the arcade. This changed to a partially glazed gable roof system after the designers observed at the St. Louis Center that the fully glazed barrel-vaulted roof caused too much heat gain and glare upstairs. Moreover, the sky went black at night, creating an unpleasant effect. They decided they preferred a white ceiling to reflect light at night.

However, in order to get an open-space bonus enabling the developer to build additional square footage in the building, the arcade had to be open or fully glazed to a forty-foot-wide swath of sky. But to build a forty-foot-wide glazed roof, the designers had to overcome the building's thirty-foot-wide column bay, which was determined by the parking garage below ground. Another issue was that a fully glazed roof would be in violation of the state energy code.

The architects' solution was to use eave skylighting, maintaining a forty-foot-wide space open above the thirty-foot column bay. The gable and pediment form was in keeping with the vocabulary of local traditional architecture, so not only did this choice satisfy the lighting, zoning, and energy code, it was also more in keeping with the neighborhood context.

Studies for identifying the entry to Lechmere's, an innovation for an anchor store in a typical "introverted" mall.

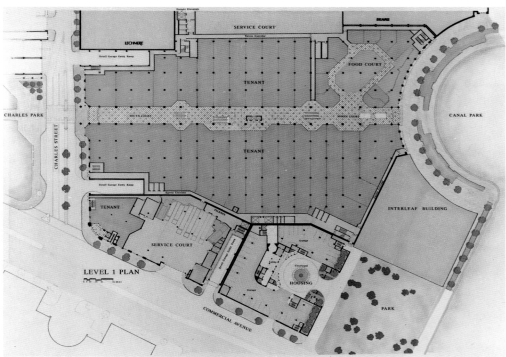

LEVEL 1 PLAN

CONSTRUCTION
Summer 1988–Fall 1990

Construction is fast-tracked to meet a schedule of anticipated completion of Lechmere's store by Summer 1989, and of the mall by Fall 1990.

"Projects of this type are always under construction before the plans are done," Steven Karp points out. "There is never the luxury of going out to bid." Speed of construction was critical to this project, since the interest on the developer's construction loan was very high. Rather than delay the project for the prolonged study required for the permanent underground structure, a temporary garage was built to provide the necessary interim parking.

One innovation that speeded up construction was the use of a building system that allowed the retail section to be built at the same time as the below-ground parking. The steel frame was put in place from foundation to roof, rather than by the traditional method of building one floor at a time.

"The risk of waiting a year for completed drawings is greater than starting early and playing catch-up," says Karp. "You can always change the plans to a certain degree, but you can't afford to delay construction once you've got an approval; the economy changes too fast."

How does that work with the city's design reviews? Karp explains that by that point in the process the city and developer had developed a strong confidence level with each other. "If I really believe in something, I'll go in and fight, and I know the planning board is going to give me a fair hearing. And where changes are reasonable we'll make them, too. This is not something where I expect to win every point. It's a give and take."

Above: Artist's view of the finished complex with the Charles River and Boston skyline in the background.

Opposite page: The project under construction, top, and the final plan, bottom.

OBSERVATIONS

The day the developer stood in front of the Canal Park fountain and said proudly, "This is my front door," the process had come full circle.

- A strong real estate market stimulated by economic growth helped the City of Cambridge shape this development according to its own vision. The success of this project is largely due to the fact that people in city government believed in the urban design plan and were committed to implementing it through the guidelines. "The State of Massachusetts's local governments have a tradition of standing up for what they want," comments architect James Batchelor. "The citizenry is very vocal. Extensive public participation in the process was an effective counterbalance to the economic interests which typically dominate large developments." The result was a classic public/private partnership to revitalize the city.
- The developer/architect team eventually got both the retail formula and the urban design diagram to work, but timing had a lot to do with it. "Ten years ago all the necessary pieces were not yet in place. One thing led to another; it was an evolutionary process," observes developer Steven Karp. Many factors were out of the team's control. For example, the successful renovation of an adjacent neighborhood brought a large population of office workers to the area and created a market for both the shops and luxury housing.
- The public/private partnership based on the PUD/Special Permits Process was mutually beneficial. "The city got both the land and the money to build a great park as a trade-off for permission to build CambridgeSide. Having a more-or-less clear image of what the community wants helps developers know what they are getting into and helps architects by providing something to work from," says the city's urban design director Roger Boothe. "The guidelines have earned the grudging respect of developers by being reasonable and consistent."
- The master plan process is essentially the front end of the building design—it lengthens planning and schematic design. "This ultimately benefits a

project: the longer you study something, the better it gets," believes urban design consultant Dennis Carlone. "This was initially a speculative project that didn't show enough concern for the context," says Boothe. "The developer was thinking of the site as an object and looking in, rather than imagining himself inside the place and looking out." Architect Brad Edgerly remembers what it was like to mediate between the client and the city: "NED often put a building where someone else put open space. How do you cope with that?"

• Reinventing urban retail centers will help suburban malls, too, according to developer Karp. "We are learning that hundreds of acres of parking don't make sense; that sites should be smaller, and the quality of the development better. What's going on inside has to be integrated with the outside world, and the design can't be too faddy. The mall should be a comfortable and inviting environment but not overpower the stores."

• Looking at the site photo is revealing: It shows the proximity to downtown Boston, the residential neighborhood, an interstate highway, and the captive office population. "From the city's point of view, the neighborhood patterns generated the development of the site more than the highway access," comments Batchelor. "Extending the existing street grid was incredibly important to them, to give the community access to the river, where there had once been an industrial wasteland. They were also sensitive to the concerns of local shop owners, who were worried that too much competition from CambridgeSide would drive them out of business and that they would not be able to afford the rents there."

• This development catches people's eye not just because it is a park with new buildings, but because it is a whole new neighborhood, says Carlone. "There was a reason for the buildings and the park, a symbiotic relationship between the built form and the open space, as in old cities. Urban design is really designing the experience of being in a city. By providing a framework of activity, the place becomes a real destination."

Artist views of the completed CambridgeSide complex

METROPOLIS

A MIXED-USE DEVELOPMENT

In this case study, a limited competition was used to commission a high-profile design for a master plan for a mixed-use complex and first-phase office tower on a prominent site in downtown Los Angeles. Although timing was a critical factor (to start construction of the tower before growth-control regulations went into effect), when the developer selected Michael Graves as the winning architect, he was first asked to redesign his master plan. Graves's design also had to satisfy City of Los Angeles urban design guidelines to qualify for city assistance in implementing the project. However, these guidelines were only formulated in detail in response to the Graves proposal. The final master plan evolved in a process of negotiation between the city, architect, and developer in which the quality of the design of the tower was an important factor. In booming cities like Los Angeles, distinctive design is almost a necessity for speculative projects, but high-style buildings are not enough to create good urban places. This project illustrates how the urban design process can reconcile the developer's desire to distinguish a project and the public's interest in rebuilding blighted downtown areas.

PROJECT OVERVIEW

Project Master plan for 2,600,000 sf mixed-use office, retail, and hotel complex and design of the first-phase office tower.

Architect Michael Graves, Architect, Princeton, New Jersey.

Client Parkhill Partners, developer, Los Angeles, California; City Centre Development Partnership, owner, Los Angeles, California.

Charge To accommodate the client's economic requirements and design agenda as well as the city's urban design and development guidelines.

Issues ✔ Using a competition to commission an exceptional design and speed up the process to start construction before growth-control regulations went into effect.

✔ Provision of a memorable architectural image to mark the entry to the city from the freeway as well as enhancement of the pedestrian environment.

✔ Commissioning a high-profile design to "sell" the project in a competitive environment both for permission to build and for leasing.

✔ Interdependence of the fast-track building design and the master plan process.

Duration Master plan: nine months from competition to initial submission to city; building design: two years to anticipated completion of working drawings (December 1987–January 1990).

Budget $650 million for entire complex.

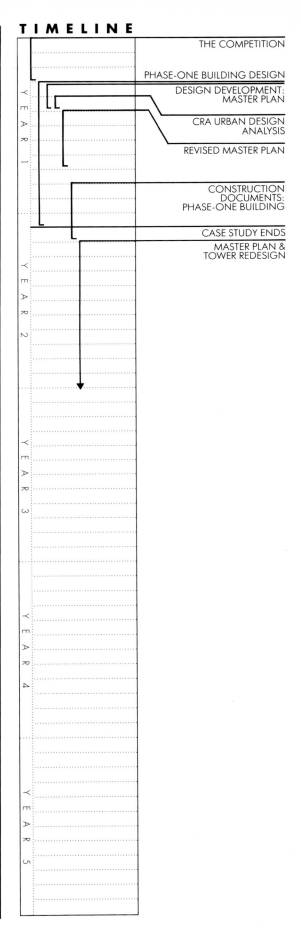

TIMELINE

- THE COMPETITION
- PHASE-ONE BUILDING DESIGN
- DESIGN DEVELOPMENT: MASTER PLAN
- CRA URBAN DESIGN ANALYSIS
- REVISED MASTER PLAN
- CONSTRUCTION DOCUMENTS: PHASE-ONE BUILDING
- CASE STUDY ENDS
- MASTER PLAN & TOWER REDESIGN

YEAR 1
YEAR 2
YEAR 3
YEAR 4
YEAR 5

BACKGROUND

The way in which Michael Graves developed a master plan for the Metropolis mixed-use complex (originally called "City Centre"), which also served as the framework for the fast-track design of a thirty-story office tower, illustrates the larger process by which new large-scale development is taking place and changing the character of downtown Los Angeles. Once a sprawling, provincial city without a real urban focus, in the 1980s Los Angeles emerged as an international economic and cultural capital. *New York Times* writer Robert Reinhold recently described Los Angeles "as a powerful world engine of change, arbiter and innovator in styles of art, architecture, clothing, hair, food, music, and pop culture, not to mention movies." Population has soared, office buildings have multiplied, and real estate prices have skyrocketed.

Now many people are deciding that growth is not such a good idea if it means worsening traffic jams, overflowing sewers, and polluted air. In 1986 Los Angeles voters approved a plan to cut in half the allowable density of most future commercial and industrial buildings. A slow-growth movement known as "Not Yet New York" was getting a lot of attention in the city. What is happening in California, where fifty-seven cities and eight counties have voted to limit growth, is the beginning of what appears to be a national trend. The public's environmental concerns are becoming a factor private developers and their architects must take into consideration.

But in the 1970s downtown Los Angeles was still a depressed area, home to a substantial homeless population. In response, the Los Angeles Community Redevelopment Agency (CRA) conducted a planning study to revitalize the central business district. When the CRA's Redevelopment Plan for the Central Business District (the Plan) was adopted by the Los Angeles City Council in 1975, no one could foresee that it would be used to control mushrooming growth rather than to stimulate redevelopment of unwanted land. During 1988 there were over thirty proposals, Metropolis among them, for major projects seeking permission to build in downtown Los Angeles.

THE REDEVELOPMENT PLAN

The Metropolis master planning process took place within the context of the Redevelopment Plan's objectives for the central business district (CBD)

planning area. These included:

- To help prepare the central city for its share of regional growth.
- To organize growth and change to revitalize deteriorated areas.
- To create a 24-hour, people-oriented urban environment and an integrated transportation system that enhances the pedestrian environment.
- To achieve design excellence based on how people use the central city.
- To provide housing close to employment.
- To promote cooperation among business, special interest groups, and public agencies in the implementation of the Plan.

Rather than tear down existing buildings to achieve its objective of "eliminating and preventing the spread of blight," the Community Redevelopment Agency encouraged property owners and tenants to remain and become part of the revitalization effort. The CRA would provide assistance in securing parcels, demolishing structures, swapping parcels within the project area, and relocating tenants, when necessary, to assemble areas for development. To qualify for such help, a developer was required to conform to the Plan's criteria and enter into a "Development Agreement" with the CRA. One incentive for landowners to participate was that parcels that did not conform to the Plan would become subject to acquisition by the CRA by means of eminent domain.

Among the CRA's requirements for land it sells or assists in rehabilitating is architectural review of any development plans. CRA staff reviews projects at concept, schematic, and design development phases of work and throughout construction, to ensure that the projects are built according to the approved designs. Evaluation of proposals is in terms of conformance to the intent and purpose of the Plan, in particular, to achieve excellence in the design of public open-space amenities.

The CRA had prepared general parameters for the development of the Metropolis project site, but specific design guidelines were written in response to the Michael Graves scheme after it had been submitted for preliminary design review. Evaluation of the proposal was less according to strict criteria than in terms of the general intent of the plan, which was determined through a process of negotiation between the CRA, the architect, and the developer.

Aerial view of downtown Los Angeles

THE SITE/THE CLIENT

The Metropolis project coalesced around the site, which encompasses an entire block (approximately 276,000 sf) between Eighth and Ninth streets, the Harbor Freeway, and Francisco Street, in the northwest portion of the South Park Development Area of the Plan. The site has excellent access to the freeway as well as to mass transit. Francisco Street, the major frontage, links several new developments in the area, which include the Citicorp Plaza office and retail center (which had shifted the center of downtown Los Angeles toward the South Park neighborhood), a major expansion of the Los Angeles Convention Center, and two planned commercial developments across the street.

In 1983, there were two major landowners on the block: Mayfair Plaza Associates and Harbor Plaza Holding Associates. Mayfair owned the larger piece, but did not have street frontage. They had asked the CRA to help them assemble the parcel by condemning the existing structures; the CRA had refused since Mayfair's holding had not entitled them to such assistance. Harbor Plaza Holding Associates had commissioned a design for the "Harbor Plaza" building, a twenty-eight-story granite-and-glass office tower with five levels of above-grade parking, to be built on their land. But the parcel ended up being too small to develop a building of sufficient density to be economically feasible. Subsequently a Japanese firm had bought the land, in an effort to assist the developer.

James Miller, a partner in Harbor Plaza Holding Associates, got the idea to combine the two sites and develop a mixed-use complex. With Ronald Lushing, Miller formed the City Centre Development Partnership (CCP) and by January 1988 had bought out both interests, also acquiring the Harbor Plaza plans and specifications. By August 1988 CCP had purchased the last integral piece of land on the block. Only five small parcels remained, which they anticipated acquiring through negotiation or with the assistance of the CRA.

City Centre Development Partnership formed Parkhill Partners exclusively to develop the project. In addition to Miller and Lushing, the development team included John Vallance, who would manage the planning and approval process; William Cook, a construction manager who would provide preconstruction services; and Barbara Harris, who would bring marketing and property management expertise.

NEED FOR A MASTER PLAN

Parkhill wanted to use the Harbor Plaza building plans, which had already been reviewed by the Los Angeles Building Department and so might have been exempt from a recently enacted sewer ordinance limiting new construction. Zoning for the site allowed a floor area ratio (FAR) of 6:1; however, an FAR of 10:1 would have been allowable, if the Redevelopment Plan's conditions were met. Any development of the block would depend on CRA approval of the proposed land use and density, and assistance with site assemblage. This required Parkhill to submit a master plan and enter into an "Owner Participation Agreement" with the CRA before applying for the first-phase building permit.

The developers wanted the master plan to make a strong architectural statement for two reasons. First, having a "star" architect would help them sell the project to the city as a civic enhancement. At the time, there was so much competition for permits and for tenants that having an outstanding design was a virtual necessity as a marketing tool. Second, because Metropolis would be the first development seen from the Harbor Freeway approach to the city, the direction of arrival from the airport, the developers wanted it to be "a memorable experience, to be noticed," in Jack Vallance's words.

DECISION FOR A COMPETITION

In light of the slow-growth movement, it was very important to the owners to get the master planning process going quickly and to start construction by the end of 1988. While seeking suggestions for a list of appropriate architecture firms, the developer was advised to hold a competition. "Given our strict parameters on turnaround time, the competition was a way to avoid going six months down the road with someone before discovering we didn't like them and also to have a few alternatives to consider," says Vallance.

THE COMPETITION
December 1987–February 1988

The five-week competition is for a master plan for the block, incorporating the Harbor Plaza tower. The winner will take the master plan through the approval process and receive a commission for the design of the phase-one office tower. Parkhill is impressed with the Michael Graves presentation but does not like all aspects of his approach and asks the Graves team to revise its submission. The developer is enthusiastic about the second scheme and Graves wins the commission.

PLANNING THE PROCESS

Parkhill hired architect Edward Wundram, a competition consultant, to administer the competition and engaged the deans of both the UCLA and USC Schools of Architecture to serve as advisors on the merits of the designs. City Centre Development's three principal partners were the jury. The winner was to receive two commissions: The first was for the redesign of the façade of Harbor Plaza; and the second was to complete the conceptual master plan for the site and take it through the approval process. Parkhill retained the right to hire another architect for the remaining buildings, in case the operator of the proposed hotel or retail components wanted some say in the design of those phases.

The five-week competition was to begin in mid-December 1987 and to conclude on January 22, 1988. Ten firms were invited to compete and five responded. The day before the competition began, all the architects met with the developer for an orientation. A week after, two firms dropped out: one had too much work; the other wasn't comfortable with the rules. Three firms remained: Murphy Jahn & Associates; Michael Graves, Architect (MGA); and John Andrews International. Each was paid a $25,000 honorarium.

The first design for Metropolis (then called CityCentre), showing the prominence of the site as a gateway to the city.

THE PROGRAM

The multiuse development initially included approximately 2.1 million gsf consisting of 1.2 million sf of office space, 275,000 sf of retail space, and 175,000 sf of residential space, as well as a 400,000 to 500,000 sf first-class, convention-oriented hotel. Phasing of the development was critical to the developer from a financing and marketing perspective since a project of that scale cannot be built or leased all at once. The master plan was to take into account a fairly complex four-phase schedule:

Phase 1: Completion of the former Harbor Plaza tower in 1988.

Phase 2: Completion of the retail component and some residential space in 1989–90.

Phase 3: Completion of the second office tower and the remaining residential space in 1991–92.

Phase 4: Completion of the hotel component, which would be developed by others within the guidelines established by the architect of the master plan.

Harbor Plaza. The program stated that the existing plan and site location of the Harbor Plaza tower were to be integrated into the master plan, unless a strong case could be made that a new building would not delay the anticipated start of construction, November 1988. Before the competition began, the developers decided to allow three options for dealing with the tower: first, simply redesigning the exterior skin; second, redesigning the top and base as well; and third, not using the original plans at all.

Retail Component. Particular attention was to be given to linking the retail component with existing retail space in the Citicorp Plaza complex and planned retail space on adjacent sites. The developers saw the retail component primarily as an internalized "destination" site, "drawing people to downtown Los Angeles who otherwise might not come." The project and its architecture were intended to play a large role in attracting a major anchor store that would be an especially strong drawing force. The master plan was to envision the transformation of Francisco Street into a pedestrian-oriented environment conducive to storefront retail activity.

Although the Los Angeles zoning code required that all parking be on-site, which was the developer's preference as well, CRA requirements, not yet adopted by the city at that time, stated that 40 percent of code-required office parking must be provided off-site. The amount of parking required on site, therefore, was negotiable.

Because this was a speculative project, cost was also an important factor. Estimated building costs for the various components were provided, although the architects were instructed to be conscious of cost but not overly concerned. The most critical factor was timing. The developer, aware that the schedule for approvals was tight, had committed full time to this one project in order to push it through as fast as possible.

THE ARCHITECT

The work of Michael Graves, Architect, has won numerous awards and has been included in exhibitions throughout the United States and abroad, although it is essentially a small, informal firm based in Princeton, New Jersey. Since 1962, Graves has divided his time between practice and teaching at Princeton University. Michael Graves's signature style is evident in all of the designs produced by the diversified practice, which in addition to urban design and architecture includes furniture and decorative arts. The seventy-member staff includes nine associate architects.

When the invitation for the Parkhill competition arrived just after Thanksgiving, many of the Graves staff were on vacation and the firm was already swamped with work. But the opportunity seemed too good to pass up. MGA Associate John Diebboll was made job captain. After the firm won the competition, associate Eric Regh joined the team to head the phase-one office tower design team.

THE MICHAEL GRAVES SUBMISSION
December 1987–January 1988

Graves and Diebboll spend their holidays on charrette and produce the competition design. Diebboll then enlists the help of a few staff members to prepare the presentation, which must consist of a model, four boards, and a narrative report including photographs of the model.

MGA presented its submission on January 19, 1988. The following description is based on the submission narrative:

Planning Concepts

• Francisco Street would be widened into a boulevard with a landscaped central median to serve as an axial link between the Citicorp Plaza and Convention Center, with Metropolis as "the fulcrum." A shuttle service could transport pedestrians to the various developments along this link.

• The primary pedestrian entrance to the retail mall would be located at Eighth Street, to serve as a link to nearby retail developments and to take advantage of existing circulation patterns. Eighth Place would be relocated to align with the development's central rotunda, where both parking and pedestrian entries to the retail anchor would be located.

• The complex would be organized around two pairs of twin towers at either end of the site and a central rotunda that houses the retail anchor store. This massing would create "a portal" to frame the view of downtown Los Angeles when approached from the west along the Harbor Freeway. Graves's strategy was "to allow

a legibility of the various components within the development, as well as identification of the site from a distance, both entering and leaving L.A."

• For the site across Francisco Street, Graves proposed to build a tower similar in size and massing to another development planned for that

block, to frame the view of the Metropolis rotunda from the axial approach along Eighth Place from Figueroa Street. The rest of the site would be low-rise housing with retail space at the ground-floor street edges and parking in a central garage. Entry to the apartments would be from a rooftop garden on the garage.

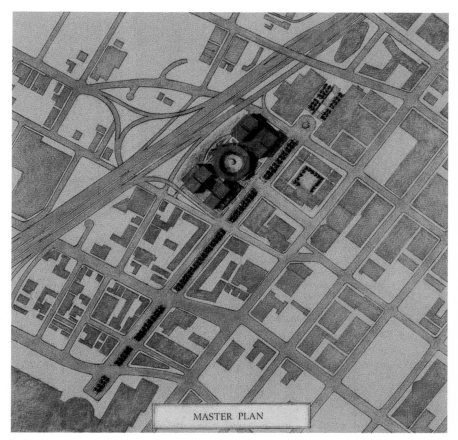

MASTER PLAN

The master plan from the competition submission

Architectural Concepts

- The four towers would all use the same floor plate and structural grid as the Harbor Plaza building, now Tower A, in the north quadrant of the site. Tower A and its matching unit, Tower B, would house offices; at the lower levels would be a retail mall and parking.
- Access to the office lobbies would be from the mall, which would lead from Eighth Street through the towers to a three-story anchor store housed in the rotunda. The rotunda form would give the anchor store a special identity from the freeway and the street. Above the retail anchor store in the rotunda would be fourteen stories of housing.
- Tower C, in the western quadrant, would be built in phase three as an office building with its own underground garage. The southern tower would house the hotel and be built in phase four. Between these towers and on axis with the Eighth Street mall would be an outdoor garden at ground level. Service would be provided by a driveway running beneath Tower C and connecting Eighth and Ninth streets.

Harbor Plaza. The tower would be incorporated in the complex with the same form, structural grid, and core as in the existing plans, but with its orientation on the site shifted by five degrees. A new base was designed, incorporating a portion of the retail mall in order to help tie the phase-one development into the existing retail activities along Eighth Street. The architects also designed a new top and façade for the building.

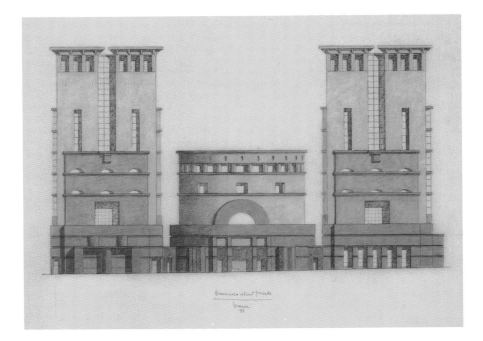

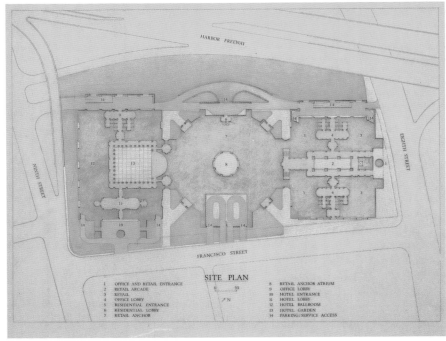

From the competition submission. Elevations facing Francisco Street, top; site plan, bottom; proposed façade for the phase-one office tower (formerly Harbor Plaza), right.

harbor plaza office tower

Materials. The same structural steel system designed for the Harbor Plaza building would be used throughout. Exterior materials would be selected from Kasota stone, ocher or red sandstone, and red granite. Windows in the office building would be typically either 5'-0" or 7'-9" square. Special glass curtain wall windows would occur within the façades in several locations.

As the competition required, the submission provided both a breakdown of construction phasing and construction cost estimates.

Context. Scalar elements would be used to relate the development to both the highway observer and the pedestrian, identifying the overall composition as well as its components. The entire complex would sit on a continuous base, which would also help to unify the various parts. The base would house parking, but on the three sides facing streets it would also contain public spaces and the pedestrian and vehicular entrances to the complex.

The towers were designed with vertical bay windows at either end, which read as "luminous columns." This element was intended to enhance the image of the towers as a gateway day and night.

The architect's choice of materials, colors, and forms subtly refer to traditional Southern Californian architectural themes. The submission narrative states ". . . the earthen tones of the buildings' stone façades are not historical quotations but come from the same regional roots that characterize local buildings from the early Mission Style through the Art Deco buildings of the '20s and '30s."

AERIAL PERSPECTIVE

Above, from the competition submission: Aerial perspective, top; model of the project facing Harbor Freeway, bottom.

Opposite page: Section looking northwest, top; Ninth Street elevation, bottom; perspective sketch of the mall interior, far right.

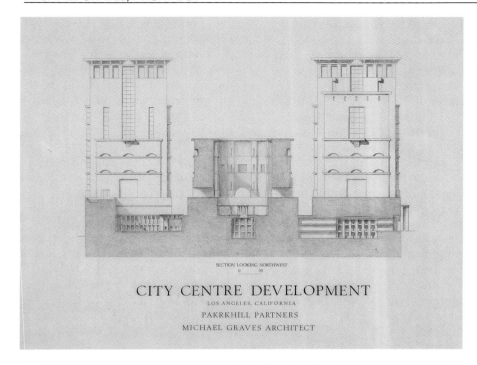

SECTION LOOKING NORTHWEST
0   30

CITY CENTRE DEVELOPMENT
LOS ANGELES, CALIFORNIA
PAKRKHILL PARTNERS
MICHAEL GRAVES ARCHITECT

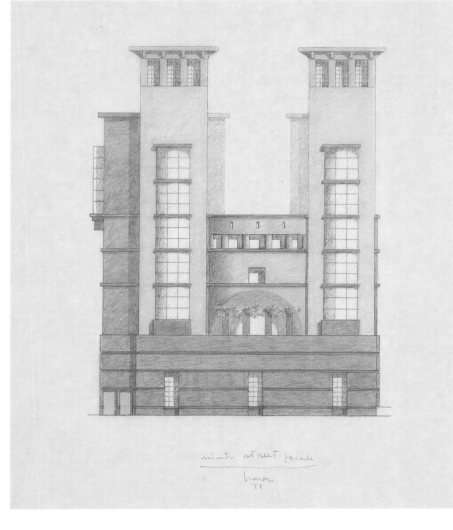

ninth street facade

graves
'88

THE JURY'S RESPONSE

MGA started out the least favored of the competitors. The developer was concerned that the firm could not work within the constraints of a spec office project. Although City Centre Development (CCP) was positively impressed by the team's presentation, and there was good "chemistry" between them, CCP's people did not understand the architect's approach.

According to John Vallance, the developer felt that the MCA proposal was too "closed in," too "medieval"; CCP had wanted something more open, "more Southern California." At this stage, however, they were looking less for the perfect solution than for general ideas, the character of a proposal. They felt that one of the other two submissions was very "high tech" and not tied to the character of Los Angeles; the other they thought was too similar to existing buildings in the city and not a significant enough statement.

Graves was given one month to design a new scheme. The firm was not yet the winner. If CCP liked the second scheme, it would award Graves the commission.

HOTEL COURTYARD

REVISED SUBMISSION:
February 1988

The developer felt that since later phases would be designed by other firms, the master plan could not be rigidly symmetrical. But phasing also gave MGA more freedom, as they would not have to utilize economies of scale (of similar buildings). The revised Graves scheme allowed for a greater variety of buildings. The central rotunda, which the architects and developer agreed did not work, was eliminated, thus simplifying planning. The residential component, which had been nearly double the level stated in the program, was reduced to the specified amount.

In the second submission, the retail anchor store was housed in a crescent-shaped building opening onto a plaza, which formed the roof of a building housing parking and an underground retail arcade. The Harbor Plaza tower was rotated 90 degrees on the site, and the two other office towers were combined in the southern quadrant, rising from a common base. The hotel was moved from the south to the eastern quadrant, facing the retail crescent across the roof garden.

The client was enthusiastic about the second scheme, flew the team to Europe to receive the investor's approval, and awarded the commission to MGA. Work getting the master plan through the approval process would be compensated on an hourly basis; the fee for the redesign of the tower's exterior skin would be based on a percentage of construction costs. CCP would handle landscaping and graphics.

MGA hired a local firm, Kober, Rippon and Associates, as a consultant to expedite the approval of the project by city agencies and to produce construction documents for the skin. Parkhill also wanted local representation.

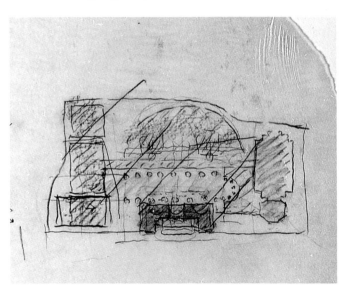

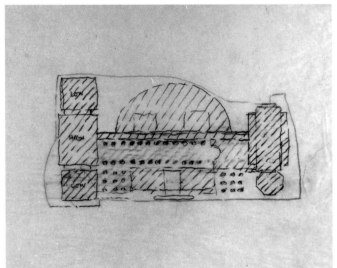

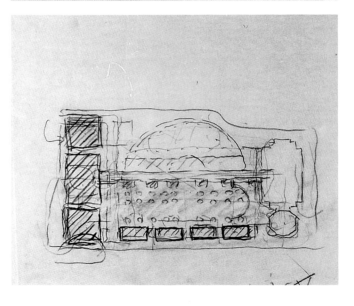

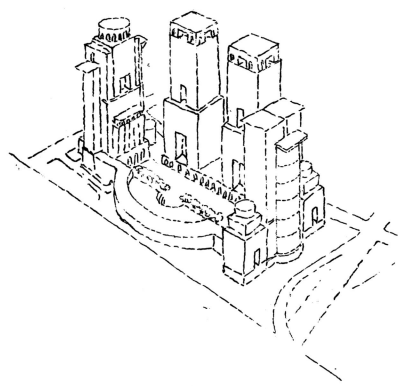

Opposite page: Studies for the revised master plan show a greater variety of buildings.

Left: Axonometric sketch illustrates revised design concept.

Below: Third floor plan.

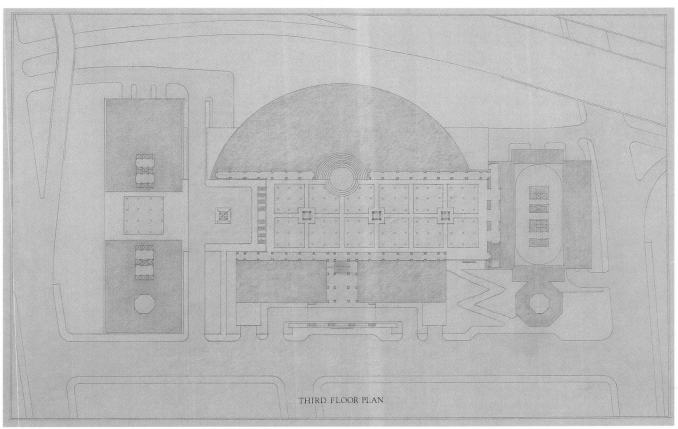

THIRD FLOOR PLAN

DESIGN DEVELOPMENT: MASTER PLAN
March–April 1988

MGA studies the master plan further in response to the comments of the two architecture school deans who continue to advise the developer on the project's design. At this time the CRA initiates a design review of the proposal and prepares preliminary design guidelines for the site. The CRA staff develops six alternative schemes that it feels improve the MGA proposal. MGA revises the master plan to incorporate the guidelines in principle.

Parkhill asked the two deans who served as design advisors during the competition to comment on Graves's second submission. Although they responded separately, the deans concurred on certain key points. They agreed that the retail arcade and restaurants should be at the ground level, rather than underground as MGA had proposed, in order to animate the central plaza.

Both deans felt the plaza was an important element in the overall project that should be used as an "activity generator, not just a static plaza." In their

Alternative schemes study the master plan concept and respond to comments of the two architecture school deans.

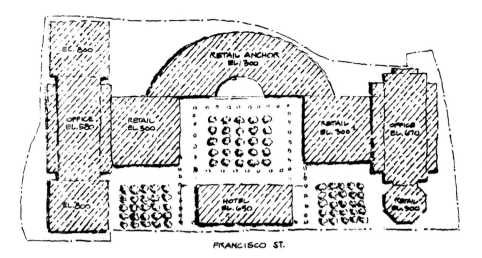

FRANCISCO ST.

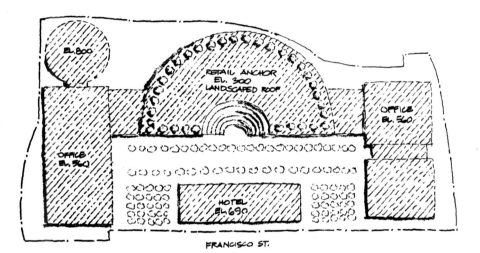

FRANCISCO ST.

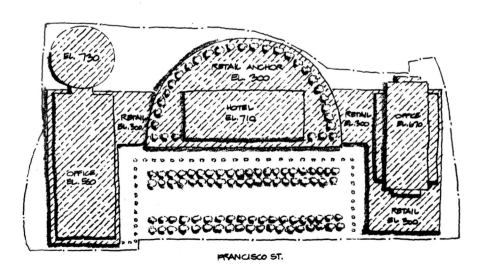

FRANCISCO ST.

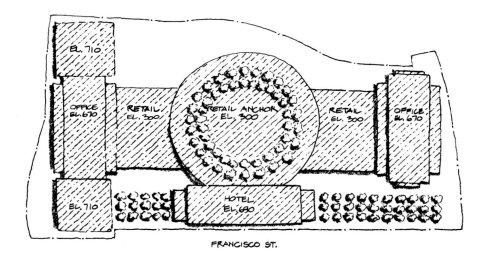

FRANCISCO ST.

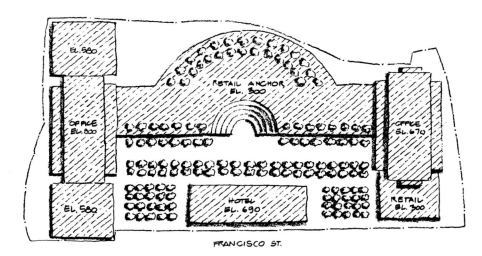

FRANCISCO ST.

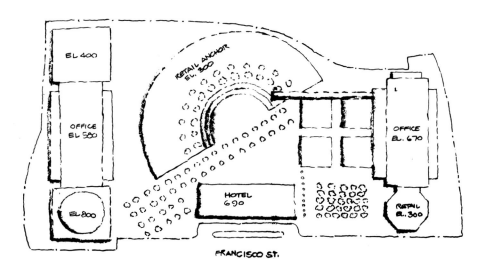

FRANCISCO ST.

opinion, the close proximity of the two towers at the southern portion of the site would block afternoon sun into the central plaza—an issue they felt warranted further study.

The deans also suggested more study on the prominence, accessibility, and "activity draw factor" of the semicircular structure, the arcades, and the terraces. Another shared concern was that the numerous curb cuts proposed for Francisco Street would weaken the project's ability to serve as a pedestrian thoroughfare along the edge, linking the Citicorp Plaza and the Convention Center. They also felt that the entry plaza at the corner of Francisco and Eighth streets seemed "forbidding." One solution proposed was to extend the central courtyard out to this corner to strengthen the tie to the Citicorp project.

Parkhill asked Graves to respond to these comments and to study the master plan concept further. MGA produced six alternative schemes for distributing the mixture of uses and open-space components within variations on their original massing concept. At the same time, the team met with the CRA urban design staff to initiate a preliminary design review of the MGA proposal.

CRA REVIEW

The Graves team refined the second competition scheme without major changes and submitted it to the CRA for review. The phase-one tower was now located at the corner of Francisco and Eighth streets and included a retail "pavilion" to mark the entry to the development. A central garden approximately twenty feet above grade was on axis with the office towers at either end of the site. The southern office tower was the tallest of the four buildings. The hotel access drive opened directly onto Francisco Street.

PRELIMINARY GUIDELINES

Following the initial meeting, the planners put together a set of guidelines for the site "to focus the master planning process towards the objectives of the Central Business District Redevelopment Plan." These guidelines outlined specific requirements and issues to be addressed.

Planning Issues
• The impact of the development on peak-hour traffic congestion.
• The scale and location of the proposed retail component from a marketing perspective.
• Development of housing elsewhere in the district, instead of on this site, which is not located in the Plan's target area for housing development.
• Provision of 25 to 40 percent of code-required parking (one parking space per 1000 sf of office) off-site [the exact percentage to be negotiated].

Land Use. The dominant land use should be for offices. Street-level frontage along Francisco Street was to be devoted to retail uses. Retail components should be oriented to the street rather than to an interior space. Parking structures should be screened from view or, preferably, be located below grade.

Vehicular access. Vehicular access should be primarily from Francisco Street and designed to minimize conflicts with pedestrians by using as little frontage as possible.

Built Form
• Provide a diversity of building forms.
• Towers should enhance views of the downtown skyline.
• Orient the street level of buildings toward Francisco Street and the towers to respond to the freeway.
• Give special treatment to the corner of Eighth Street and Francisco Street.
• Establish Eighth Place as an axis to the project from Figueroa Street.
• Landscape Francisco Street and provide pedestrian amenities.
• Visibility into street-level stores is mandatory.
• A hotel component, if any, should be oriented toward Francisco Street.

Public Open Space
• Provide accessible public open spaces located at grade level.
• Secondary public spaces may be interior courtyards, but must also contribute to an active pedestrian environment.
• Provide special paving, landscaping, and lighting of pedestrian areas.

Right, from the CRA submission: Model of the revised master plan.

Opposite page: A section looking northeast, top, and the first floor plan, bottom.

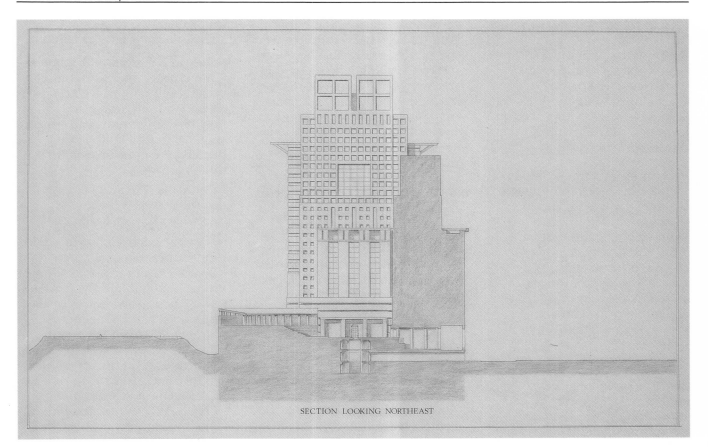

SECTION LOOKING NORTHEAST

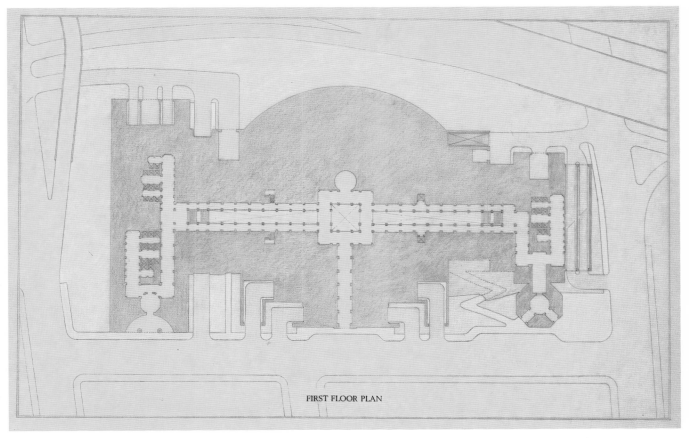

FIRST FLOOR PLAN

URBAN DESIGN ANALYSIS: April 1988

The design staff of the CRA Planning and Urban Design Department, led by David Riccitiello, felt that the MGA proposal could be improved and suggested the following six alternative schemes:

Scheme A flips the positions of the hotel and retail buildings, to integrate the retail components more closely with those along Figueroa Street and Citicorp Plaza. The first-phase tower's pavilion is turned toward the corner. The south tower is shifted to allow more afternoon sunlight into the garden. Vehicular circulation is internal to the site.

Scheme B maintains the basic elements of the plan as submitted, but the garden is relocated to grade level and incorporated with the hotel drop-off. Pedestrian access to the buildings is oriented toward Francisco Street.

Scheme C shifts the hotel and the first-phase office tower to respond to existing pedestrian patterns. The hotel terminates the axis along Eighth Place, and the retail building is oriented to the freeway. The south tower is stepped to allow afternoon sun onto the grade-level garden. Internal vehicular circulation is separated from the garden so that retail and hotel uses can spill onto it. Ground-level retail spaces off of an arcade surround the hotel and garden and lead to the retail building.

Scheme D orients all buildings and pedestrian entries toward Francisco Street and all vehicular access toward a garden that faces the freeway. The hotel and retail spaces are combined into one highly visible structure.

Scheme E also combines the hotel and retail spaces into one building. Buildings open onto a garden at grade level, off Francisco Street and visible from Figueroa Street and Citicorp Plaza. This open space mitigates the impact of possible large-scale construction across Francisco Street. Vehicular circulation is around the garden. The south tower is shifted to allow afternoon sun onto the garden.

Scheme F is similar to Scheme E but creates two office buildings at the south end, which could be phased in both timing and height. The internal road system is on axis with Eighth Place, dividing the open space into three parts.

In sum, the CRA staff suggested that the architects make the following changes to the plan:

- Place the central plaza at grade.
- Internalize vehicular circulation.
- Shift the south tower to allow more sunlight into the garden.
- Allow pedestrian access to all buildings along Francisco Street to be from this street.
- Flip the hotel and retail structures to improve visibility of the retail stores.
- Create an open space along Francisco Street by combining the hotel and retail structures.
- Reorient the buildings to respond to the existing circulation flow.
- Consider the impact of future projects on adjacent sites on the proposed master plan.

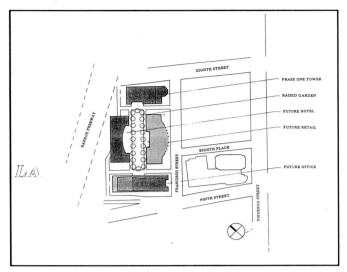

Scheme A

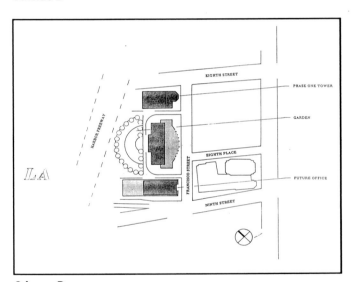

Scheme B

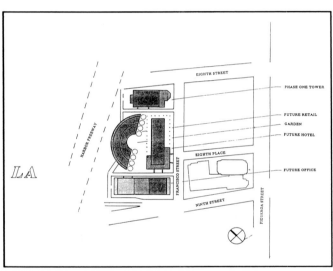

Scheme C

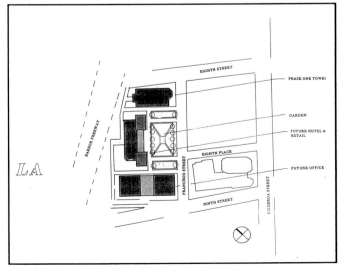

Scheme D

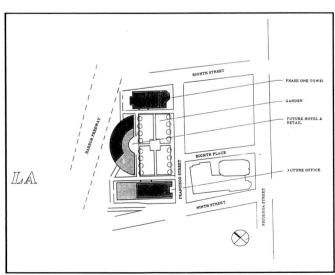

Scheme E

Scheme F

REVISED MASTER PLAN
May–August 1988

The CRA analysis shows the Parkhill and Graves team what its concerns are, but the developer does not think CRA has improved on the MGA scheme. The CRA does not expect to have actual control, but leverages its position to influence the final product. MGA revises the master plan to accommodate the CRA recommendations in principle. The plan is approved by staff, enabling the developer to enter into negotiations for a development agreement with the CRA and ultimately to apply for a building permit for the first-phase tower.

The most significant concession won by the CRA was in getting all vehicular circulation to occur in the center of the site, below ground. Neither the developer, the architect, nor the CRA staff really had liked the idea of the first six levels of building being a garage. Parkhill decided to build an underground parking garage at an additional cost of approximately $16 million. Four to five levels of parking would be totally integrated for the entire project.

Concessions were also made regarding pedestrian circulation. The "pavilion" was redesigned to become a more visible pedestrian entry to the development from the northeast corner. The octagonal structure was to have been strictly a retail component, announcing the beginning of the central plaza and the mall. It grew to be eight stories high, with the two lower stories open and the six above

used as offices, forming a porte cochere and serving as the entry to the office tower.

Parkhill did not agree that the retail component was too large. The developer's team brought in their own retail marketing consultant to strengthen their arguments that Metropolis would complement the CBD Redevelopment Plan's objective for retail development in the area. However, Parkhill did agree to increase the number of storefront shops along Francisco Street.

MGA moved the hotel to the south end of the site, improving its visual connection to the Convention Center and the freeway. They included a stepped form, which permitted more afternoon sunlight into the garden. The automobile drop-off was kept apart from Francisco Street and the shops. The second office building was split into two lower buildings, each with larger floorplates, oriented to Francisco Street. These provided an open passageway to the garden and decreased morning shadows on it.

The garden increased in length to consist of five pieces terraced with the slope of the site. The north terrace was made level with the first tower's lobby (five feet above the street level) and the central terrace with the second floor of retail. The south terrace was placed at the level of the first floor of the retail stores and the hotel lobby where it would serve as the automobile dropoff.

FINAL DESIGN
The revised scheme did not work, however, since the hotel had to be built before the office

towers, and construction phasing was to be from north to south on the site. By the summer the team had found a formula that satisfied everyone. In this scheme, the hotel is returned to the Francisco Street edge of the site. A wide, sloping arcade passes through it up to the garden. The garden is level with the street at the north end of the site but eight feet above the level of Francisco Street where it meets the arcade. The arcade borders the garden and connects all of the buildings; it will serve as an entry loggia for stores or offices. Small shops line the Francisco street-edge, surround the base of the hotel, and thread back to the mall. The two office towers are relocated at the site's southern end and are designed to be combined into one building, if the idea proves marketable.

In August the CRA staff accepted MGA's master plan. One issue for the Graves team was to embed the master plan with conditions to guarantee that their design concept would survive in future phases of development, designed by other architects. Because the garden was one element of the design that the architects did not want changed, they specified that one piece of the garden and the portion of the arcade linking it to the first tower and entry pavilion would be built during phase one, establishing a solid framework that architects of later phases of the development would be compelled to follow. Although MGA provided general guidelines for colors and materials, the general character for the rest of the project would be established by the design of the phase-one office tower.

The design submitted to the CRA for final approval in August, subsequently revised: Upper lobby and site plan, top; the phasing plan, bottom.

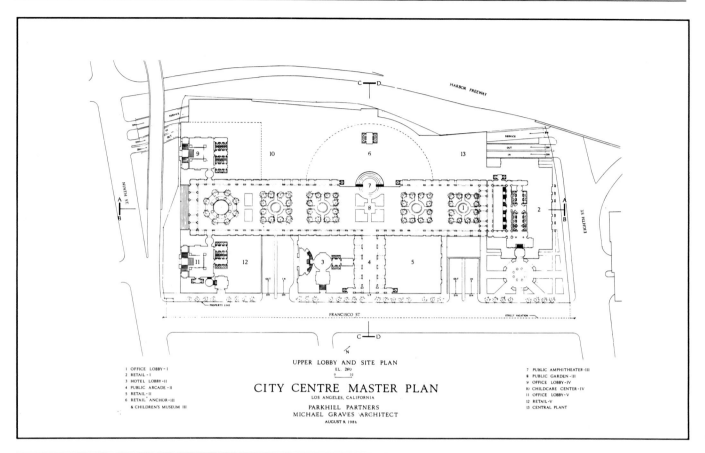

UPPER LOBBY AND SITE PLAN
EL. 280

CITY CENTRE MASTER PLAN
LOS ANGELES, CALIFORNIA

PARKHILL PARTNERS
MICHAEL GRAVES ARCHITECT
AUGUST 9, 1988

1 OFFICE LOBBY - I
2 RETAIL - I
3 HOTEL LOBBY - II
4 PUBLIC ARCADE - II
5 RETAIL - II
6 RETAIL ANCHOR - III
& CHILDREN'S MUSEUM III

7 PUBLIC AMPHITHEATER - III
8 PUBLIC GARDEN - III
9 OFFICE LOBBY - IV
10 CHILDCARE CENTER - IV
11 OFFICE LOBBY - V
12 RETAIL - V
13 CENTRAL PLANT

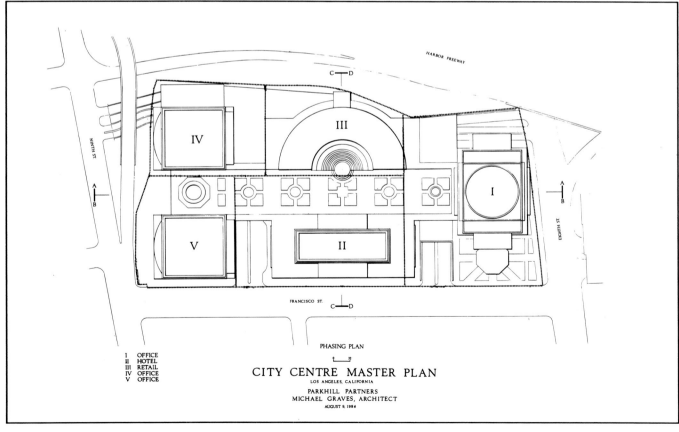

PHASING PLAN

CITY CENTRE MASTER PLAN
LOS ANGELES, CALIFORNIA

PARKHILL PARTNERS
MICHAEL GRAVES, ARCHITECT
AUGUST 9, 1988

I OFFICE
II HOTEL
III RETAIL
IV OFFICE
V OFFICE

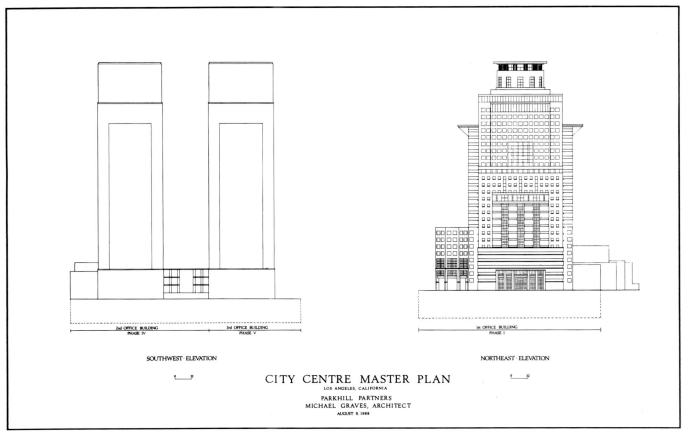

2nd OFFICE BUILDING
PHASE IV

3rd OFFICE BUILDING
PHASE V

1st OFFICE BUILDING
PHASE I

SOUTHWEST · ELEVATION

NORTHEAST · ELEVATION

CITY CENTRE MASTER PLAN
LOS ANGELES, CALIFORNIA
PARKHILL PARTNERS
MICHAEL GRAVES, ARCHITECT
AUGUST 9, 1988

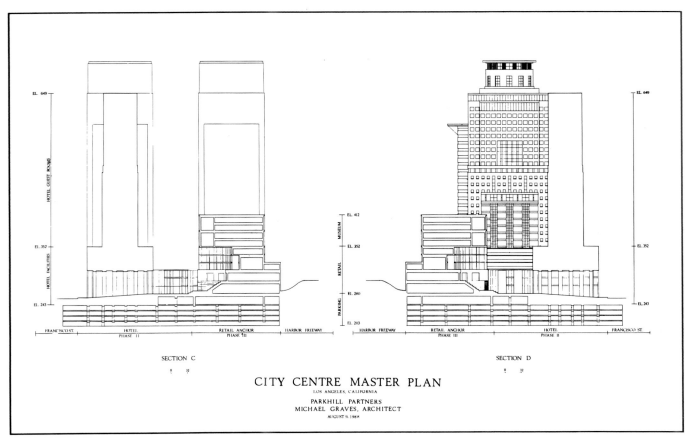

SECTION C

SECTION D

CITY CENTRE MASTER PLAN
LOS ANGELES, CALIFORNIA
PARKHILL PARTNERS
MICHAEL GRAVES, ARCHITECT
AUGUST 9, 1988

PHASE-ONE BUILDING
March–December 1988

Design of the master plan and the first-phase tower occur simultaneously; one influences the other. The master planning process is, in a sense, an extended schematic design phase for the tower, which evolves into an entirely new building. In turn, the master plan reflects the reality that one building is progressing faster than the others.

After the competition, Parkhill realized that the Harbor Plaza tower's position on the site, with its long side fronting the freeway, did not make sense in the context of the whole block master plan. The developer was willing to move the building if the foundation permit could be saved. For the competition, MGA had first rotated the building 5 degrees and next 90 degrees. Architect Eric Regh explains, "Over the course of about a month and a half, we analyzed one design issue after another. The developer kept agreeing to incremental changes until we had touched every building trade and it wasn't worth trying to save the existing plans anymore." Meanwhile, it turned out that the permit process had not been completed previously, so nothing was forfeited.

In response to the developer's comments on the competition submission, MGA revised the design to "lighten up" the building's façade, using larger areas of glazing on the upper levels and reinterpreting the masonry concept with terra-cotta. When the CRA staff reviewed the building design, they recommended moving the entry pavilion toward the corner, relocating parking access to the south of the tower, screening cars from view at street level, and reconsidering terra-cotta as a cladding material (which the CRA thought was an unrealistic choice because of its high expense).

MGA did relocate and enlarge the pavilion. Discussions with the CRA also led to the developer's decision to build an underground garage, perhaps the single most important factor influencing both the first tower design and the master plan, according to Eric Regh. The architects had to redesign the tower's footprint, bay size, and circulation not just in terms of the constraints imposed by its own garage, but also in terms of what would work for parking for the rest of the site.

Opposite page, from the "final" CRA submission: Elevations facing southwest and northeast, top; a section through the complex at midblock, bottom.

Right and overleaf: Façade studies for the first-phase office tower.

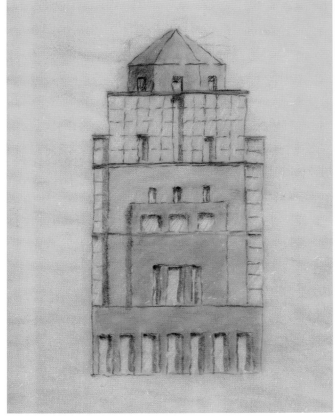

The central plant was another "control point" in the design of the master plan. This outbuilding—adjacent to the tower and fronting the garden—was part of phase one so that it could be expanded later to supply chilled water for phases two and three.

The arcade was key in integrating the master planning and building design process. The 2'-6" module it was based on also established the proportions and dimensions of the other phase-one buildings, making the arcade the element unifying the tower, entry pavilion, central plant, and garden.

INTERIOR LAYOUT

Marketing consultants joined the architects in convincing the developer that the existing plan's floor plate was too small, that there were too few elevators, and that the windows were on the wrong module for the typical office interior layout. Eric Regh took about a month to develop an alternative elevator and service core that could be adapted to serve either side of a floor equally well, giving smaller tenants more options. This idea was seriously considered but ultimately abandoned.

However, the building MGA designed does have eight different cores and fourteen separate floor plates, quite unusual for a thirty-story spec office building. There is also great variety to be found on any given floor plate, resulting from the wide range of window types (nine), with up to three to four different types used on some floors. The architects acknowledged that such nuances are expensive, but they felt that the variety of spaces would attract more tenants. Parkhill agreed, but only after first asking leading interior design firms, Gensler and Associates/Architects, PHH, Walker Associates, and Cole Martinez Curtis Associates, to test the floor plans with typical office layouts. These studies of the usability of corners, column locations, and window sizes confirmed the marketability of the unusual plans.

ELEVATIONS

Graves's early sketches and model established the major components of the elevation composition in terms of mass and void. MGA staff architects worked within this composition and figured out a geometry of windows that would satisfy both the massing and the interior requirements, selecting from among windows that read vertically or horizontally to enhance Graves's design concept. For example, from the eighteenth floor up, larger windows, 7'-6" square rather than the typical 5'-0" square, are used to make the upper portion of the building "read" lighter. At the "wings," spandrel windows are used to make the building seem thinner.

In response to the interior designers' studies, MGA made the pattern of windows slightly more uniform. At the fourteenth floor, however, the design concept prevailed. A "little house" is superimposed on the façade at this level. Eric Regh describes it as "a reduced piece, at a smaller scale, of what's going on in the rest of the building." In order to make the visual metaphor of the house work, the cornice piece there had to be larger and heavier than on other floors, requiring less glass in the wall. Parkhill agreed to this variation, even though to accommodate it required offices on that floor to be fifteen feet wide.

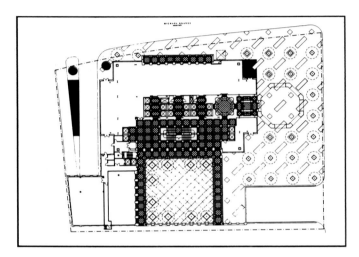

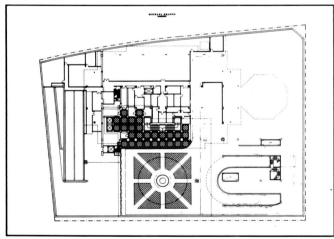

Plans for the first-phase office tower

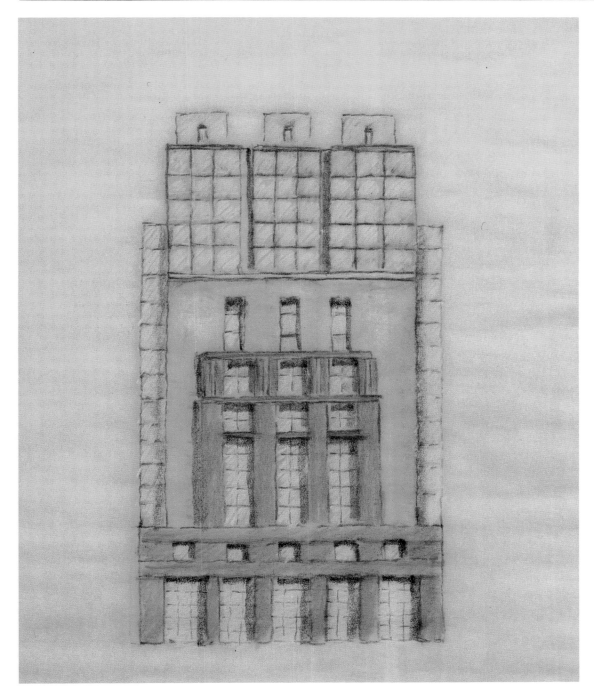

CONSTRUCTION DOCUMENTS:
October 1988

Local architects Kober, Rippon and Associates produced the working drawings for the tower based on MGA's very complete design development set. For the interior portion of the tower, MGA itself produced the working drawings. When the construction documents were 75 percent complete, in mid-December 1988, the local architects filed a set of drawings with the building department for review. Documentation was planned to be complete by the end of January and construction was scheduled to begin six months later.

However, during early 1989, changes were proposed to the master plan (including the addition of an art museum), which postponed the building permit approval process for the tower. Subsequently, the design of the tower went through numerous reworkings as well, and even the name of the project was changed—to Metropolis from City Centre. However, at that point this case study had already been completed.

OBSERVATIONS

The challenge here was how to rebuild the inner city fabric while at the same time allowing a "world class" architect to make a significant statement.

- Although the stated purpose of the competition was to commission a distinctive design quickly, it was actually used to select an architect. Having so many program options (e.g., how to handle the tower) complicated the exercise and made it difficult to compare and evaluate the different schemes. "The more we can get a clear program, the better the schemes will be," commented one architect.

- The developer's eventual request for a revised submission from Michael Graves might have been difficult for a less financially secure architect to accommodate. According to architect John Diebboll, this situation is not uncommon for "celebrity" architects, who are often tested by clients who have high-visibility projects but are not seeking to build long-term relationships. The developer wanted a lot: an architect who could both produce "world-class" design and work within the constraints of a speculative project. Graves was able to be flexible without weakening his own architectural ideas.

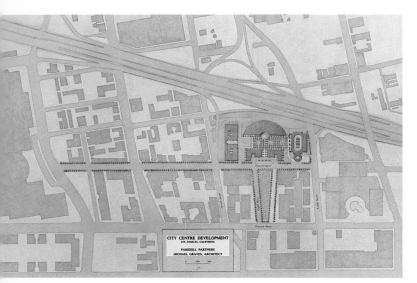

The master plan, c. August, 1988, above, and the first-phase office tower façade, opposite. The design continued to evolve during the following year, as new uses were included in the complex and new urban design issues emerged.

- In competitive markets, distinctive design is almost a necessity; however, high-profile buildings alone do not create good urban design. Major buildings in prominent sites define the character of the public realm. The redevelopment plan's density bonuses gave the city leverage in shaping the development to meet its needs, yet urban design guidelines were specifically formulated in response to the developer's proposal—the city established the policy context, but the architect/developer team put the diagram on the table. This working situation reflects the difficulty of controlling the design of new buildings in the midst of downtowns with strong real estate markets, as it is hard to predict which land will be developed for what purpose, and when.

- Architect John Diebboll says that in some ways putting together the plan was "like putting together a Chinese puzzle. There is only one way that idea can go together; in order to make a change, the whole thing would have to be completely different." The master plan was the medium for negotiation over whether the development would be designed by shaping blocks of spaces or by shaping blocks of mass. Thinking in terms of urban design, the city and the architects saw the plan as a sequence of outdoor rooms formed by buildings. The simultaneous design of the tower provided a counterpoint to this process. The building design process was driven by two potentially conflicting goals: for the building to be successful as a sculptural object and for it to work in terms of how it formed one wall of these rooms. Without the benefit of strict guidelines or the perogative of design review to control future phases of the development, the architects came up with an ingenious means to protect their concept for the character of open space in the project: to build restrictions into the formal plan itself.

- The developer's original intent in repackaging a conventional building was to improve its marketability without forfeiting permission to build before slow-growth regulations went into effect. This impending construction slowdown caused an acceleration of the development process. Once the master plan process led the architects to look at the building in the context of the block rather than simply the site, however, the design process could not stop at the building's skin, and the basic architecture ended up being reevaluated. Ultimately, the breakneck schedule did have to be adjusted, but both the project and the city have undoubtedly benefitted from the more thoughtful approach to the master plan and, ultimately, the phase-one building's design.

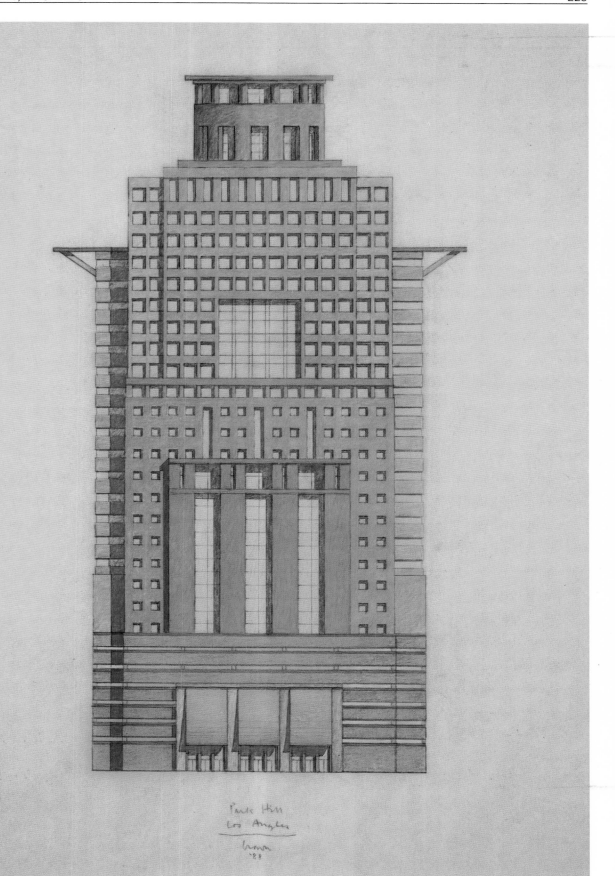

Park Hill
Los Angeles

Graves
'88

The work of Andres Duany and Elizabeth Plater-Zyberk (DPZ) reflects a new traditionalism in urban planning that looks to the American small town as a design model for an alternative to suburban sprawl. DPZ believes that a walkable community with stores and jobs close to housing not only provides a lifestyle many people want but also makes financial sense. To achieve this aim, DPZ employs an unconventional design process: They plan new towns by assembling all the key participants in a project for an intense one-week work session they call a charrette, held on the site. Their aim is nothing less than to redefine the American suburb. To do this, DPZ challenges prevailing practice and changes the rules—they write their own building and zoning codes. In June 1988, DPZ conducted a charrette to design the new town of Kentlands, in Gaithersburg, Maryland. For this project, DPZ for the first time planned to integrate a mall with a traditional-style new town. This case study takes a close look at DPZ's process as a model for what town planning might be like in the future.

<table>
<tr><th colspan="2">PROJECT OVERVIEW</th></tr>
<tr><td>Project</td><td>Master plan and guidelines for the development of a 352-acre new town including a 1.2 million sf mall, 900,000 sf of offices, and 1,600 residences.</td></tr>
<tr><td>Planners</td><td>Andres Duany and Elizabeth Plater-Zyberk, Town Planners, Miami, Florida.</td></tr>
<tr><td>Client</td><td>Joseph Alfandre & Co., Inc., Rockville, Maryland, developer, with Melvin Simon & Associates, Indianapolis, Indiana, mall developer.</td></tr>
<tr><td>Charge</td><td>To plan a residential development with the sense of community of a traditional small town.</td></tr>
<tr><td>Issues</td><td>✔ "Charrette" method to shorten design time and involve decision makers early in the process.

✔ Integration of a new regional mall with the town.

✔ Reducing the need for automobiles by mixing residential, retail, and commercial activities in the same neighborhood.

✔ Encouragement of social interaction and a sense of community through the design of public spaces.

✔ Utilization of building and urban design standards to implement the land plan.</td></tr>
<tr><td>Duration</td><td>Schematic design: one-week charrette, June 1–7, 1988; new town to be built over ten years.</td></tr>
<tr><td>Budget</td><td>$200 million for the entire development.</td></tr>
</table>

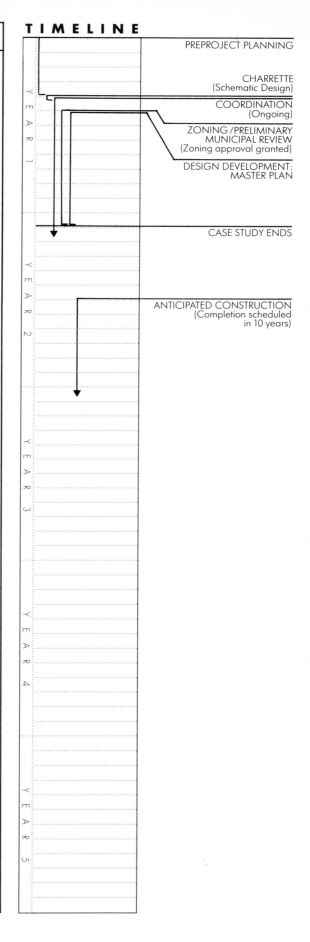

TIMELINE

PREPROJECT PLANNING

CHARRETTE
(Schematic Design)

COORDINATION
(Ongoing)

ZONING /PRELIMINARY
MUNICIPAL REVIEW
(Zoning approval granted)

DESIGN DEVELOPMENT:
MASTER PLAN

CASE STUDY ENDS

ANTICIPATED CONSTRUCTION
(Completion scheduled
in 10 years)

YEAR 1

YEAR 2

YEAR 3

YEAR 4

YEAR 5

BACKGROUND

Planning a large-scale residential development by conventional means can take months if not years. First studies are conducted, next design concepts are developed, and then a plan is subjected to endless reviews by marketing strategists, financiers, public officials, and concerned citizens. This process is time-consuming, expensive, and risky, as costs rise and circumstances change. Yet prolonged study alone often does not improve the quality of a subdivision, the design of which instead usually is driven by the developer's need to maximize profit. Designs aimed at short-term cost savings can lead to long-term social ills. Suburban developments that lack a defined civic center and are organized around pods of lookalike buildings can be alienating for residents and do not foster a sense of community.

The husband-and-wife architecture team of Andres Duany and Elizabeth Plater-Zyberk believes the problems of suburbia can be solved "in the design of integrated communities using the traditional small town as the model." They refer to eighteenth- and nineteenth-century towns as models to shape environments that are built to human scale, where streetscapes are more important than individual buildings, and which have a sense of place. As developers have realized that these ideas also make financial sense, such "traditional" developments have come into vogue, and are now even in danger of becoming their own formula, according to urban designer Jonathan Barnett.

DPZ is unusual, however, in its approach. They design new towns, complete with building and zoning guidelines, during an intensive one-week planning session they call a "charrette," held on the site itself. Why design a town in seven days? Andres Duany explains that, "with the charrette we can be more effective because the people who have a say in any one part can give their opinion right away; we never get more than a couple of days off track. The

charrette generates incredible energy. It's not just faster and more efficient; it's better." This case study of DPZ's process to design the new town of Kentlands shows that how a plan is conceived is in many ways as important as the final product.

THE CLIENT/THE SITE

Developer Joseph A. Alfandre lives and works near the site of his proposed new town in Gaithersburg, Maryland (current population: 30,000), a suburb of Washington, D.C. Alfandre's family are prominent local developers, and his own company has earned a solid reputation as builders of quality housing. In early 1987, with the backing of his father as a silent financial partner, the thirty-six-year-old developer purchased the 352-acre Kent Farm, on the western edge of Gaithersburg, for $41 million. Alfandre envisioned building a mixed-use development on the site, including homes, a regional retail center, a commercial center, and public amenities.

Kent Farm was among the last undeveloped parcels in affluent Montgomery County. It was bounded on three sides by highways and on the fourth by an estate owned by the National Geographic Society, which is preserved as a bird sanctuary. The farm had been owned by the Kents since 1942, when they had bought it from the Tschiffely family, who in 1852 had built a manor house on the property. This mansion and its outbuildings inspired Alfandre to restore the buildings as a landmark and to model his development on a traditional village.

Out of concern that the farm would be subject to piecemeal development, the City of Gaithersburg formed a neighborhood task force and conducted a major planning study of the site. Gaithersburg mayor Edward Bohrer said, "The city wants this property to be protected for future generations." Alfandre commissioned Baltimore-based RTKL Associates to produce a master plan for his project, which was coordinated with the city's effort. The mayor and Gaithersburg City Council welcomed Alfandre's comprehensive approach and agreed to approve a special mixed-use zone to enable the plan to be implemented.

But Alfandre was not satisfied with the approved master plan—it did not reflect the "villagey" idea he had in mind. Then David Wolfe, the marketing consultant on the project (who specializes in planned adult communities), referred Alfandre to Duany and Plater-Zyberk. The following week the *Atlantic Monthly* ran an article by Philip Langdon featuring the firm's work. Within two weeks Alfandre and Andres Duany had met and drawn up a contract for a one-week charrette.

The Kent Mansion

THE ARCHITECTS

Andres Duany and Elizabeth Plater-Zyberk met as architecture students at Princeton and formed their partnership (DPZ) in 1980, not long after completing their professional training at Yale University's School of Architecture. Based in Miami, Florida, the firm won national recognition for its design for the highly successful Seaside development in Florida. DPZ's practice includes architecture as well as town planning, but charrettes are keeping the staff of twenty-five very busy. In the year preceding this project, DPZ had designed nine large developments from Texas to New Hampshire. In addition to running their practice, both partners have taught at Yale, Harvard, Princeton, and the University of Miami.

Key members of DPZ's team for this project included partners Andres Duany and Elizabeth Plater-Zyberk; William Lennertz as project manager; Charles Barrett, Ray Chu, and William Dennis as project designers; and Estella Garcia as project administrator.

Aerial view of Kent Farm

PREPROJECT PLANNING
February–May 1988

DPZ begins by assembling the design team. Next, the team evaluates the program and available data on the site and studies the region's architecture and town-planning traditions. With Alfandre and his key staff, DPZ visits London to look at models of planned towns.

SCOPE OF SERVICES

The project was organized into three phases of work: preparation and programming, design charrette, and coordination. The objective of the charrette phase was to design a master plan, identify building types that fulfilled the program, and write an urban and architectural code that defined those buildings in terms of building envelope and construction detail. These codes and the master plan would be prepared using CAD. DPZ was also responsible for arranging national press coverage.

During the coordination phase, DPZ's responsibilities included providing assistance for the public review process, coordinating with the civil engineer and other consultants, advising the developer in the hiring of other architects and preparing procedures for reviewing their work, and coordinating the Homeowners' Association regulations prepared for the town.

THE TEAM

On each charrette only about a third of the participants are from DPZ's Miami office. Others are "grafted on" from previous charrettes, new members "to keep things from getting stale," and local professionals who are sympathetic with the concept.

This time the team included architect Tarik El-Nagar, from Indiana; civil engineer Richard Chellman and two of his staff, from New Hampshire; and landscape architects Douglas Duany and Kathy Poole and architect and Harvard professor Alex Krieger, all from Boston. Local architects included Dhiru Thadani and Patrick Pinnell, whose firm, Cass and Pinnell, would help carry out the project following the charrette. A core group of ten designers would stay for the entire week and a second wave would arrive to start work on day four.

The design team was amplified with members of the developer's staff, surveyors, institutional planners, market researchers, traffic specialists, and publicists. To develop the mall, Alfandre entered into a joint-venture partnership with Indianapolis-based shopping-center builder

Melvin Simon & Associates. Leon Nitsun and Herman Renfro, architects for Melvin Simon, participated in the charrette.

PROGRAMMING

The contract stated that before the charrette was held, the developer would join DPZ on a visit to London to look at examples of projects with mixed commercial, retail, and residential uses. According to Alfandre executive Steve Wilcox, however, the group went to England together before signing the contract, more to test their chemistry than to look at models.

Wilcox recalls how during their walks around planned communities such as the 1926 Welwyn Garden City and the Hampstead Garden Suburb, Andres Duany would explain what made those places feel good. "He would point something out and say, 'This is a terminated vista' or 'Could that be your office building? Could that be your mall?' " They also visited urban theorist Leon Krier, an advocate of city planning based on human scale. The trip convinced Alfandre to go ahead with the charrette.

The design team's preparation included an evaluation of the previous master plan, existing codes, and the program. The program consisted of up to 1,600 residential units with a broad mix of sizes and types, a 1.2-million-square-foot regional mall with four department stores, a Main Street shopping area, 900,000 sf of commercial office space, a cultural center, and public parks.

The mall, to be on the periphery of the town, was a "given." The developer wanted it to improve the project's profitability and the mayor of Gaithersburg wanted it to provide a financial base for the city. Another given was an elementary school. Alfandre had agreed to donate land for the school as one condition for the city's approval of the previous master plan.

LOGISTICS

Once the date for the charrette was set, DPZ project manager Lennertz and Monica O'Neal, coordinator for Alfandre, organized the event. They transformed an old barn on the estate into a design studio equipped with a dozen makeshift drawing boards and wired to run computers, photocopiers, telephones, lights, slide projectors, a telefacsimile (fax) machine, and even an espresso coffeemaker. A small library of architecture and town-planning books was also set up. Tables for buffet-style meals and meetings were arranged in the hayloft.

Snapshots taken during the team's visit to England

CHARRETTE
June 1–7, 1988

DAY 1: June 1

The charrette is open to the press and the public. The official kickoff is a press conference/orientation meeting at the barn. That afternoon, the design team visits local models for the new town. After a public lecture by Andres Duany in the evening, the team gets down to work.

8:00 A.M. Joe Alfandre officially begins the charrette by announcing, "The Mayor's vision is that Gaithersburg will have a Main Street—we are building that." For the first time DPZ will plan a town that includes a regional mall. Andres Duany says, "We don't know the shape of the mall yet, but we do know it will be the center of the town. We want the end result, the Town Center, Main Street, and mall, to be seamless, to flow together."

Local architect Patrick Pinnell provides an historical perspective, reflecting on the design of Annapolis, Maryland. He will lead the group on a tour of the best urban spaces in the area. "Today we will look at local planning traditions, such as diagonal avenues converging on a circle, and how to combine these with a grid street layout. These ideas are appropriate, but even more important is to use them as a model for *how* a plan is conceived and put together. Our method isn't new; it's a reincarnation of the type of process used during the 1690s by Nicholson to plan Annapolis and in 1798 by L'Enfant and Jefferson to plan Washington, only now it is being compressed to seven days."

Afternoon. The design team piles into a van for a tour of Annapolis, Georgetown, and Washington, D.C. On the way,

they compare drawings of town plans such as Oak Park, Illinois; Seaside, Florida; Frank Lloyd Wright's Mile Square Proposal; and Leon Krier's ideal neighborhood based on ten minutes of walking distance. Pinnell explains that they are analyzing sizes and numbers: How big is 350 acres, for example? "It's the size of Athens at the time of Socrates and Plato, the size of Shakespeare's London," he observes.

The van stops frequently as the group examines the ingredients that create intimate urban spaces, such as outbuildings, porches, and alleys. DPZ architect Bill Lennertz says they do this to "share images, so when we refer to the feeling of a particular street we all know what we're talking about." They analyze how the Annapolis Statehouse, sited within a traffic circle, commands the vistas along the roads leading to it. Engineer Richard Chellman measures the width of streets and the circumferences of street corners, details that distinguish streets in old towns.

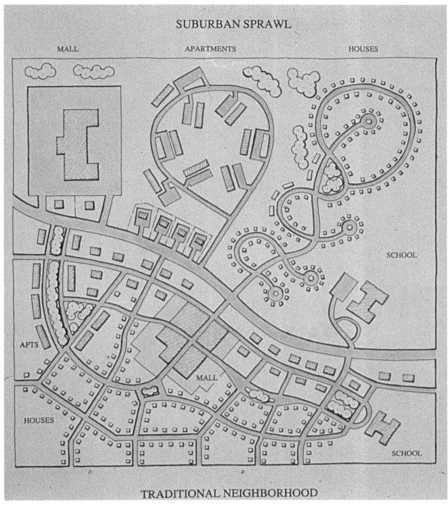

SUBURBAN SPRAWL

MALL   APARTMENTS   HOUSES

SCHOOL

APTS

MALL

HOUSES

SCHOOL

TRADITIONAL NEIGHBORHOOD

7:30 P.M. Alfandre hosts a dinner reception at the community center for 100 guests, including businessmen, public officials, and preservation groups. Andres Duany gives a slide lecture on town planning and explains DPZ's planning principles (an important first step in every charrette).

Duany critiques subdivisions organized around clusters of buildings, where streets arranged "like bowls of spaghetti" make it hard to find addresses, create traffic jams on nearby roads, and form barriers for pedestrians. He explains what make cities like Paris and London so livable and points out that such urbane places could not be built in the United States without changing zoning laws. Ironically, he tells, people drive to neighborhoods like Georgetown just to walk around. He concludes, "We have two missions here at Kentlands: to create a new town and to change the way the world is planning." He invites everyone to visit the charrette and offer suggestions.

Clockwise from top left: The orientation meeting; diagram of a typical subdivision; an early scheme for the mall; the group touring Annapolis.

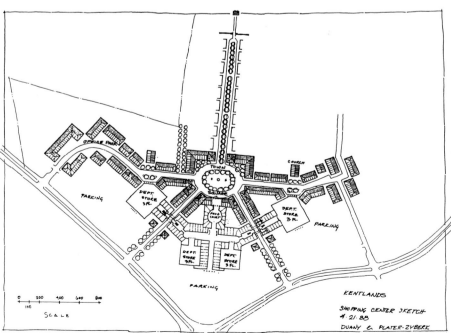

KENTLANDS

SHOPPING CENTER SKETCH
4·21·88
DUANY & PLATER-ZYBERK

10:00 P.M. Eager to get to work, the architects return to the barn. How do they get the character that only history creates? "You only achieve variety when different people work on things," Andres Duany says, "so every part of the town will be designed by several different teams, for a sequential blending of ideas that reproduces the not necessarily compatible discourse that produces real towns." Initially, teams of two to three designers become experts on one corner of the site, starting with the mall, the old estate buildings, and the overall master plan. Later they will trade tasks.

That night they decide that the old estate buildings, now called the Homestead, will form the core of one neighborhood and be a focal point of the town. A round-robin is started to design the shape of this core—the same drawing is passed from one designer to another.

Preparing for the next day's meeting with the mall developer is the team's top priority. Plater-Zyberk, Krieger, and Andres Duany work with Simon architects Nitsun and Renfro to design a scheme that accommodates the developer's criteria: Three of the department stores have to be visible from the adjacent highway, parking has to be close to the building and extend about 400 feet, and inside the mall all stores have to be visible from each other. The group overlays sketches of one idea on top of another as they talk. Work ends at 1:00 A.M.

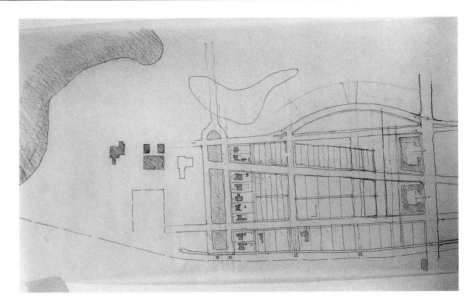

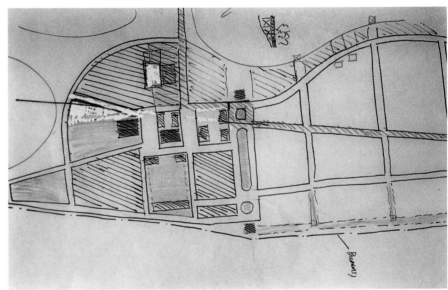

Early sketches for the Homestead area

DAY 2: June 2

The designers' day begins with a tour of the site in the rain. Basic elements of the master plan are put into the computer. A key meeting takes place with the mall developer, targeting the issues to be resolved during the week. Transportation officials review engineering standards for the street grid. The teams switch assignments for the mall, the Homestead, and the master plan.

8:00 A.M. Rain is falling, but the architects are anxious to get a feel for the site and ride around its forests and fields in a pickup truck. Working on the site proved to be a great advantage. "If we needed to know whether a particular tree was worth saving, we could send someone out to look at that tree." says Pinnell.

All master plan drawings will be produced with CAD, and architect Tarik El-Nagar has been put in charge of running the computer system. This morning he finishes setting it up and begins putting in those parts of the master plan that are known. DPZ's Bill Dennis analyzes yesterday's observations to come up with a "townhouse typology" including generic floor plans and elevations. These are put into CAD format; they will become the building blocks for setting plat dimensions.

10:00 A.M. This is DPZ's first charrette with an engineer on the team, but Andres Duany is sure that Chellman will play an important role. This morning Chellman and Duany meet with an official of the county department of transportation to discuss engineering standards for laying out streets at right angles. The grid street pattern is an essential element in DPZ's planning concept. Duany points out that curvilinear streets are

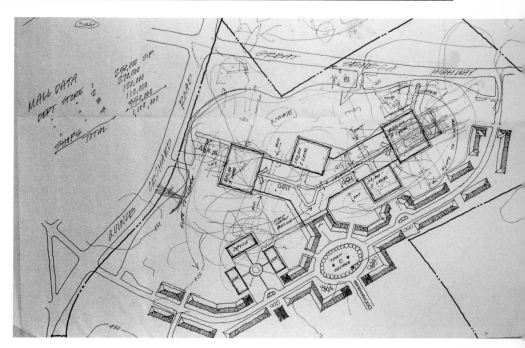

designed for the convenience of drivers, not pedestrians.

The team assigned to design the mall works intently in preparation for the afternoon meeting. Alfandre is not the majority partner in the mall, and Melvin Simon & Associates' approval is crucial. The team must tackle the following problems:

- How to avoid a ring road and "sea" of surface parking.
- How to connect the mall with the Main Street shopping area.
- How to combine the mall with other uses.
- How to provide strong, visual identity for both the mall and the town from the road.

The architects propose that the mall be connected to the town with a pedestrian bridge, and that it be served by a system of roads—a utility ring road, Main Street, and an alley to back-street parking. There would be offices and shopping on Main Street as well. They question how much parking is really required and whether it can be in a garage.

Top to bottom: An early study for the mall; the team at work in the barn/studio; Tarik El Nagar runs the computer.

3:00 P.M.: Mall Meeting. Jerry Garvey, a vice-president of Melvin Simon & Associates, runs the meeting, along with Elizabeth Plater-Zyberk. It soon becomes clear that the major stumbling block is the parking situation. Garvey does not want to build a garage that would hide parking from view.

A dialogue ensues:

Plater-Zyberk: "Malls aren't just regional centers but local centers too. Here's the killer question: Can you imagine housing on top of a mall, as in an old town center?"

Garvey: "I'm an adventuresome guy, but that's tough. Are we talking about a mall with housing or a town with a large shopping area?"

Plater-Zyberk: "But is the tail wagging the dog? When you drive along do you have a sense of arriving in a town or in a mall? A mall is a regional place, not just a regional building. We want to create a place where people go and might end up shopping too. In suburbia, where there is no place to go, the mall provides a community focus, so you need more activities there."

The architect suggests that other uses, such as a garden center or a library, could be included. She stresses how important it is that residents be able to walk to the mall. "We're throwing on the table the extremes our thinking is taking, to find out how much further we can go, under what conditions you would allow change."

Garvey tells Plater-Zyberk, "Keep going. Your overall concern for image and architectural integration is a tough sell, but not impossible."

Although the meeting ends without resolving key design

These two pages show mall studies dealing with parking, access, and the link to the town.

Two early views: From the town square, below, and a section through the mall with a foot bridge to the square, opposite page, bottom.

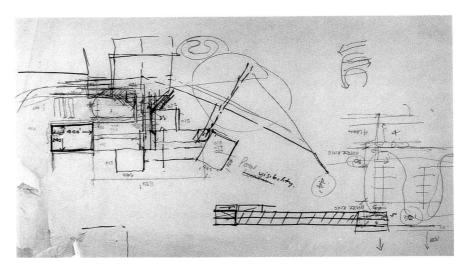

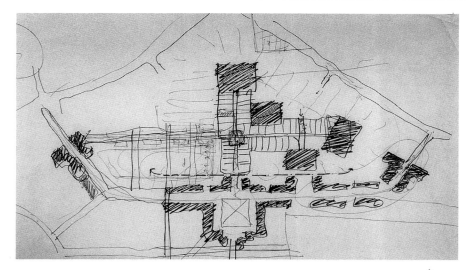

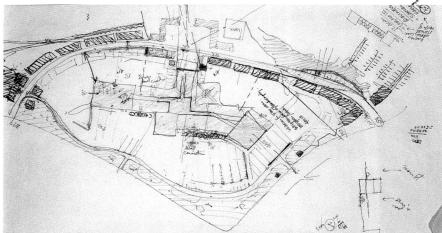

issues, Garvey praises the charrette and tells the Mayor, "It's a very efficient way of getting things done. I'm encouraged by the process."

5:00 P.M. The architects review the design of the historic core with Alfandre. They propose to make the Homestead into a cultural center, the town's centerpiece. The developer likes the idea and decides to donate the mansion to the city.

Alfandre and Andres Duany also meet with Annapolis-based marketing consultant David Wolfe to discuss the town charter. Duany feels that "Kentlands should not just look like a town, but function as one too," with democratic institutions. However, he insists on a system that gives the developer control until the project is nearly complete. This is needed so Alfandre can fully implement his ideas and make adjustments if land-use problems arise. By the end of the week Wolfe writes a draft set of "townowner" bylaws. "This is more than a building project," he says, "we're changing society."

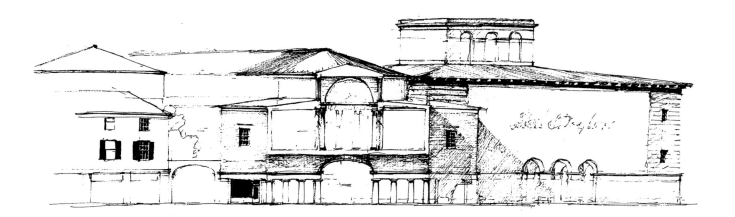

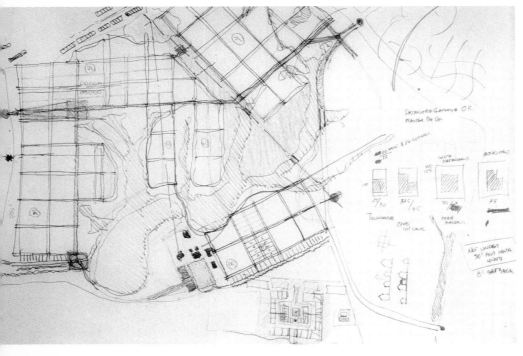

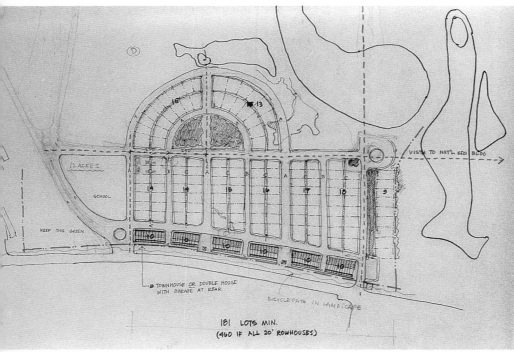

Preliminary street and plat layouts

6:00 P.M. The team gathers to review their work and Plater-Zyberk summarizes the mall meeting. After dinner is served in the barn, Andres Duany switches team assignments.

Completing the street layout—a key element of the overall urban design—is now top priority. The streets establish neighborhoods, vistas, and focal points—they define the character of the development. DPZ designs streets as "outdoor rooms," not just voids between buildings. The team works hard to create a hierarchy of streets, block sizes, and open spaces that will impose a sense of order. Later, building footprints and the location of trees will be specified to reinforce the streetscape. Work ends at 2:00 A.M.

DAY 3: June 3

Engineer Chellman has a breakthrough on how to solve problems with the wetlands. Local builders give their support to the concept. City officials agree to allow on-street parking. A revised scheme for the mall emerges, but the developer is not yet convinced it is right. The neighborhood planning group visits and voices its concerns. The second team arrives after dinner and the scheme is subjected to an intense internal critical review.

10:00 A.M.: Wetlands. Chellman had discovered that the existing topographic survey was inaccurate. In plotting a new map, he had learned that the wetlands on the site are more extensive than anticipated, cutting large areas of the site off from each other. This poses a serious obstacle, since DPZ's intent is to develop the town so that all its parts are integrated. Another problem with this situation is that a lengthy approval process is required by the Army Corps of Engineers for permission to fill in more than five acres of wetlands. This morning Chellman comes up with a strategy to split the site into two parcels, each of which has fewer than five acres of wetlands to be filled in. The pattern is complex, and it will take the engineer a few days to fully evaluate which portions of the wetlands are worthwhile using and how they must be managed according to the law.

12:30 P.M.: Local Builders.

Andres Duany and Alfandre meet with five local homebuilders to discuss unit types. The developer describes his intent to achieve the traditional town theme by mixing small, medium, and large houses on a block. "We want the neighborhoods to connect," he says. Duany explains that builders will have to adhere to a set of design standards so that every home will blend into each of the five proposed neighborhoods. The builders are quick to respond: "Do people in single-family homes want to live across from town homes and quadraplexes?" Duany's answer is: "It's been tested and it works."

Before leaving, the builders express basic support for the concept. Duany asks the builders what the local norm is for minimum units and learns it is 22 feet wide. Duany agrees to make this the basic planning module. Lots will be 22 feet wide for townhouses, 44 feet wide for attached houses with a side yard, and 66 feet wide for individual houses. All buildings will be designed to fit in these sized lots, so the plan can be constantly adjusted. Plats can be assembled for larger parcels or broken down into smaller ones.

3:00 P.M.: Mall. The architects

develop a design for the shopping center that blends an old town center and a suburban

mall. The design makes one long building appear like several smaller ones, but it requires underground parking. Alfandre feels it is too soon to be so specific. Andres Duany argues for continuing to work on certain

points, for example, how public squares and gateways fit in. "Will Simon go for them?" Alfandre responds. "If I were Melvin Simon & Associates I'd say it's too early in the game. Let's not blow it for ourselves."

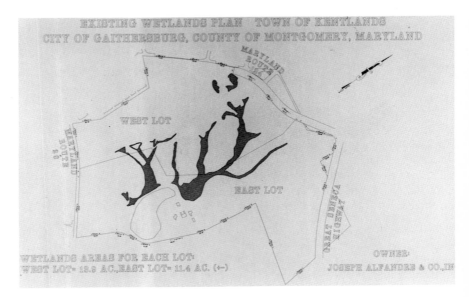

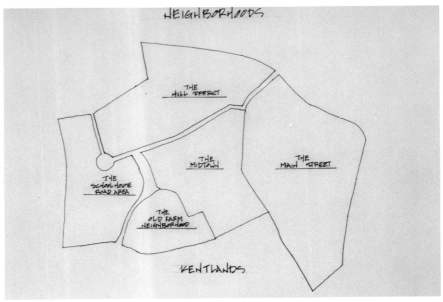

Plan study showing the extent of the wetlands, top, and diagram of neighborhood areas, bottom.

5:00 P.M.: Infrastructure. The next meeting is with the mayor and the city manager along with staff from the public works department, the planning commission, and the electric company for a review of infrastructure and ordinance issues. Topics discussed include how wide and curved the roads can be, where electric transformers will be placed, what paving materials the streets will have (brick, asphalt, gravel, and cobblestone), and where people will park. DPZ wants to plan utilities under paved midblock alleys, but the public works department will not allow it. DPZ wins one small victory; permission for on-street parking.

6:30 P.M. After a difficult day, the team walks the site for inspiration. Landscape architect Douglas Duany points out the native plants and places that will become landscape features. Both the street layout and parks are designed to take advantage of existing trees. Dinner is waiting in the barn when they return.

7:30 P.M. The Kentlands plan violates parts of the previously approved master plan, and members of Neighborhood Four, the neighborhood task force, visit for a presentation by Andres Duany. They voice concerns over the mall's size and its lack of covered parking. But the group is excited about how the town will look, pleased to be involved so early, and relieved when Duany agrees to avoid locating apartments next to a neighboring town-house development.

10:30 P.M. The second wave of designers arrives. Everyone gathers for an overall review, where there is intense criticism of the work. They make up a list of drawings to complete and assign new teams to various tasks. Work ends at 1:30 A.M.

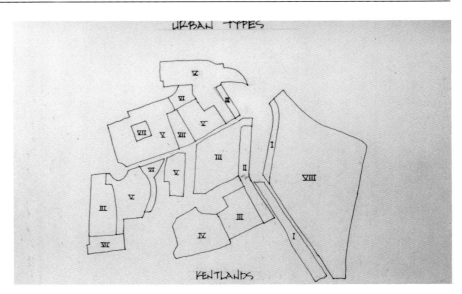

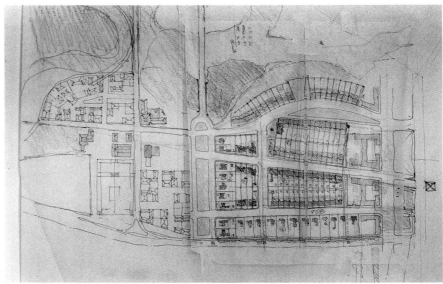

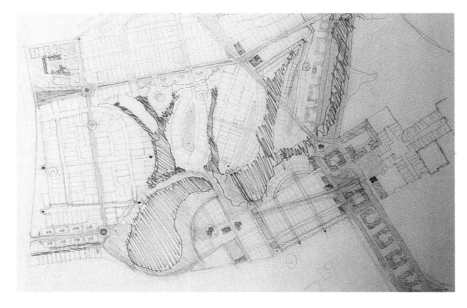

DAYS 4 AND 5: June 4–5

The weekend brings two heavy work days. The focus is now on refining the neighborhoods. A conflict arises and is resolved over the character of the Homestead. The developer approves the master plan, including the mall and the proposed office building type. By Sunday night the plan is totally in the computer, but the designers have not gotten much sleep.

Master Plan. With the street layout now generally blocked out in the computer, the focus shifts to the character of the five neighborhoods. Each fits the topography and has its own range of housing types. The designers constantly refer back and forth between the street layout and the generic housing types to test plat sizes and relationships. Town houses, mansions, and small cottage-style houses are mixed in each neighborhood to help ensure variety. However, reality is never far away—Alfandre executive Steve Wilcox constantly calculates the feasibility of various mixes of units, based on the number of units-per-acre of varying density.

According to DPZ's Bill Dennis, the generic housing types are based on historic examples and local vernacular patterns but have been adapted to fit the site. "We take the best of what we find and hope we make it into a better model," he says. "It's urban design, not architecture (i.e., the behavior of buildings— how they act—is more important than what they look like)."

Clockwise from bottom left: Preliminary street layout; planning streets, plats, and house types; diagram showing areas of urban types; Type VI, a five-bay, zero-lot-line house; Type III, a Georgetown house.

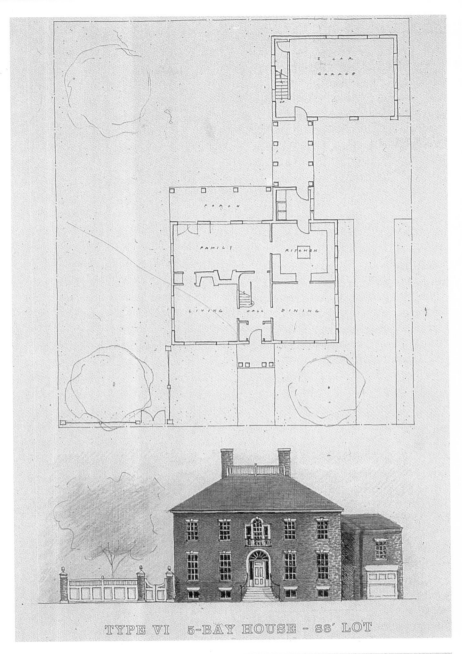

TYPE VI   5-BAY HOUSE - 88' LOT

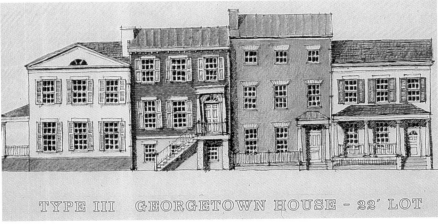

TYPE III   GEORGETOWN HOUSE - 22' LOT

The Mall. The architects have been determined to make the mall fit into the town center and now, after making many sketches, they have a scheme they like. The mall's axis is rotated from east-west (as proposed by Simon's architect) to north-south. This allows a direct pedestrian connection from the mall's entry to Main Street, leading through the town center to the Homestead (a five-minute walk). The mall's food court will be located at the entry as a magnet to draw pedestrians into the shopping center and shoppers out toward the town.

Local architect Dhiru Thadani develops an office building type that is planned at right angles to the mall (on the east-west axis). The offices are sited "to tell people driving by that there's a town in there," says Andres Duany, who admits that the offices began "as a cynical reaction to the mall, but . . . came out looking quite nice."

The Homestead. Architects Patrick Pinnell and Charles Barrett have developed concepts for the Homestead and they cannot agree: Should it be centroidal like Annapolis or modeled on an old farm settlement? Pinnell wants to create the effect of a circle using existing elements and develop a formal procession from the downtown area. Barrett wants to extend the existing fabric by linking the buildings and yards with low walls and wandering walkways. Andres Duany must mediate and chooses the latter proposal, which suggests how old farms become seeds for towns that grow up around them. The team decides to call the Homestead area the Old Farm Neighborhood and locate housing for the elderly there, close to cultural and civic activities.

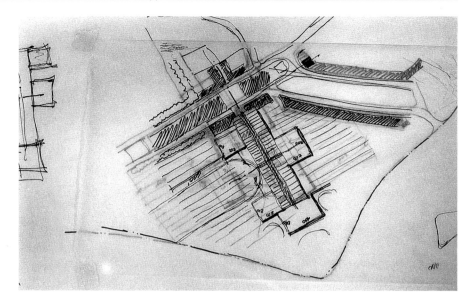

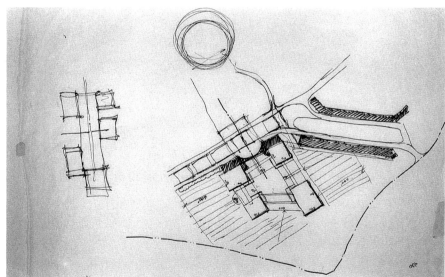

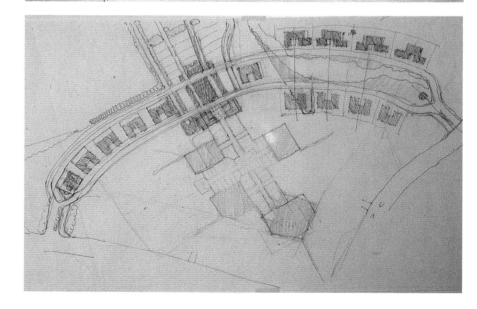

Public Spaces. The design of common areas including lakefronts and parks takes advantage of high points in the terrain for views and orientation. Upon entering the town from the south, there will be a view of the manor house across a lake through parallel rows of trees. Another vista is from the Old Farm Neighborhood north to the town center. Wetlands are protected in a belt of parkland that winds throughout the town, a concept modeled on Boston's Fenway Park. The shores of the site's largest lake will also be fully accessible to the public and a restaurant is strategically sited overlooking it. These spaces are tied together in what Andres Duany calls "an orchestrated sequence of events" aimed at providing a pleasing pedestrian experience.

Duany notes the importance of working on a team in this kind of setting: "At the same time someone is designing a street, someone else is designing a tree, and an engineer is making sure that type of street and tree won't disrupt the way water drains."

Approval. On Sunday afternoon Alfandre reviews the project. He agrees to go ahead with the mall and the office building prototype. The team now moves full speed ahead to get the entire plan into the computer, which they accomplish by midnight.

Opposite page, top to bottom: The mall, rotated from the east-west to the north-south axis; study for a less linear plan; plan showing the mall with office buildings sited on the north-south axis.

This page: A centroidal plan for the Homestead area, top, and an alternative modeled on an old farm village, bottom.

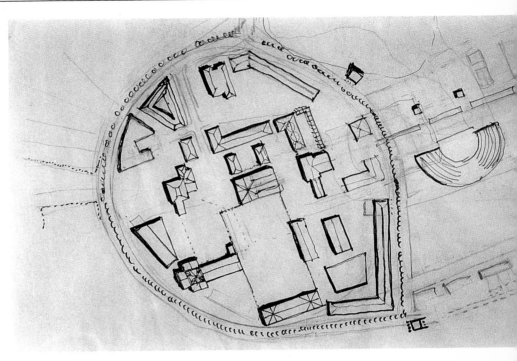

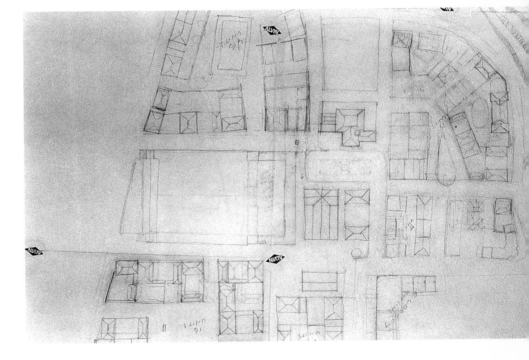

DAY 6: June 6

The biggest problem over the weekend has been coordinating all the pieces; the biggest distraction was that so many people kept coming and going. The plan now emerges in detailed renderings of specific buildings and vistas. Members of the county school board discuss the proposed elementary school but decline the developer's offer to pay for its design. The pace of work quickens.

9:30 A.M.: Elementary School.

Andres Duany and Alfandre meet with representatives of the county school board. The twelve-acre elementary school site commands a key focal point in the design. The building is planned to be integrated with a traffic circle: Through traffic is routed in the center of the circle and bus drop-off is at the periphery. In this way the school will be part of the town fabric.

Alfandre wants control over the building's appearance and offers to pay for architectural fees in exchange for the right to select the architect. The school board has its own specifications for buildings, however, and the group rejects his offer. The developer proposes a joint venture but is turned down. One school board representative explains, "They may not want you involved; there's a sense of too many strings." Duany suggests a compromise: Team up one architect who specializes in schools with one approved by Alfandre. The group agrees to present this option to the full school board.

Agreement on the mall is reached with Melvin Simon & Associates vice-president Jerry Garvey over the phone. It will be integrated with the town center. The town will be visible from the highway, with its own exit; there will be no parking lots between

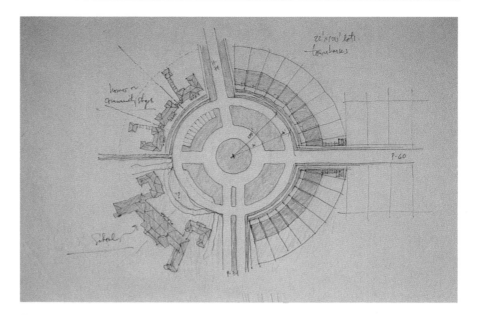

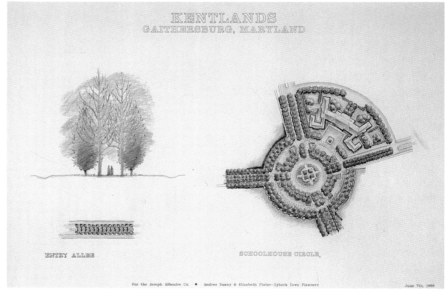

KENTLANDS
GAITHERSBURG, MARYLAND

ENTRY ALLEE

SCHOOLHOUSE CIRCLE

For the Joseph Alfandre Co. • Andres Duany & Elizabeth Plater-Zyberk Town Planners

June 7th 1988

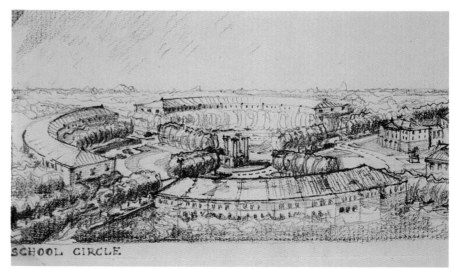

SCHOOL CIRCLE

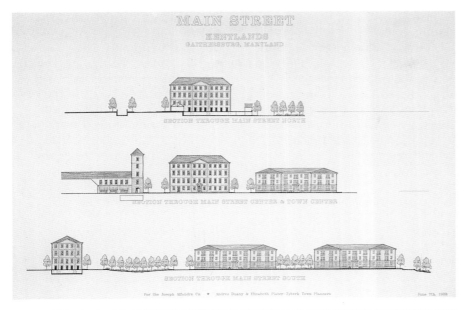

Opposite page: Views of the schoolhouse circle plan.

Main Street elevations, top, and a bird's-eye view of the town center, bottom.

the mall and town; and the mall's townside facade will front directly on Kentland's Main Street and form a public square.

11:00 A.M. Alfandre's staff has put together a pro forma program that shows that the plan is still 500 units short and encroaches on too many wetlands. Andres Duany and Plater-Zyberk take turns working at the computer with Tarik El-Nagar, laying out plats, counting units, and conferring with local architect Thadani, who is now developing apartment building types.

Afternoon. The plan is emerging in intricately rendered drawings. The five neighborhoods are: The Old Farm Neighborhood, which looks like an eighteenth-century town; Midtown, which is modeled on a nineteenth-century town; Main Street, which includes a twentieth-century shopping center; the Hill district, where the hilltop is preserved as a park and streets and lots are sited to take advantage of the slope; and the Schoolhouse area.

Along Main Street there will be both apartment and office buildings. The five-story office building type is designed with a large floor plate to accommodate corporate needs; however, it will be linked with single-story structures, behind which there will be parking. These low buildings will house smaller tenants as well as create a comfortable street wall and screen cars from view. Lots are reserved in the main square for civic buildings such as a library, church, post office, and/or meeting hall.

DPZ's copyrighted architectural and urban design standards are attached to each plat of land as the means to implement the land plan. The rules are straightforward. Buildings can be any style but must include traditional elements, such as pitched or hipped roofs, vertical-oriented windows, porches, and balconies. Building materials must be ones that age well, such as wood, brick, or stone. No aluminum siding is allowed. Traditional proportions are also precisely prescribed for the buildings' form, the street width, the lot size, the setback, and the yard sizes.

A separate urban design code will be written for the Old Farm Neighborhood. This area will be set off on three sides, to serve as a gateway or filter from downtown. Streets will be lined with native trees and paved with a combination of cobblestone, red brick, and asphalt. The civic buildings will be set off with a certain look, such as blue metal roofs, to identify them as public facilities. A walled garden will be renovated and existing trees supplemented. According to architect Patrick Pinnell, the image the team has in mind is the "contrascape"—a neighborhood that was just beyond the old city walls in medieval times.

Road standards, top, and a street rendering, bottom.

Evening. DPZ's Bill Lennertz comments, "The craziness is just beginning." There is an 11:00 P.M. deadline for drawings that need large-size photocopies. Many drawings still have to be done by hand, including streetscapes, illustrations of public squares and parks, and vignettes of what Pinnell calls "instant monuments"—memorable focal points that contribute to the city's authenticity.

The studio is buzzing with activity and there are many observers on hand. The enthusiasm is contagious. People are running on sheer adrenaline and fight fatigue by drinking espresso and playing soothing classical music tapes. Design continues while final drawings are being made, but the main effort is concentrated on documenting the work. Work continues all night.

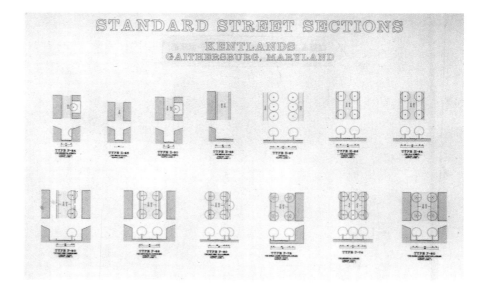

DAY 7: June 7

Work continues up until the very last moment, as 300 guests crowd into a rented tent. Andres Duany presents nearly one hundred slides describing how the new town will look. Public reaction is enthusiastically supportive and the long road to implementation begins.

Morning. By midmorning the team is back at work. There is still much to be done before the evening presentation. The boundaries of the town center keep shifting and as a result the landscaping features of that area are still being designed. The land plan must be modified to fit in fifty-five more units. Alfandre worries about density and considers the trade-offs of providing the elderly housing in the Old Farm Neighborhood or not. The mall façade is being designed.

Afternoon. Andres Duany takes the finished drawings outdoors to photograph them. The film must be developed in time to put together a slide show before 6:00 P.M. Landscape architect Kathy Poole sits in a quiet corner of the barn writing the landscaping criteria—it is over thirty-six pages long and specifies over 350 native species. The charrette begins to wind down.

4:00 P.M. Andres Duany gives local builders a preview presentation. Robert Mitchell, the county's most prominent builder, asks pointed questions but concludes that "People are ready for something like this." Duany feels it is important to the process that builders agree to conform to the team's guidelines. He says, "Builders will be exempt from the design code if they buy a large enough parcel. They'll only have to go by the street grid. It's very hard to impose zoning. We would prefer not to zone, to let history do that and just zone the envelope."

KENTLANDS

TOWN CHARTER

(Declaration of Covenants, Conditions and Restrictions)

PREAMBLE

WE, THE DEVELOPER AND ALL TITLEHOLDERS who come to own Real Property subject to this Charter within the community of Kentlands, located in the City of Gaithersburg, Maryland, affirm and subscribe to the purposes and provisions of this Charter and concur as to the considerable importance and value of the Mission and Goals of Kentlands, as set forth in this Preamble, to all Titleholders and Citizens of Kentlands.

WE AFFIRM THAT the central purpose of this Charter is to beneficially protect and enhance the general health, safety and welfare of the Citizens of Kentlands and to promote opportunities for enrichment of the quality of life of each Citizen of Kentlands, and further, to make substantive contributions to the City in which we live and own Real Property.

WE FURTHER ENDORSE AND PLEDGE our support for and commitment to the provisions of this Charter and the following objectives that have materially influenced the Town Plan for Kentlands and the design of the Kentlands Citizens Council, the internal governing body for Kentlands:

1. To satisfy the intents of the Town Plan that, in its conception, was directed towards the goals of protecting and enhancing the value of each Titleholder's financial investment in Real Property in Kentlands.

2. To provide for the human habitation of the lands comprising Kentlands in ways that minimize adverse environmental impacts and that otherwise serve to protect and enhance the wholesomeness of the human and natural ecosystems that operate within Kentlands, and in particular, to creatively promote and effect measures that lead to a lesser reliance upon private automobiles than has been customary in modern communities.

3. To provide for each Citizen and all residents of his* household unique opportunities to enjoy a social environment that enriches personal and family life through community congeniality and the operation of an overall spirit about Kentlands that it is an especially emotionally and spiritually rewarding place to live. In particular, Kentlands has been conceived to uniquely provide opportunities for individual, personal growth to better enable each person to more fully fulfill his and her human potential.

4. To foster a strong sense of inter-connectedness between Citizens in support of the idea that for a community to be able to give its utmost to its individual constituents, its individual constituents must give their practical utmost to their community.

The "Townowners Charter"

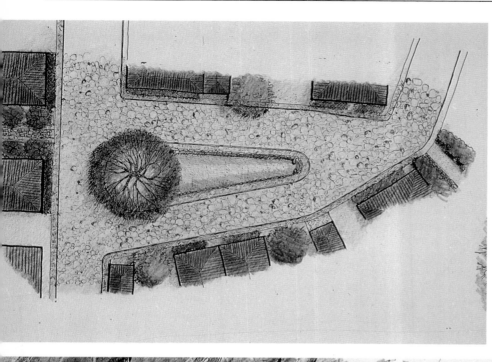

From the final presentation: Views of the Old Farm Neighborhood, opposite page; a garden, above; and a streetscape showing paving detail, bottom.

6:00 P.M.: Finale. Three tents have been set up on the front lawn of the mansion. The presentation begins with Alfandre's symbolic presentation of the Kent estate buildings to the town. Andres Duany improvises his ninety-minute presentation and shows nearly 100 slides, which were developed just a few hours earlier. Inside the tent the mood is buoyant. "It really turned out better than I had ever imagined," beams Alfandre.

The charrette concludes over drinks and dinner outdoors, as a brass band plays. The design team has become a closely knit group through sharing this experience. Good-byes are anticlimatic; however, for some

the whole process will start all over again in just a few weeks in another town.

COORDINATION
June 1988—(ongoing)
Public hearings began in July, and by February 1989, zoning approval for the mixed-use district was obtained. DPZ continued to refine the master plan throughout the fall and winter. At the same time as the zoning review, the first section of the development was submitted for schematic design review by the city. The final plan would be submitted for concurrent review, with approval expected by June. By early March, Alfandre had already staked out which plots he

planned to build himself, as "seeds" for the development. Ground breaking for construction of the Old Farm Neighborhood was scheduled for July. The land designated as the school district was sold, with construction scheduled to begin in August, pending approval of the wetlands, street engineering, and fire safety plans. The mall design evolved throughout the ensuing year as well, but no anchors had committed to the space by the spring, making it premature to concentrate on the architecture. As of the spring, still to be pinned down were which public services are to be provided, although a post office and library will definitely be included.

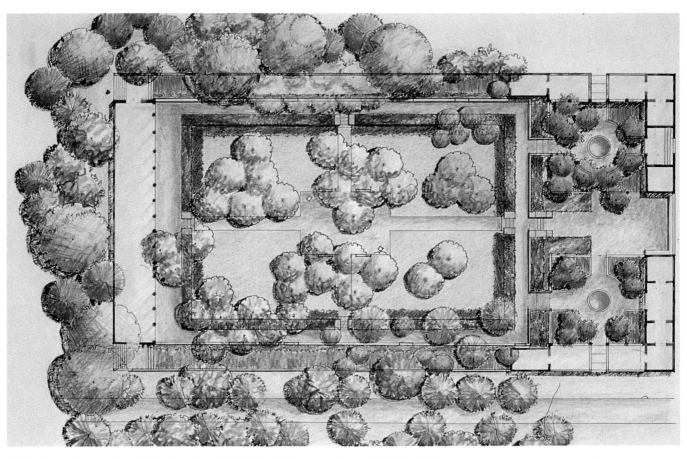

LAKE TERRACES

KENTLANDS
GAITHERSBURG, MARYLAND

A key feature of the Kentlands plan is the design of the public realm. From the final presentation: A carefully planned vista, opposite page; the Secret Garden, above; and the graceful terraces, left.

OBSERVATIONS

"Working by committee isn't all bad."—Roger K. Lewis, architect

• The charrette concept depends on participation for success, according to Andres Duany. "That's why we began with an open lecture on principles. It's very important for people to understand that it is more efficient to do this through a group rather than as individuals. Things happen that never would have without people to interact. In theory, the work could be done in fifteen days by five people, rather than in seven days by ten. But we want the collision of hands and ideas and sequence of people working—not together, but sequentially, the overlay of designer on designer. And this way costs less than conventional methods once you figure the travel expense, meeting time, and time lost before an error or problem is caught, let alone resolved."

• The success of a charrette also depends on strong project management. Throughout the process individuals or small teams worked on separate tasks, occasionally joining to form a larger group. Periodically the entire team would meet for a review of work, a discussion, or a presentation. Because meetings with consultants and key participants were scheduled in rapid succession, the material to be discussed had to be completed on time by the appropriate team member. Reporters and visitors constantly came through the site asking questions. None of this could have worked without good coordination and organization. DPZ's role included much more than design. Alfandre notes, "They helped broaden my vision and helped me assemble the necessary team to achieve that vision."

• By bringing together designers and public officials to discuss regulations and proposals, the charrette fostered a mutual authorship of ideas that facilitated reaching a consensus, even when it involved a departure from standard practice. However, unlike other small towns, Gaithersburg has control over its zoning; this process could not have happened with a larger bureaucracy. While it is interesting to consider the charrette as a model for the public planning process, it probably requires a single powerful patron with both the money and the drive to pull it off.

• The role of the developer in this sort of process is crucial. They must not only be willing to take risks and have long-range perspective, they must also be ready to commit to the plan so that the basic concept remains intact during implementation. "The charrette exceeded our expectations in terms of the amount of detail and the participation and enthusiasm it has caused," says Alfandre executive Steve Wilcox. "We did everything 'right,' and our attitude was, if this doesn't work, what would? We're still not sure this concept will fly and we'll have to test it with additional market research. I don't think at this time we can give a parcel to a builder with these restrictions and have anyone want to buy it. But if we need to make changes, we'll get back in touch with DPZ and work out something we could all agree on. We won't abandon this plan."

• The charrette generated a contagious enthusiasm. Gaithersburg mayor Edward Bohrer said afterward, "This has been one of the most engrossing weeks of my life." Yet many questions remain to be answered—for example, how the mall will be incorporated and what the impact of traffic will be on local roads. Residents will still need cars to shop since there are no convenience stores in the neighborhoods. The location and type of civic services is vague. Most critically, there is hardly any provision for affordable housing. As *Washington Post* architecture critic Benjamin Forgey put it, "This is a relentlessly upscale project." Mayor Bohrer tempered his own enthusiastic support of the charrette and Kentlands by borrowing a phrase from President Reagan: "Trust but verify. We will be watching."

• One week may be long enough to develop a schematic plan full of innovative ideas, but it is not long enough to think through complex issues such as creating a truly balanced community. Nevertheless, the importance of the process and the plan it produced is that it provided people with a vision. The fact that there is such a strong working relationship between the developer, architect, and city officials means that the value of the process will go beyond showmanship and will endure, helping make that vision become a reality.

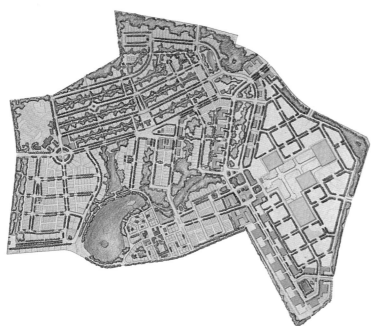

The final master plan, left, and
a bird's-eye view, below.

CREDITS AND SOURCES

The architects whose work appears in this book have kindly provided drawings and photographs of their projects in process. The owners and developers of these properties were equally generous in lending material for publication. In addition, drawings and photographs have been provided by individuals and organizations; the material is reprinted with permission.

DESIGN IN PROCESS

p. 14: Photograph by Robert P. Matthews; courtesy of Princeton University.

p. 18: From *Harper's New Monthly Magazine*, October 1877.

THE VILLAGE CENTER

Sketches and photographs by William Rawn; courtesy of William Rawn.

p. 25, bottom, and p. 26: Reprinted from *Brewster, A Town Remembered*; courtesy of The Brewster Historical Society.

pp. 30 and 31: Photographs courtesy of University of Virginia/University Relations.

FIRESTATION FIVE

Sketches, drawings, and photographs courtesy of Susana Torre Raymond Beeler and Associates.

p. 55, center left: Firestation at York, Pennsylvania, c. 1799, drawn in the 1850s from memory by Lewis Miller. Courtesy of the Historical Society of York County.

p. 55, bottom left: Photograph by A. Pierce Bounds for the National Endowment for the Arts, from *The American Firehouse* by Rebecca Zurier (Abbeville Press, 1982). Now part of The American Firehouse Project archive at the Library of Congress. Courtesy of the Prints and Photographs Division, Library of Congress. (See also p. 55, bottom right, and p. 58, left.)

p. 55, center right: From *The American Firehouse* by Rebecca Zurier (Abbeville Press, 1982). Courtesy of Chief Steve B. Campbell, with thanks to A. Pierce Bounds.

p. 55, bottom right: Photograph by Theresa Beyer, from *The American Firehouse* by Rebecca Zurier (Abbeville Press, 1982). Courtesy of the Prints and Photographs Division, Library of Congress. (See p. 55, bottom left.)

p. 56, left: From *Our Firemen: A History of the New York City Fire Department* by Augustine E. Costello (New York: A. E. Costello, 1887). Courtesy of the Picture Collection, New York Public Library.

p. 56, right: From *Harper's New Monthly Magazine*, October 1877.

p. 58, left: Drawing by Theresa Beyer, from *The American Firehouse* by Rebecca Zurier (Abbeville Press, 1982). Courtesy of the Prints and Photographs Division, Library of Congress. (See p. 55, bottom left.)

p. 58, right: From *Fire Engineering Magazine*, June 1945 (Pennwell Publishing, Tulsa, Oklahoma). Used with permission.

p. 59, left: Courtesy of Venturi, Rauch & Scott-Brown.

p. 71, bottom left: Photograph by Timothy Hursley, The Arkansas Office. Used with permission.

WASHINGTON COURT

Sketches, drawings, and photographs courtesy of James Stewart Polshek and Partners.

p. 89: The article, "Battle Over Cornices and Lintels Rages in 'Village' " by Richard Severo (*New York Times*, 28 August 1984) copyright © 1984 by The New York Times Company. Reprinted by permission.

p. 93, bottom left and right, and p. 95, top left: Copyright © Paul Warchol Photography, Inc.

p. 95, top right and bottom: Copyright © Jeff Goldberg/ESTO. Used with permission.

LEWIS THOMAS MOLECULAR BIOLOGY LABORATORY

Sketches, drawings, and photographs courtesy of Venturi, Rauch & Scott-Brown. Additional drawings and documentation courtesy of Payette Associates, Inc.

p. 99, top: Photograph by Tom Bernard; courtesy of Venturi, Rauch & Scott-Brown.

p. 99, bottom: Photograph by Robert P. Matthews; courtesy of Princeton University.

ADDITION TO ASU COLLEGE OF ARCHITECTURE AND ENVIRONMENTAL DESIGN

Drawings and photographs courtesy of The Hillier Group; Architecture One, Ltd., Phoenix; and the College of Architecture and Environmental Design, Arizona State University, Tempe.

pp. 128–29: Photograph by Lourdes Sodari-Smith; courtesy of Arizona State University.

p. 137, right: Courtesy of Arizona Biltmore, Westin Hotels & Resorts.

p. 147: Photograph by Okland Construction Company; courtesy of Arizona State University.

AETNA HOME OFFICE RENOVATION

Drawings, photographs, and documentation courtesy of Jung/Brannen Associates, Inc., and Aetna Life & Casualty.

pp. 170 and 171: Photographs © 1986 and copyright © 1987 by Richard Mandelkorn. Used with permission.

CAMBRIDGESIDE

Drawings and photographs courtesy of Arrowstreet Inc.

pp. 174 and 175: From *City of Cambridge: The Greenbook*. Reprinted with permission by the Cambridge Community Development Department.

p. 177 and p. 192, top: Courtesy of Aerial Photos International Inc.

METROPOLIS

p. 199: Copyright © Fred Emmert, Airviews, 1986. Used with permission.

p. 201; p. 204, top and bottom; p. 205; p. 206, bottom; p. 207, left top and bottom; p. 209, bottom; p. 212; p. 213, top and bottom; and p. 225: Photographs by William Taylor; courtesy of Michael Graves, Architect.

KENTLANDS

Drawings, photographs, and copyrighted standards courtesy of Andres Duany and Elizabeth Plater-Zyberk, town planners. Additional photographs and drawings courtesy of Joseph Alfandre & Co., Inc.

p. 232, bottom: Photograph by Matt Hamblen/*The Montgomery Journal*. Used with permission.

INDEX